Peter's Lullaby

*A song without words
that held a little girl's life together*

by
Jeanne Fowler

✳✳✳ DAISY CHAIN PUBLISHING ✳✳✳

Peter's Lullaby

Daisy Chain Publishing
1890 Crooks Road
Troy, Michigan 48084

ISBN 0-9771975-0-6

Library of Congress Control Number: 2005932154

Printed in the United States of America

First Printing, October, 2005

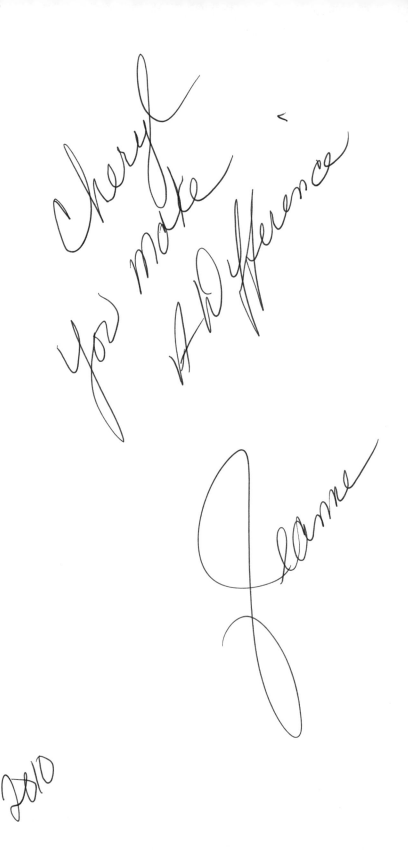

Cheryl

You make

A Difference

Jeanne

2010

A special thank you to everyone who helped make this book possible. The lengthy list, which continues to grow, has too many names to mention here. You know who you are and I appreciate every one of you.

Jeanne

Front Cover Illustration:
"The Patchwork Girl"
oil acrylic and lace on canvas
by
Jeanne Fowler

"When I left the slave farm in 1964, I left the hatred and brutality behind. I patched my life back together with all of the good pieces I had left."

Back Cover Photo
Stephen Lengnick, Plum Street Studio

Aunt Bea Duquette
(June 8, 1913 - April 18, 2000)
from an oil on canvas portrait by Jeanne Fowler

To Bea and Doody Duquette,

the foster parents who taught me how to love. If it hadn't been for my brief time with them, I would never have learned how to love my own children. Aunt Bea, your love was stronger than any beating I ever got.

To my son, David,
and my daughter, April,

you are my life. God did a beautiful job when he gave me the two of you. You are the reason I lived.

Contents

Introduction viii

A Note About Accuracy..ix

1. Eating Boogers..1

2. A Girl Named Georgie..9

3. The Fairytale Princess...16

4. Dancing Blue Flames...21

5. Bea And Doody 24

6. Goodnight Georgie...29

7. Christmas Surprise..34

8. Beady Little Eyes 40

9. Comfortable And Adequate.....................................45

10. Crying Over Spilled Milk......................................52

11. Gruesome Finger Painting 59

12. The Bum Got Up...66

13. Crocodile Tears...71

14. Quite A Hero...78

15. I Guess I Was Angry...85

16. I'm A Little Tea Pot..92

17. Just Too Sick 97

18. The Bravest Thing...103

19. Candy From A Baby 110

20. DO YOU LIKE KITTENS? 115

21. THE HUMAN GATE 121

22. A DOLL OF MY OWN 128

23. BEHIND THE EIGHT BALL 135

24. SPARKLING SNOW..........................140

25. TREAT YOU LIKE A GIRL 145

26. DUCKING DONUTS 150

27. THE ATTIC 159

28. I DREAM OF JEANNE 167

29. MY FIRST DATE...........................174

30. TICKET TO RIDE 181

31. DIME, CLIP AND PHOTO...................186

32. ANOTHER GEORGIE DEEP INSIDE 193

A Letter to Heaven.............................201

The Need for Mommies 202

Where are they Now? 204

Abuse In Perspective 208

What Has and Hasn't Changed...................209

Resources 212

"Michigans" 213

About the Author.............................214

Introduction

I started researching my past in order to find the siblings I lost 50 years ago. Success came in 1998, when five of us were reunited in Plattsburgh, New York. I'm a private person, and I wasn't an activist or a writer, nor did I start out to write a book about my horrific childhood. I might not have written this book at all, but on November 2, 1999, the *Detroit Free Press* carried a story that galvanized me into action.

The story was about a licensed foster mother and her little nine-year-old mentally challenged boy. He was found naked and tied to a bucket in the basement of her immaculately clean home. She had a spotless record with the welfare system, even though one of the children she had cared for had died in 1993 and another had died in 1995, both under suspicious circumstances. Then in October 1999 another of her charges turned up with retinal and cranial bleeding, possibly caused by shaken-baby syndrome. It was during the course of investigating this shaken-baby case that the police discovered the boy tied to the bucket and arrested the mother.

Reading these articles took me back to my childhood, to where I had been tied naked to the wall of my mother's immaculate house with a bucket between my legs. The police and social workers had known for years about my situation, but until my brother Peter was found dead, they had done little to protect us. Once I was "rescued," I spent 12 years in the foster-care system, much of it as a slave on a foster farm, where I was beaten regularly with a rubber hose. Over our screams and cries, the silence of the people in a position to help us was deafening.

The little, mentally challenged boy in Detroit who was tied to the bucket will probably never be able to write his story, nor can my dead brother ever sing his sad lullaby again, but my voice can still be heard. Now it is time for me to bear witness about Peter's little song of hope. I hear Peter's lullaby in my head every day. By reading this book I hope that you may be able to hear Peter's lullaby for the first time.

A Note About Accuracy

It has been emotionally difficult but rewarding to go back into my sad past to write this book. I have made every effort to portray every person and event honestly and accurately. Many events that happened before I started school are seared into my memory forever, while other events are composites of hazy memories of tortures too numerous to keep straight. I have used court, welfare, autopsy, and medical records to fill in some of the details. I have interviewed many of my family members in order to put my early record into a coherent and accurate story.

I found that many sources of information have problems. Children who have been tortured all their lives are not reliable persons to ask about details of their daily lives. My parents, who were arrested for murder, on the other hand, knew many of the details, but had reason to hide the horror they had inflicted. The Child Protective Services workers, who stood to lose their jobs if the extent of their oversight regarding the murder became known, had reason to change some of the facts or "lose" the files. A foster parent bent on exploiting or mistreating a child is not a reliable source of information either. Some of the people in this book are dead or missing. I'll never be able to ask them what happened or why. The court records, friends, and family will have to speak for them.

In the final analysis, I was forced to use my common sense to settle the inevitable conflicts in our various stories. I have also checked my recollections against police psychological profiles of typical perpetrators of the crimes described. I have also talked to both perpetrators and victims of similar crimes for insights. A couple of psychologists were consulted to help explain the feelings and motivations of the people depicted. I have talked with many friends, relatives, and government sources to maintain accuracy that this story deserves. After the age of seven, my memories are substantially more accurate and detailed and, thus, have given my impressions more weight.

I have tried to let each person's actions speak for themselves. I have no hard feelings toward anyone. I would hate to cause the slightest pain or embarrassment to the people in my life, so I have changed a few names to protect the privacy of the good people in this book.

Chapter One

Eating Boogers

I HUNG IN MY CLOSET sobbing and hyperventilating. I was in a great deal of pain. I slumped forward. The tattered strips of blood-and sweat-soaked cloth held my raw, scarred wrists. My shoulders hurt something fierce. I turned my head and strained as hard as I could to hear Peter singing. His song didn't come. Even his moaning had stopped. I found it impossible to pass into the semiconsciousness that passed for sleep in my world.

Just after sundown a policeman threw open the closet door. The kitchen light blinded me. The policeman took out his pocketknife. He used it to cut the strips of cloth holding me up. My naked body collapsed onto the floor. The policeman scooped me up and handed me to a neighbor lady. The lady helped me into some clothes that she found in the bedroom.

Once I was dressed, the nice lady gently laid me on Jill's bed. I hurt all over. I knew that I shouldn't be in a bed. This was cause for a severe beating in our home. But I was too tired and I hurt too much to go back to my closet. I was sort of happy to be in a bed. It had been over a year since the last time I had been in one. I closed my eyes and tried to sleep.

My five-year-old sister Jill was in the living room, and she was screaming in terror. The commotion got me so very frightened that I got out of Jill's bed and rushed into the living room to protect my sister.

Our house was filled with firemen, neighbors, and the police. I didn't know what was going on, but I was very frightened. Every time anyone came near us, Jill and I both screamed. We then hid behind the couch and hugged each other.

A policeman bent over and extended his hand to me. "Don't be afraid little girl. You are safe now, and no one will ever hurt you again."

I remembered his exact words that day and I guess I always will. I thought, "My, what an odd thing to say."

I declined to take his hand. I knew that he would drag me out from behind the couch if I did. I didn't want to go with him, and I didn't like all the commotion going on in our house. I crawled backward away from his outstretched hand and eased my small trembling body behind the heavy, floral-pattern drapes. Jill was still there hiding and shivering, so I took her skinny little body into my arms.

I heard footsteps on the wooden front porch. I let go of Jill and crouched down until my left ear was on the carpet. In that position I could just barely see the bottom few inches of the front door as it flew opened and a new man rushed into our living room. I could see his shoes and gray pant legs. He wasn't a uniformed policeman or a uniformed fireman. His shoes were new and shiny, even though they were covered with raindrops. My dad was still sitting on the couch. I glanced over to his feet. Dad wasn't wearing any shoes, and he only had one gray sock on.

I knew that the policeman who had promised me that no one would ever hurt me was still standing at the end of our old, beat-up couch, because I could see his wet shoes.

The man in the suit spoke, "Well, what do we have here, Harold?" His tone of voice seemed to indicate that he was now in charge

The uniformed officer replied, "The toddler in the kitchen looks to be in bad shape. He may not make it. Dad here says he doesn't know 'nutten.' Says that we need to talk to mom. Says that she's at work. That boy over there holding the infant called mom before we were called. She's supposed to be on her way home. We have two small girls hiding behind the couch. The one girl looks banged up pretty bad. It looks like we have torture chambers in the bathroom, the bedroom, and in the closet. There is also a note on the kitchen table from somebody named 'V.' It apparently explains the plans for today's torture."

The man in charge thought for a moment and then asked, "How far away is mom and when was she called?"

The officer replied, "I don't know. I didn't ask."

The man in charge inquired, "Well, where does she work?"

Dad softly replied, "She works at the Kool-Aid factory over on South Pulaski. She should be home by now."

The man in charge asked, "What's the mother's name?"

Dad softly replied, "Veronica Burowsky."

"Okay, Harold, get those kids away from the evidence and tape off the bathroom, closet, bedroom, and the kitchen. Then stick all of the kids in squad cars. Call in while you are down there and have someone go over to the Kool-Aid factory and pick up the mother. Get a description of her car, in case she comes here and doesn't stop. She may not stop when she sees all the squad cars."

Police Officer Harold walked out into the rainy night. He was gone for a couple of minutes. When he got back, his shoes were covered with mud. Then he walked out of my sight. A few minutes later he came back and stood at the end of the couch. In the reassuring singsong voice that grownups reserve for talking to children he said, "Okay, little girls, it's safe to come out now. We'll protect you."

I wasn't buying any of that! Jill and I didn't budge or make a sound.

Officer Harold tried several more times to talk us into coming out, but we didn't respond. Finally he became frustrated, went over to dad, and ordered, "Off the couch!"

Dad stood up and moved out of my sight. Then Officer Harold picked up the end of the couch and pulled it away from the wall. He then slowly parted the drapes and found Jill and me huddled together. Officer Harold picked me up, but I had my tiny arms around my little sister, so she came with us. Jill, crying softly, had wrapped her arms around both the drapes and me. Our little chain of humanity managed to pull the curtain rod off the wall. The noise startled us, and we started to sob. One policeman came over and grabbed onto Jill. We screamed and screamed but to no avail. The two men gently pried us apart.

Dad was standing in the middle of our normally immaculate living room in his neatly pressed blue slacks, a T-shirt, and one sock. The room was in a shambles. The couch was now in the middle of the room, jammed up against an ambulance gurney. Two boxes and a metal cylinder cluttered the floor. There was bright-yellow plastic tape across all of the doors in the house. All I could think was that mom was sure going to be mad when she saw this mess.

Police Officer Harold carried me across the living room. I was sobbing. Everyone else, including the police and medics, had eyes filled with tears.

Little Peter was on the kitchen floor, with three men hovering over him. One man had placed a clear-plastic mask over Peter's nose and mouth. A tube connected the mask to a battered but shiny metal cylinder. The men had shed their heavy coats, which were in a pile on the La-Z-Boy chair. The men around Peter were all dressed the same. They had on heavy rubber boots, white T-shirts, and wide, red suspenders holding up their big, old, bulky pants.

Officer Harold went over and pulled a neatly folded, old, gray blanket from the gurney and wrapped it loosely around me. "Don't be frightened. It will be okay. No one will ever hurt you again."

I wanted to believe him. I wanted to believe the nightmare was finally over for us.

As we walked out on the porch, I took one last look at Peter. I walked down the steps, out into the sad summer drizzle, and to the car. I watched the flashing reflection of the red police lights in the puddle next to the car. Tears rolled down my face. I think the warm drizzle was God crying too. I pulled the scratchy, old, gray wool blanket tight around my body, but I still couldn't stop shivering.

The police officer placed me on the cold, green vinyl back seat of a police car and sat down next to me on the seat. He said, "You are safe now."

I sat in the car with Officer Harold for a long time. One more police car showed up. Then mom arrived by taxi. She was in her wet, stained Kool-Aid uniform. Mom was crying, which was hard for me to understand. I had never seen her cry before. Mom came running past the car. I ducked down. She must not have seen me, because she raced into the house. Officer Harold followed her in. After a long wait, he returned to my car and got in. We slowly drove away from the house. Once we got onto the highway, I noticed that the late-night streets were nearly deserted. When we got to the jail, a nice lady took me to a cell. She sat on the bed with me for several minutes. She said, "Don't be afraid. I'll be right down the hall. I won't lock your door, so you won't be trapped."

As soon as she left, I hobbled over to the cell door and grabbed the bars of the cell. I shook them as hard as I could. Sure enough the door wasn't locked. I got back into the bunk and cried. I hurt so badly. After what seemed like a very long time, I became very thirsty. I hadn't had anything to eat or drink since the day before. I could see the matron sitting at her desk through the bars of the cell door, so I meekly asked her, "Can I have some water?"

Mom, who was down the hall, overheard me and yelled, "My daughter needs a drink of water! Can't somebody see she's thirsty!

What the hell is wrong with you people? Let me get my daughter a drink of water!" She rattled her door viciously, but it didn't open. Thank God for that.

I was stunned by mom's sudden show of concern for my welfare. I knew that she wouldn't have given me anything to drink on this night if the police hadn't come.

The matron came in and gave me a small glass of water that I held in both hands. She sat with me while I sipped the cool water. I was shivering uncontrollably. "Your mother is locked up. She can't hurt you any more," she said.

I wanted to believe the matron, but mom was an incredibly strong person who could do anything to anyone and no one could stop her. I think the matron could see that I was exhausted, so she gently tucked me into the prison cot. It felt so good to have a bed and covers. I hadn't had either in so long. I was less frightened, but my body hurt from the thrashings of the last few days. My head hurt from tight punishment braids, but I certainly wasn't going to take my hair down and make mom mad.

This jail had every thing that I dreamed of ever having—a bed and toilet of my own. Best of all, the lights in the corridor stayed on all night. That was great because I hated the dark. It seemed like such a luxury, that I never wanted to leave. The jail cot was the softest, most wonderful bed I could imagine, and I finally drifted off into an erratic sleep.

In the morning they brought me eggs, juice, and a chocolate-covered donut. I ate the donut with great gusto because it had been two days since I had eaten. I wasn't sure about the runny eggs, but I wolfed them down also.

Then they took me to St. Bernard's Hospital. A nurse gave me some candy and told me that everything would be all right. She seemed like a nice lady, but I had my doubts. She told me that a man was going to ask me some questions. I just stared blankly back at the nurse. I didn't respond to her much, because mom had warned me about strangers. They did horrible things to little girls.

They took photographs and X-rays of my body then fed me lunch and placed me in a well-lit, comfortable hospital room with a large window to look out. There were trees and birds in the courtyard. It was a beautiful sight. That night I was served my meal in bed, and I thought, "Wow, this is great!" For supper that night I ate a large tray of scrumptious hospital food, including some springy, red Jell-O. I had more fun playing with the Jell-O than I did eating it. The only bad part of the hospital was that there was no lock on the door to the hall, and I was afraid mom would come and get me.

A psychiatrist came and talked to me several times that first day. The psychiatrist explained to me that Peter was dead and had gone to heaven. I asked him when Peter would be coming back. He gently explained that Peter wasn't ever coming back. I started to cry. I didn't know how I could go on without my brother to help me. I felt more alone at that moment than I had ever felt hanging in my closet.

I ached for Peter. I couldn't hear him singing his lullaby.

When I woke up the next morning, I was given breakfast, which I ate very fast.

That night I left the light on in the bathroom and the bathroom door ajar. A soft ribbon of light illuminated the door to the hall. I stayed awake as long as I could, watching that unlocked door. I listened to the sound of everyone walking the hall. I was waiting for the attack that I was sure was coming.

The next afternoon, after the police talked to me again, I was checked out of the hospital and sent to the dormitory of the children's home, where Jill was. The orphanage was full of children. A nun helped me to stand in line to get a tray of food. I ate my meal very fast, and then I sat and watched the other children.

After lunch, the nun told me that I might be coming to live here with them. I sure hoped that she was right. I couldn't imagine anything better than that. The hospital and the jail had been wonderful compared to my home, but the orphanage was the best place yet. I really loved eating with all of these other children. I hoped that I could stay here forever. I wasn't choosy. Just as long as I didn't have to live with mom again.

The orphanage had a large room full of single beds. That night I asked the little girl in the bed next to mine what I could expect in this place. She said, "If you're caught picking your nose here, the nuns will go around with a large plate and each kid will blow his nose on that plate. Then you will be forced to eat the whole plate full of boogers as punishment." The girl was undoubtedly pulling my leg with this institutional legend, but I took it as fact. With her dubious warning as my only guide, I embarked on my new life as a ward of the Chicago courts.

I looked with considerable distrust at the nuns, and I was very careful not to pick my nose. I was trembling in fear and anxiety. One of the nuns held me for quite a while before she gently laid me on my bed. I cried a lot for my brother, and I worried about mom coming to get me in the middle of the night. There was something frightening about the orphanage. My fear just wouldn't let me sleep peacefully. In my world I only knew two safe ways to sleep. I knew how to sleep hanging on the wall, and I knew how to sleep kneeling beside the refrigerator. The bed seemed strange and dangerous. Lying down wasn't at all comfortable. What if mom came in the night and caught me? The risk was just too great. I got on my knees under the covers.

When the lights went out I was delighted to discover that there was a wonderful green "EXIT" light over the door. I positioned myself in such a way that I could watch it. It was so much better than the blackness of the closet in mom's house. I watched that "EXIT" light most of the night. I thought to myself, "Maybe the green glow will chase the monster away." From that day forward, I would never willingly sleep in a dark room again.

I still couldn't sleep because I missed Peter so much. His lullaby had always reassured me that we had survived. Now there was no lullaby, and it was impossible to sleep. I started to sing Peter's lullaby to myself, "Aah, Ah, Aaaah, AAH, Aah, Ah, Aaaah, AAH, Aah, Ah, Aaaah, AAH."

I sang Peter's lullaby for quite a while. Then the door under the "EXIT" light opened, and a lady walked in. I was trembling in fear that mom had come for me! I was relieved that it was just one of the nuns. She had heard Peter's lullaby but didn't understand. She thought that I was moaning in pain. She came over and held me for a while. "Shush, there, there, it will be okay," she said. Then she placed me on my back and tucked me in.

I was very uncomfortable lying on my back in a bed. As soon as the nun left I got back on my knees and started to sing my brother's song very softly so that I wouldn't attract any more unwanted attention from the nuns. I soon fell into an exhausted sleep.

Next morning, the nun came and got Jill and me. She took us out into the garden and down a path to the cemetery. She said, "Your brother is dead. Peter has gone to live with Jesus our redeemer. He is in a much better place where he will be happy and no one will ever hurt him again. You will not see Peter again for a long time, but when you get to heaven Peter will be there to greet you." She pointed to a basket full of flowers and said, "I brought you here where your brother is buried so you could say goodbye."

It would be over 50 years before I discovered that the nun was not telling me the truth that day.

Jill and I cried when we learned that we wouldn't see Peter again.

That night an older girl at the orphanage said, "You're too old to be adopted. Only healthy white babies get adopted. Old white kids like you are 'damaged goods.' No one will want you. I've been here three years and no one has even talked to me."

I was no good, at the age of six, just like my mother had told me. I was very sad. I thought, "What if we act real sweet, and then someone will want us." I sure hoped that I wasn't too old to be adopted.

I would have loved to rest and heal for a few more days, but I was told that I had to go to the inquest. I guess that back in 1953, justice was swift.

The next day, a stern police lady in a big, black car came for Jill and me. "My name is Officer Rita Meany. You can call me Rita," she said. "I have come to pick up you two girls and take you to the inquest."

When we got to the inquest, I was none too thrilled to be surrounded by so many pushing and shoving police officers, nurses, social workers, investigators, newspapermen, and curiosity seekers. After so many months of hanging by my wrists in a dark closet, I was completely overwhelmed with the attention.

The police lady had all of us kids sit with mom while we waited for the inquest to begin. Mom held infant Donna on her lap and cooed to her, "I missed my precious little girl so much. Did you miss me?"

I was frighten by the hubbub in the hall, especially when a man in a rumpled, gray suit set off a flash bulb in my face. He pushed a button and the hot bulb flew out and skittered across the floor. He loaded another and flashed another picture.

I tried to concentrate on what I needed to tell the people at the inquest.

Chapter Two

A Girl Named George

I WAS BORN in Plattsburgh, a small industrial town in upstate New York. Now, by upstate I don't mean Albany or Schenectady, I mean the cold, primitive, wild far-northern part of upstate New York. The small town of Plattsburgh is 20 miles north of Lake Placid and 20 miles south of the Canadian border. It is nestled between the ruggedly verdant Adirondack Mountains and the shores of clear, blue Lake Champlain.

George Trombley was a hard-drinking, tough man. His wife, Alice, was beautiful and an even harder drinker. He made a fortune running rum over the nearby Canadian border during prohibition. As the Roaring Twenties came to a close, they settled down as one of the richest families in town. George and Alice had four daughters: Francis, Geraldine, Margaret and Veronica.

George owned a nightclub called the Lido, and he had a penchant for the showgirls who worked there. The marriage of Granddad George and Grandma Alice eventually failed. The wildest and most beautiful of his daughters was Veronica. Near the end of the Depression, when everyone else was broke, Veronica had a flashy car and money. In an era when good girls didn't, Veronica did. She was very popular, but she was not the kind of girl you could take home to mom. Veronica spent the war years hanging around her father's nightclub, where she drank heavily and picked up men.

Veronica Trombley always wore her long, dark hair gently cascading in front of her left eye like the popular pre-war movie star Veronica Lake. During the Second World War, the war department felt that this over-the-eye hair style would endanger the female "Rosy the Riveters," who were pouring into the factories to do war work, so they started a publicity campaign against the Veronica Lake hair style. By 1943 the Veronica Lake hair style had gone out of fashion, but Veronica Trombley maintained the Veronica Lake look until well after the end of the war.

Veronica wanted to be a mother. She eventually had seven children by five different men. Unfortunately, she wasn't a good mother. Veronica abused and neglected these children until someone in the family came along and took each child away. It became a pattern in Veronica's life.

During the war years, Veronica bore three children, and her perfect hourglass figure was just slightly heavier. Veronica was no longer stunningly beautiful, but rather just very pretty. The war years had not been good for her reputation either. People talked about her sleeping around, drinking, and the child abuse.

Plattsburgh was, and is, a small, tolerant town where people didn't pry into other people's business. Everybody knew what was going on in town, but they tried not to get involved. The decent people of Plattsburgh knew that Veronica Trombley was a beautiful, spoiled, rich girl who would sleep with almost anyone. They also knew that Veronica was a child abuser who had all of her children taken away. Her reputation repelled women, but her beauty attracted many young men.

One day, Red Calahan came into the Lido for a few drinks. He met Veronica and offered to buy her a drink. Everyone in town knew Veronica's reputation, but when Red looked at Veronica through the bottom of his cocktail glass, he only saw a beautiful, wealthy, unencumbered, easy woman.

Soon Veronica was pregnant with me. All of my older siblings had already been removed. Unfortunately for me, Veronica was having babies and abusing them faster than relatives could be found to take them.

Months before I was born, mom and Red were suspected of attempting to burn down the Lido, so Red left his pregnant girlfriend and skipped town. Even though Red was probably my father, I never met him.

Since Veronica's beautiful body was not yet showing, she knew that she could attract another man. She was especially interested in Peter Burowsky, a returning soldier who had hired on as granddad's new bartender.

This wasn't the first time that Peter had worked for George. During the Depression, Peter—who was young, hungry, and desperately poor—would often walk the three blocks from his small tenement to the nearby Margaret Street commercial district to wash windows and help his family to get by. Granddad George, the crusty, old ex-bootlegger felt sorry for this spunky young boy whose father was dead, so he would hire Peter from time to time to wash the many windows of the Trombley business.

After the war, Peter's first stop was to his mom's house. Peter's second stop was the Lido to get a beer.

Peter remembered Veronica from his window-washing days. The budding young girl was hard for him to forget. Veronica started spending many hours every day drinking at the bar and chatting with the handsome, young bartender.

Peter Burowsky was a tall, trim man. He was thin, but not to the point where you would call him skinny. Peter's thick hair was jet-black. He had a gentle voice and a charming, winning demeanor. Peter was a natural bartender. He had a real talent for making drinkers have a good time and spend money.

Peter never shouted or even talked with a loud voice. He was graceful and had a soft walk. He could come into a room without anyone knowing that he was there.

After a brief romance, Peter and Veronica were married on August 25, 1946, in a civil ceremony.

Six months later, on February 1, 1947, Veronica went into labor. Peter rushed his new wife through the icy streets to the Plattsburgh Hospital. When I was born, I weighed 7 pounds, 14 ounces. I was strong and healthy, which was a good thing because I would need all my strength to survive the coming years.

A couple of months after my birth, on April 6, 1947, I was baptized Georgianne Burowsky.

I had three older siblings, but they had been taken away by the time I came along. The oldest child was known as "Pug." I never saw my five-year-old brother Pug, because mom's sister Gerry and Granddad George took care of him.

The next-oldest child was Debbie. Veronica's third child was given away at birth. I was mom's fourth child, but I was the only one living with her so I was sort of an only child for the first 13 months of my life. On March 31, 1948, my little sister Jill was born to Veronica and Peter. Jill was mom's fifth child. All five of us had different fathers.

When mom had her first child, Pug, no one was sure who his father was. Veronica was married when she had Debbie, but her husband tragically died in a mining accident a few months after the wedding. The other fathers, including mine, were gone from Veronica's life so fast that even their names are now only rumors. Peter Burowsky, Sr. was mom's second husband and my stepfather.

I believe that my name, "George," which was handed down to me from my granddad, was an unfortunate name for me to inherit. I think that in mom's confused, angry mind, I was interchangeable with my granddad. Mom now had a little "George" to torture. From the very start, she beat me with a seething passion.

My first childhood memory is of being beaten. I doubt if it was my first beating, just my first memory. I was about three years old. I remember laying face down on the cold, parquet dining-room floor in our house. My eyes were less than six inches from a gleaming chrome table leg. Although my wide-open eyes were filled with tears and terror, I was able to recognize a very distorted, pale-beige image of the rest of my naked body in that table leg. I could also barely see the reflected form of my tormentor and the big black belt as it smacked loudly against my body, again and again.

I remember concentrating on that table leg. Maybe it numbed the pain a little bit as the belt cut savagely into me. I cried and screamed as loud as I could. I just hoped that my screaming might attract dad, granddad, or one of my aunts. They might make mom stop thrashing me. No one came to save me that day. The blows worked up my body. I also kept my head near that chrome table leg to protect my face.

After the beating stopped, mom pulled my right arm away from my side and tied a ragged strip of powder blue bed sheet to my wrist. She did the same to my left arm and each of my legs. She grabbed my long auburn hair, twisted it tightly in her clenched fist, and yanked me to my feet. She dragged me backward across the floor to the bedroom, trailing streamers of fluttering cloth from my limbs. A plastic sheet was placed on the bed, and I was roughly thrown onto the middle of it. The loose end of one of the strips of cloth was securely tied to the ornate walnut pillar of the four-poster bed. My other arm was yanked out to the side, and the strip of sheeting was tightly tied to the other post. My feet were tied to the bed's footposts. A strip of electrical tape was stretched across my mouth so that I couldn't open it.

And then she was gone, and I was all alone, staring at the ceiling through tears of pain and fear. I opened and closed my hands and wiggled my toes to pass the time. Quite awhile later, my arms and legs were numb, but they weren't yet numb enough to allow me to collapse into a painful sleep. Then came the footsteps that jarred me into an alert but helpless tension.

My body convulsed in fear, because I knew that footsteps could mean danger. I tried in vain to move my arms and legs. My taped mouth couldn't even open up to scream. The door opened slowly, and through my tears I could see it was my father standing in the doorway. He had a slender, curved knife in his hand. He looked up and down my battered, helpless body. I closed my eyes as he brushed my long red hair out of my eyes and kissed me on the forehead. His breath smelled of alcohol. Dad used the knife to cut through the knots that held me down. I crawled into his arms, and he carried me to the couch.

He said softly, "You really made mom mad today, didn't you?"

I said, "Uh huh. I try not to make mommy mad. I'll be better daddy."

He said, "Good girl."

I thought that maybe if I was a better girl and learned how to take my punishments better, mom wouldn't be so mad at me all the time.

Father got me a crisp carrot from the refrigerator. My little hands were too numb for my fingers to close, so I held it in both hands. When I brought it up to my mouth it tasted delicious to a starving little girl. Since I couldn't hold a glass of milk in my trembling hands, he gave me one of my sister Jill's bottles of milk.

Dad sat down in his easy chair with a bottle of beer in his hand. He continued to drink beer after beer as the summer sun went down. He didn't bother to turn the lights on. He just sat in his chair and drank. I watched the sunlight fade and the shadows lengthen. The street lights came on, and my imagination ran wild. It was very dark outside. God, how I hated the dark! Our living room seemed gloomy and sad because the pale blue drapes were always drawn. Thankfully the headlights from cars occasionally lit up the room a little bit. From my perch on the couch, I could barely see dad as he drank. When I was with dad, this was the best part of my day, but I still felt alone and frightened.

After a while, I went to the refrigerator and stole another carrot for myself. Since I never knew when I would get to eat again, I stocked up on food when I could. I hoped that mom wasn't counting the carrots because if she was, I would get another beating. She loved to see how long I could go without eating.

I ravenously devoured my stolen food, then I got a bottle of beer for daddy. I wanted to make him happy because he was my only hope of escaping mom's tortures. I carried the beer in both hands; my arms still ached from being tied. I was still trailing strips of torn sheets from my ankles and wrists as I hurried to the living room. I scampered over to daddy with a beer.

He said, "Thank you, Georgie. You're a good girl."

I always loved it when dad was home and mom was away. Sometimes when I was alone with dad, he would untie me, feed me, and even let me play. I loved to watch cartoons on the television with dad. He even let me climb on the furniture, because he didn't really care what I did. Mom would never let me do any of those things. Daddy sometimes said nice things to me. It made me feel that he would save me someday. I soon fell into a fitful sleep on the couch. I awoke for a moment as dad picked me up and carried me to the bed.

He tied the torn sheets that were still around my wrists back to the bedposts. The strips of cloth were now considerably shorter than before he had cut them. He had to painfully stretch my body in order to get enough slack to tie the knots, and it hurt a lot. I begged him not to do this to me, but he continued to replace all of the bindings and the tape around my mouth.

He said, "Georgianne, your mother punishes you because you're bad. She'd be mad at all of us if she came home and you were untied."

Tears poured down my face as dad went to the kitchen to get another beer. He came back after a while and kissed me on the forehead. Then he said, "Be good, Georgianne. Your mother will be home soon."

I couldn't reply because my mouth was taped closed, so I just stared at him. He then went to his room and closed the door.

My wrists and ankles were already covered with raw wounds from months of being bound. The fresh scabs reopened and began to bleed. The cloth of the bindings soaked up the trickle, and soon the bleeding stopped.

By the time mom arrived home, dad was in bed asleep but I was wide awake. I could hear her going to the bathroom. As I lay there, my body convulsed with the fear of my impending beating. I felt that I must have been very bad. I was really terrified of receiving a thrashing while tied face up on the bed. I knew that I couldn't close my legs or hide my face from the belt. The hours of stark terror waiting for the next beating was just as bad as the beating would be.

The bedroom door opened slowly, and my mother stood there examining my vulnerable, bruised body. In her hand she had the same heavy belt she had used on me earlier in the day. She wickedly smiled down at me as she gently swung that belt back and forth in the air. "Good night, Georgie," she said. Then she suddenly turned, walked to her bedroom, and shut the door.

I was so relieved that she didn't hurt me that the muscles in my bladder relaxed, and a warm puddle formed under me. It was so dark and I was so scared that I didn't think that I could sleep, but my arms soon became numb enough for me to fall into a restless, fitful slumber. I was finally released the next morning, and I tried to stay out of the way and not make a mess.

My mom was a meticulous housekeeper who didn't like to have anything out of place. This included Jill and me, so once we were big enough to crawl, we were often tied up. Usually we were just secured, but sometimes we were beaten before we were bound, and sometimes we were beaten while we were bound. I would soon learn that if I cried too much, I would be struck until I stopped.

Chapter Three

The Fairytale Princess

JILL AND I WENT HUNGRY on many occasions. Often our entire day's food was a single cold hot dog with no bun. We ate sporadically because one of mom's favorite punishments was to withhold our food and water for periods of up to two days. When we were finally fed, we ate like wild animals. When we would play in the yard, I was usually obsessed with finding food.

One day Jill woke me up whispering, "I am hungry."

"Me too," I groggily replied.

We both tiptoed into the kitchen so that we wouldn't wake up mom. That's the last thing in the world we would want to do.

"I don't think mom is home," I whispered to Jill.

"Uh huh," she replied

We both scrounged for food, but we didn't find any. No milk. No bread. Not even a box of cereal.

I looked at my sister's sad eyes and suggested a dangerous scheme: "We could go to the store and steal candy."

"Oh no," Jill cried. "Mom would be mad."

I put my small arm around her and said, "Not if we don't get caught."

Jill replied, "The man watches the candy. I'm scared."

I said, "Maybe we'll get an apple or banana. If we stay away from candy, maybe we won't get caught."

Jill tried to sound brave and hesitantly said, "Okay, I guess."

I just knew that we would get caught, but I was hungry and had little to lose. After all, I was beaten nearly every day, so I might as well have some food to eat before the next beating.

I was scared and trembling as we quietly tiptoed down the stairs and slowly worked our way into the convenience store next to granddad's club. Actually, Jill was even better at survival skills than I. She had a natural charm and beauty that was beguiling and innocent. Who wouldn't trust that smiling, poker-faced cherub with nerves of steel. Jill, street-wise far beyond her years, took her small doll up to the store owner and showed it to him. He probably knew that both of us were candy thieves, so he tried to watch his merchandise as he looked at the doll. While the shop owner was distracted, I stole two bananas and was quickly out the door. I waited behind the Lido for Jill. In a minute she was by my side. We hugged and sat on the ground to eat our purloined breakfast. Jill and I were hungry, crafty, feral children who survived by our wits. We were good, really good. We over-matched the store owner this day.

We knew better than to take our trophies home, because mom might be up. We ate slowly, savoring every bite. We were happy to have eaten and even happier that we got away with stealing our breakfast. As we tiptoed back upstairs, our eyes met and Jill smiled. Without saying a word we just headed for our beds, triumphant.

A few days later, Jill and I stole candy from the corner grocery store again, but this time we were caught. When the store owner told mom about it, she was furious.

Mom threw me into the kitchen. I lost my balance and skidded on the floor. I looked up and saw her eyes filled with rage.

Mom yelled, "Steal from the store and make me look bad. I'll show you what happens to little girls that try to make me look bad."

The black belt struck my legs. I screamed and tried to get away from her, but my legs could get no traction. The belt struck again.

"I'm sorry, mommy, "I sobbed. "Please, I'll never do it again."

She would not hear my pleas. She just kept screaming and hitting me. When she got exhausted, she dropped the belt and walked out of the kitchen. I squirmed into a corner and tried to rub my legs to ease the pain. We went without food for two days after that.

No one knew how hungry we were, because mom seldom let anyone into her apartment. I think she was afraid people would turn her in for child abuse. She had already lost three children, after neighbors and concerned relatives turned her in, and she wasn't about to lose two more. We were her favorite playthings, and if she played a little rough, well, that was her business. We were her kids after all.

Mom loved the idea of having children. In the summer of 1949, she became pregnant again. Dad was only lukewarm to the idea of another child and all of the commotion it would cause.

One day, dad even confronted mom about the child abuse. The argument soon escalated into a fistfight, during which dad punched mom in the face and in her pregnant stomach. Granddad called the police, and Peter was taken to jail.

A couple of days later, Peter was sentenced to 90 days for beating his expectant wife. The authorities thought that it would be better for mom if dad were sent out of town, so Peter Burowsky was sent to Albany, New York, to serve his time. Albany was two hours south of Plattsburgh.

Mom told her sister, "I hate Peter. That bastard nearly killed me. I hope he rots in jail. I swear I'll kill him if he touches me again."

Later that evening, mom began to get morose as she downed beer after beer. She nervously crushed out her cigarette and began to weep. "I know Peter loves me and the kids. He wouldn't get so upset with me if I didn't deserve it. I've got to go to Albany and get him out of jail. I really love him so much."

The next week, mom went to Albany and made dad promise not to hit her or interfere with the upbringing of the kids ever again. Then she got him out of jail.

Dad had served 11 days of his three-month sentence. On the way back to Plattsburgh, they made up and were in love again.

On January 16, 1950, Peter Burowsky welcomed his first son into the family. They were both thankful that the beating dad gave mom hadn't hurt their perfect new son. They named the strong, healthy child, Peter John Burowsky, Jr. Little Peter was a good-looking baby with a pleasant temperament. On March 5, 1950, he was baptized at St. Peter's church. Peter's best friend, Theodore Hudyma ("Hoochie"), sponsored little Peter's baptism. Hoochie and dad had occasionally worked together as window washers before the war. The other witness was Veronica's mom, Alice Trombley. Peter was wearing his suit, and Veronica was wearing her best tailored blue wool suit. Everyone commented on what a fine-looking family the Burowskys made. Veronica and Peter both loved to dress up in fine clothing when they were out in the public. Peter, in particular, always wore a tie whenever he could.

Even when dad was at home, he was well-dressed and merely removed his tie. Mom, on the other hand, seldom wore any clothing at all when she was at home, and neither did us kids except during playtime. One of mom's favorite hobbies was to buy fine dresses for Jill and me. For some reason, mom always liked the way that Jill looked in her dresses, but she was never satisfied with my appearance.

Most of our days were the same. Jill and I would wake up early and play in our room. Mom woke up late. She would clean the house for a while, and then she would come into our room to play dress-up with us. Jill and I had the finest clothing that was available in Plattsburgh.

One day, mom put my long, red hair in a ponytail. Then she dressed me in my pretty pale-yellow jumper with a matching hat and delicate, white gloves. The skirt was held out to my side by many white petticoats. Mom taught me to sing "Home On The Range," then she placed me in front of the full-length mirror and sat down beside me. I looked at my scrawny body and then at her nude glory. I hoped that I would look like her someday. Mom gave me a hairbrush to use as a microphone, and we sang "Home On The Range" together.

Sometimes mom was in a bad mood, and we didn't have a dress-up day. When these black moods gripped her, she loved to punch me in the face. I often had visible bruises and black eyes that mom didn't want the neighbors to see. I hated it when I was too bruised to go out and play. That meant I had to spend the day with mom.

Mom didn't want my beautiful clothes messed up, so they were always taken off me before I was beaten and tied. Dad would usually untie me when he got home from work, but he would always tie me back up for the night when he went to bed.

Except for occasional lapses, mom wanted us to be clean. She would give us hot baths with excessively vigorous scrubbing. That hurt a lot. Mom occasionally liked to give us a thrashing right after she gave us a bath. She would say, "It hurts more when you're wet, doesn't it?"

She also liked to experiment with new ways of causing pain. I remember one time when she beat me alternately with a wooden spoon and then a belt. She said, "Does this hurt more?" WHACK! She hit me with the wooden spoon. "Or does this hurt more?"—SLAP!—she asked as she hit me with the belt. I knew she was toying with me, so I didn't answer. She examined the welts and the expressions on my face for clues as to which punishment was the most severe. "Doesn't the spoon hurt the most?" WHACK! "Stop your damn crying or I'll really give you something to cry about." SLAP! "Oh yes, that's welting up nicely. The spoon definitely hurts worse than the belt, doesn't it?" WHACK! "You're daddy's spoiled little princess aren't you?" WHACK! "I'm going to beat you until you learn how to behave." WHACK!

I think I was beaten more because I had pride. I wouldn't allow myself to cry, at least, not easily. I tried to control my emotions. Sometimes I would pretend that I wasn't even there. I could look her right in the eye and never see her, because I would look right through her.

Sometimes mom would be too tired to get up and beat me. On those occasions she would throw things at me. Shoes, forks, table knives, water glasses, and plates were her favorite. Fortunately, she had a bad aim, and I was seldom hit. After each fit, she would demand that I pick up the mess right away and return her "missiles" in case she wanted to throw them again.

I don't know what made mom so mean. It undoubtedly had something to do with her fiery temperament and her drinking. I think that her compulsive neatness also had something to do with it. Mom had no idea that children were different than adults. She didn't understand that crying is a baby's way to communicate or that potty training had to be gradually learned.

Mom tried to be a good mother. She often took hours gently combing my hair and putting it up in a fancy hairdos. I enjoyed standing there as she made me look beautiful. I had many different, frilly, colorful dresses and boxes of flouncy, white, crinoline petticoats. The best part of this play was when mom would coo and cuddle with me and say, "Oh, Georgie, aren't you the most beautiful little girl in the world? Go to the mirror and take a look. Okay, that's it, turn around. Now curtsy. No, remember to hold your hem when you curtsy. Georgie, Georgie, Georgie, I can't believe it you look just like a little princess in a fairytale."

After we played dress-up for a while, mom would undress me and carefully fold my pretty dresses and put them away. Jill and I would then go back to our room and wile away the morning dressing our many dolls.

Dancing Blue Flames

ONE DAY, MOM PUT MY HAIR UP in a pretty hairdo that made me look much older. Then she brought out a new, dark, navy-blue dress with white lace around the neck, sleeves, and the hem of the skirt. It had a square-cut bodice and was quite short. When I looked in the mirror, I was so proud of the way I looked. I spun around a couple of times and then struck a pose with one arm in the air and my leg out to the side. I tried to look like the dancers I had seen on Sid Caesar's, "Your Show Of Shows."

I said, "Mommy, mommy, look at me. I'm a star."

Mom didn't say any thing. She just got a scary, far-away look in her eyes. She sat on the edge of my bed and glared at me for the longest time.

Then she said, "Georgie, you look ..." Mom stood up and continued, "Take that damn dress off this instant."

I stood there motionless and started to cry.

Mom stormed out of the room, shouting over her shoulder, "Stop that crying or I'll give you something to cry about."

I was very frightened so I yanked the dress up over my head. When mom returned, I was still lightly sobbing, I was as naked as she was.

Mom had an odd look on her face that I had never seen before or since. It was somewhere between hatred and glee.

Mom reached down and scooped me up, but instead of picking me up in the normal way, she had me in some complicated grip that held my legs against my chest. We were eyeball to eyeball, with my legs sticking straight up over mom's shoulders. Her death grip on my elbows hurt and caused me to sob. I tried to squirm, but I found that both my arms and my legs were immobilized. Mom carried me out of my bedroom, down the hall, across the kitchen, and straight to our white, four-burner Hotpoint gas range. At that point in my young life, all I knew about the range was that it was where cooked food came from.

Mom was about to teach me something new about stoves. The large front burner on the right was already burning full blast. "So you think you are hot. I'll show you hot!" I looked over my shoulder and watched the dancing blue flames as we approached the range. When we reached the blazing burner, mom held me about 10 inches over the flames. I instantly felt a blast of intense heat enveloping my body. At my height from the stove, it wasn't hot enough to cause damage, but I was profoundly uncomfortable and frightened. I looked over my shoulder and found that I could see the wavering heat waves that enveloped my body.

She quickly bent her knees and lowered my bottom into the inferno. The licking flames swirled around my legs. The pain was intense, and I screamed at the top of my lungs! The instant my bottom reached the flames, mom screamed and dropped me. I tumbled to the floor on my head. I was dazed, but I rolled over on my back to let the cool linoleum sooth my blistered bottom.

Mom rushed to the sink shouting, "Ouch, ouch, ouch." She ran cold water onto a washrag. "God damn you, Georgie, you worthless piece of trash." She held the dripping washrag up to the lower swell of her nude left breast. "Look what you made me do. By God you will pay for this. You think this is funny, but we'll see who has the last laugh."

Mom poured herself another tall drink of vodka and locked herself in the bedroom.

Mom was very depressed after the birth of Peter on April 12, 1950. She took an overdose of sleeping pills and was rushed to the hospital, where she stayed four days. With mom in the hospital, granddad went to look in on Peter, Jill and me. He discovered that we had been severely abused and took us to the hospital. Our family doctor was shocked at our condition. We had scars and bruises all over our bodies, so the doctor called the police and recommended that we children be placed in emergency foster care for our protection.

Peter, Jr. was sent to the home of Bert and Delima Burnah. They were a nice Catholic family who lived in nearby Redford, New York. The Burnahs had signed up to be foster parents, and Peter, Jr. was their first placement. Jill and I did not stay with the Burnahs. We went somewhere else, but I don't remember the people's names, and the records are now lost. All I remember is that Jill was not with me, and the people treated me with love and kindness.

On April 16, 1950, my birth mom was released from the hospital. It was her 25th birthday. She stopped in at her father's bar for a beer before going home. Granddad told her that the Clinton County Child Protective Services had taken us away. Mom drank and cried late into the night before going home to dad.

On July 1, 1950, mom was arrested for some minor offense. Granddad used his money and influence to get her off without jail time or a record. A few days later, mom and dad got permission to visit us. They were quite drunk and made a bad impression on our foster parents. Mom wanted us back and she didn't give up. Two months later, while mom was fairly sober, she arranged with Child Protective Services to get Jill and me back. The caseworker didn't think that mom was quite ready for Peter, Jr., so he was allowed to stay with the Burnahs for another year. Bert and Delima wanted to adopt Peter, but mom and dad were dead-set against it.

Jill and I were given back to mom and dad. At first, mom seemed to be much better. She didn't drink much nor did Peter, Sr., for that matter. Mom also had help from her family, the church, and a part-time housekeeper. After a few weeks, things were going so well for mom that she felt she could start to drink a little more. Mom started partying late into the night, every day.

On the housekeeper's days off, mom would wake late and spend hours cleaning the house. Mom was much more meticulous at cleaning than the housekeeper was. Mom complained loudly about the housekeeper's cleaning ability as she worked.

When the housekeeper was working, mom yelled at her about her sloppy work. Mom also didn't like the looks that the housekeeper gave her when she woke up with a hangover and yelled at us kids. Granddad was giving Veronica and Peter less money than they would have liked. For all of these reasons, the housekeeper was soon let go. Mom also apparently felt that she needed less support. She stopped going to church as well, and she started keeping her family at bay.

Bea And Doody

A FEW DAYS LATER, granddad discovered me tied to the bed, lying in my own waste. Then he found Jill hungry and crying. Granddad got so mad that he went to the Child Protective Services and turned his daughter in again.

When I entered foster care, I was obviously malnourished and had been mistreated for quite some time. There were scars and bruises on my wrists, neck, waist and ankles, as well as on my face. On July 31, 1951, the Child Protective Services entered these notes in my record:

> We received a referral from George Trombley, Veronica Trombley's father. Our investigation disclosed that Veronica Trombley's daughter Georgianne had a bottom that was black and blue with broken skin spots. The children frequently went without dinner. Grandfather reported the birth mother frequently spanked the children severely and left them alone on their beds for extended periods. When the child, Georgianne, arrived in the system, she was very upset. She screamed and clawed at anyone who came near her. Over time the welfare workers calmed her down. On July 31, 1951, Georgianne told this department that her mother was mean to her and she did not want to return to live with her.

On August 1, 1951, the police and the social workers pulled down my panties and gasped about my bruises and burns. They felt that the stress of so many children was too much for mom. It was decided at that time that Jill and I should go into foster care again. Little Peter was still at the Burnahs' foster home. A family member had adopted my sister Debbie. Mom's oldest boy, Pug, was still with Granddad George. When I arrived at my new foster home, a couple met me at the door, and the lady said, "You can call us Aunt Bea and Uncle Doody."

"Okay," I replied. I would be an adult before I discovered that I wasn't related by blood to Aunt Bea and Uncle Doody.

This small, brown-haired woman bent down close to my face, put her hand on my shoulder, and said, "How old are you, darling."

I didn't like to be touched, but I didn't run or squirm. I just gritted my teeth and held up three fingers.

Aunt Bea smiled and said, "My, what a smart girl you are."

I noticed Aunt Bea had a broad smile that lit up the room of her beautiful and clean home. A crucifix and pictures of Jesus were on several walls of the small, white farmhouse. Aunt Bea was a devoutly religious woman, who wore simple, clean cotton dresses. Although her hands were tiny, they seemed to always be busy.

Uncle Doody was a strong man of medium height and build. He looked me over with the practiced eye of a man who could tell how much lumber a twisted sapling could make. Uncle Doody was a lumber expert who worked at the Diamond Sawmill as a wood scaler.

He had a laugh that made me feel less frightened just hearing it. His hands were strong, big and frightening. He gave me a hug, and that scared me a lot. I was frightened when the nice social worker pulled away in her big car. What would these strange people do to me?

My memories of the time I spent at the Duquette foster home are good ones. Aunt Bea and Uncle Doody turned out to be very nice people. I was happy there. My world was filled with pretty dresses and sunshine. I wore ringlets and bows in my hair. I remember lace curtains on the windows and nice, clean sheets on the bed.

In the mornings while Uncle Doody was at work, I adored running out to his small red barn trimmed in white, with Lady, our big, old, gentle, black dog. When Uncle Doody would get home, he would take me with him for a walk. I held his hand as we strolled down to the barn or out to the pasture. His hands were big, warm and gentle. I would eagerly watch Uncle Doody while he milked our one cow. Sometimes he would squirt some milk our way, and the dog or I would try to catch the warm, sweet liquid in our mouths.

When I first arrived at Aunt Bea's, I was a difficult child, and I had many odd behaviors. It was difficult for me to have anyone approach me. I was not potty trained. I didn't like to take a bath, and I wouldn't go near the cooking stove. It seemed that I was afraid of everything. Aunt Bea was gentle and loving and most of all, she was patient with me.

Mom started going to church, where she made sure to talk with the priest a lot. She told him all about how she loved Jesus and Mother Mary. Every week, mom also wrote a large tithe check out to the church. She somehow convinced the priest that she had changed and that it was best for us children if we could be returned to her.

That spring, mom also met regularly with the welfare department about getting us back. When she had an appointment, mom would first put on one of her beautiful, tailored, brightly colored summer dresses and go down to the beauty parlor and have her hair and nails done. Mom usually drove a big, cobalt-blue Buick, but when she went to the welfare office she drove granddad's more impressive gold Lincoln so that they would know that they weren't dealing with poor folks. Mom was sober, well-dressed, neat and polite. Mom told the social workers that she and Peter were moving to Chicago in hopes of starting over. She said that she wanted to take her children with her.

Everyone at the welfare office was amazed that Veronica was now much better. They felt that maybe Veronica had finally changed her ways. So the people of the Clinton County Welfare Department crossed their fingers and told mom that if she checked with the Catholic Home Bureau of Chicago and got their permission, she could get us back.

The next week, mom and dad moved to Chicago. Peter soon got a good job working as a machine operator for the Rheem Manufacturing Co., located at 7600 South Kedzie. Dad's shift was from 8 in the morning until 4 in the afternoon on weekdays. Mom continued going to church, and she cultivated the priest to help her get her kids back.

My mom and dad met with the officials from the Catholic Home Bureau of Chicago and told the priest that they had quit drinking and that Peter had gotten a good job. The priest talked to mom and dad about God and about responsibility. They told him that they both loved Jesus. One day a church representative even went to the Burowsky home unannounced and found that mom kept a clean house.

On July 15, 1952, the Catholic Home Bureau of Chicago sent a letter to the Clinton County Child Protective Services. This letter said that our parents were settled in and that they were doing much better. It also said that it was time for their children to return to their parents' home in Chicago. Mom was jubilant when she was told. The next Saturday, my birth mother and stepdad drove mom's Buick from Chicago, Illinois, back to Plattsburgh, New York. The trip took 24 hours that was spread out over two days. They stayed with granddad overnight on Sunday.

On Monday morning, Aunt Bea knelt down on one knee. She looked me in the eyes and said, "You must leave now because you're going back to live with your mom and dad."

I cried and stammered, "No. Whatever I did, I promise not to do it again. Please don't make me go."

Aunt Bea's eyes filled with tears. She held me. "You didn't do anything wrong. I love you and I always will."

I desperately clung to her. She was the only love I knew. My two years here had been filled with love and kindness. I grew and flourished under Aunt Bea's gentle care. She had given me back my childhood and taught me to trust again. At the age of five I could not understand why I had to leave this wonderful home.

Aunt Bea continued, "I love you, but you have to go now. Be a good and brave girl."

Jill and I both had sad eyes in the fall of 1952, because the courts had taken us out of good homes and put us back with our birth parents.

When mom and dad arrived, dad came over, picked me up, and said, "I bet you would like some ice cream."

"No. I want Aunt Bea." My little hands desperately clawed at the air trying to get back to Aunt Bea's loving arms. I continued begging long after we had left her. I hoped that if I cried and pleaded enough that I would be allowed to stay with Aunt Bea. I was wasting my tears. I didn't know that a distant official in far-away Chicago had already decided my fate. I climbed onto the large package-shelf under the back window and sobbed. My sister Jill was also crying. She too had been torn away from a home that she loved. The tears and pleas were the only sounds heard in the car.

I eventually cried myself out. I calmed down a little and climbed down from the package-shelf. I looked around the car and was surprised to discover that mom was holding a baby. Mom told me that the baby was named Donna. I wondered if Donna would be strong enough to survive in our world. About an hour later, we arrived in nearby Redford, New York, to pick up little Peter.

Peter, Jr. was a very small two-year-old. He had a beautiful face crowned with short, blonde hair. I like to remember Peter the way I saw him that day, because his blue eyes sparkled when I first saw him. When we arrived at the Burnahs' foster home, they started crying. The Burnahs were devastated at being forced to give up the toddler. They suspected that he would be going to a hell-on-earth, but they were powerless to stop it.

Mom and dad were angry that all three of their children were crying and begging to go back to the homes they had left instead of being happy to be with them again. They stopped at the first liquor store to stock up for the long trip ahead.

By the time we got to Buffalo, mom and dad were quite drunk and their mood was foul. Mom felt that we were making too much noise with our intermittent weeping. She taped our hands behind our backs and taped our mouths shut. Peter and I lay on the seat of the car. Jill was placed lying on the floor of the back seat. My parents had achieved the peace and quiet that they desired. I was filled with apprehension.

When we arrived at our apartment in Chicago, it was late and everyone was tired. We all went straight to bed. Jill, Peter and I were still bound and gagged. We weren't untied until the next day. Our new life in Chicago had begun. I would come to remember this place forever as a house of horror.

Goodnight, Georgie

OUR NEW APARTMENT was in a large, old, two-story house that had been converted into a triplex. There was a long common hallway through the center of the house, with a door on the left where a nice older woman lived. Farther down the hall on the right was a long staircase that led to the upstairs apartment of a Japanese family.

Straight ahead at the end of the hall was the door that led to our big living room. When the couch was folded out, this room also doubled as mom and dad's bedroom. The room next to the living room was the kitchen. It was mainly memorable because all of the walls were painted a bright lemon-yellow. The refrigerator was placed in the far corner of the room, but it wasn't flush with the wall, it was cattycorner. I would become very familiar with the pie-shaped space next to the refrigerator in the near future.

When morning came, mom untied us and took us into the kitchen for breakfast. We were scared and our wrists and arms hurt from being tied all night. Our first day was just scary. We didn't know what to do. We just sat at the table and tried to make breakfast last as long as possible. Mom had some toys for us to play with, and we stayed in the bedroom and were quiet until lunchtime. Lunch came and went, but no food appeared for us. Afraid to say or do anything, we just continued to play with our toys. One by one, we all fell asleep on the floor. When dad got home, we all sat at the table and had dinner. We were very hungry and thirsty, and we ate fast, afraid it would be taken from us.

After supper, mom opened the door to the bathroom. "Peter, this is your room."

I stuck my neck into the room and glanced around. It was just a regular bathroom. There was no bed. I was perplexed. Then we went back across the kitchen, and mom opened the broom-closet door. "Georgie, this is your room." I glanced inside. It was about two feet deep and approximately four feet long. It was much smaller than Donna's crib, let alone Jill's twin bed.

"Mom, I want a bed like Jill has," I whined.

"Shut the hell up and get in there." She hit me in the stomach, I fell backwards into my "room," and she slammed the door. I stayed in that tiny closet for the rest of the night and sobbed. That night I slept in my clothes on the cold closet floor. It was late fall. Once the door was closed, my "room" had no heat, and the temperature dropped a lot. This closet was on the north side of the kitchen, and it never got any sun. The cold soon became unbearable. I had no way to keep warm except by shivering.

The second night after we arrived, I followed mom around as she put everyone to bed. First, mom roughly dropped Donna into her crib. This harsh treatment caused Donna to cry.

Jill was then sent to her bed, where she huddled under the blankets, with only her eyes showing. My little sister stared straight at the ceiling and didn't move a muscle. I wondered what she was thinking.

Mom took Peter into the bathroom and removed all of his clothing. She then twisted heavy copper wire around his wrists. I could see that this was uncomfortable for Peter, because he began to sob and struggle. Mom then stretched his little hands above his head and wired him to two water pipes that were covered with peeling white paint. The pipes were about an inch in diameter and about six inches apart. They ran from floor to ceiling beside the bathtub and directly in front of the toilet.

The sound of Peter and Donna sobbing was all I could hear as mom stripped me of my clothes. Long strips of torn bed sheets were tied to my wrists. Then I was carried to the closet. The other ends of these ribbons of cloth were hooked over a couple of bent nails that mom had pounded into the outside, north wall of the closet. My arms were held straight out to my sides like a crucifix. My mother then forced a large, speckled, porcelain chamber pot between my quivering legs. I was a very small five-year-old girl, and the sharp, cold edge of the pot was painful for me to straddle.

It was impossible to sit or to lie down. I could only stand. Then mom gently said, "Good night, Georgie," and closed my door.

Sleep was unattainable. I sobbed and screamed for many hours. No one came. I slumped in my bonds. That made the pain in my shoulders worse, so I stood up straight again. First, my fingers went numb, then my arms. My legs began to quiver, and I was afraid that

I would fall. I maneuvered the cold, sharp chamber pot from between my legs, then I just stood there sobbing and waited for morning.

Sometime during the night, I became semiconscious in a trance-like mode, where I was still standing but unaware of the world or my pain. I wasn't even aware when it was morning. When mom opened my door, she saw that I had moved my chamber pot during the night. She was furious and slapped me awake, yelling at me about the chamber pot. Then she slammed the door. I sobbed for a few more minutes or maybe hours and then went back into my zombie-like state. I was just awake enough to remain standing, but that was all.

I was released the next day and fed. I then went back to my closet. I pushed the chamber pot to one end, and I curled up on the floor. From that day on, most of my nights were spent tied up in the closet. I spent my days trying to be quiet and hiding from mom. I slept and ate when and where I could. My life was a living hell.

My brother's life was no better. Night after night, Peter was forced to stand naked in the bathroom, where he was wired to the pipes. His hands were wired over his head instead of straight out to the side, like mine were. Even though the bathroom was heated, the iron pipes conducted heat so well that they were always cold on Peter's thin body.

Sometimes mom would make us kneel all night. This was much better than hanging in the closet. Most of the time she forced me to kneel on the floor

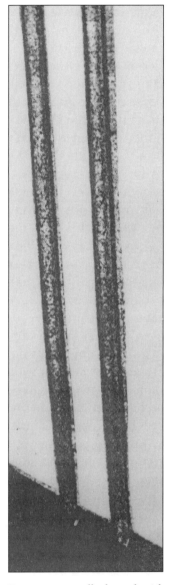

Peter was usually bound with heavy copper wire to these pipes in our bathroom.
-Chicago American, July 29, 1953-

in the small, pie-shaped space between the refrigerator and wall. The bad part of the kneeling was the rule that if you fell asleep and she caught you curled up on the floor, she would wake you with a frenzied beating. Other times, mom made us kids kneel on the furnace grate in the floor of the living room. The furnace grate was horrible because it cut into my knees, and after a few hours the pain became unendurable. In the winter the grate was even worse because of the hot air blowing through it. It was like being in the desert all day. The heat was insufferable. Sometimes I would faint from the heat, only to be beaten back awake. Sometimes we were forced to kneel on broom handles. Jill usually got this extremely painful treatment. The only torture not used on me was the pipes. Peter was the only one to be wired to the water pipes in the bathroom.

My brother and I discovered that it was impossible to cry, scream or whimper for 24 hours a day, seven days a week, no matter how bad the pain. I think that there's a limit to how much agony and fear a mind can handle. Our common dilemma was how to stay alive and stay sane.

Mom really enjoyed playing with Donna and talking baby talk to her. I remember one time when mom was in a good mood, she took Donna into her arms and cooed as she stroked her hair. "Are you mommy's precious little darling? Yes you are." Mom held Donna and cuddled her to her bosom. "Oh, what a wonderful little girl you are. Does mommy's little girl need her diaper changed?"

Although mom was a stickler for a clean house, she hated to change diapers and sometimes wouldn't change Donna's for more than a day. But this day, she set about carefully and gently changing Donna's diapers.

When she finished, mom washed up and went to the kitchen and put some water on to boil. As the water started to heat up, mom placed a bottle of formula in the pan. While the pan started to heat, mom opened a bottle of rum and took a shot straight then dropped a small but healthy shot into the warm formula. Mom took another shot. She then put some hot dogs into the same hot water for the rest of us to eat. She put each hot dog onto a slice of white bread and gave one to Peter, Jill and me. She gave the bottle to Donna. I don't think Donna liked the taste of rum very much, but she was hungry and drank it all. Donna went right to sleep. Mom got beers and a hot dog for herself and for dad, then pulled Peter gently into her lap and lovingly combed his short, blond hair. "Aren't you getting to be a handsome little man, you worthless bum," she cooed.

"Yes, mommy," he said, as he concentrated on the first food that he had eaten in days. "I wanna wadda," he murmured

"Georgianne, get up off your lazy ass and get some water for the bum!" she screamed!

"Yes ma'am," I said as I rushed to get the water. I had learned to never keep mom waiting.

Mom purred, "You are going to be such a big, strong man, aren't you?" Little Peter didn't pay much attention to her. He was too busy savoring his water and precious hot dog. She then sat down to watch television.

With both of my parents working and with help from granddad, we had some fairly nice furniture, including the wonder of the age, a console black-and-white television set. We were among the first people on the block to have one. Mom had fallen in love with television in 1948, when Granddad George had installed sets in his house and in the nightclub. As soon as television became affordable, mom and dad had to have one. Mom loved to watch Arthur Godfrey, Milton Berle, and a who-done-it called "Stand By for Crime." We soon learned it was never a good idea to disturb her in the middle of a program she liked.

Christmas Surprise

AFTER THANKSGIVING, late fall turned into an early, hard winter. Mom loved Christmas, and she began preparing for our first Yuletide back together. My mother worried and became obsessed about having a perfect Christmas for us. She spent too much money and became so anxious, that the spirit of the season was completely spoiled for her.

On Christmas Eve of 1952, children all over the world were nestled snugly in their beds waiting for Santa Claus. Our preparations were quite different. Mom first tied Donna in her crib. Then she tied Peter in the bathroom. When mom came to me, I begged her not to tie me in the closet. I should have known better. She slapped me until I quit begging. I sobbed bitterly but said nothing more as she tied me to the wall that night.

Mom said, "I want to have everything perfect on Christmas morning, and I don't want you to mess up the house or spoil the surprise of opening your presents. You understand don't you, dear?"

I didn't understand, but I didn't want her to explain it to me with her fist so I just stood there crying.

On Christmas morning, mom was very proud of how nice her house looked. Dad took our picture as we opened our presents. Donna got a Raggedy Ann doll, while Peter got a big, yellow, metal dump truck. Jill and I got matching baby dolls and carriages. Mom loved toys, and she would spend a large amount of money on toys for us. We all got tricycles, blocks, and stuffed animals. We girls were also given a Susie Homemaker Playhouse Set. It had a toy kitchen, including a stove, sink, and a refrigerator. It even had a toy washing machine and a child-size ironing board and iron. Unfortunately, I was far too physically exhausted and mentally discouraged to play with any enthusiasm that day.

I hurt terribly, but the allure of the dolls finally got to me, and we three girls played with them all afternoon. Peter played with his truck by himself. Mom and dad toasted that Christmas with rum egg nogs.

That night, mom let Peter and me sleep in Jill's bed. We even had sheets and blankets.

Mom warned, "Don't expect to sleep in a bed every night and don't wet Jill's bed, if you know what is good for you."

I hadn't spent a night in bed for a long time, and it really felt good. I stayed up late talking and playing with Jill and Peter. Then I stayed awake most of the night to make sure I didn't wet the bed. Early in the morning I had to go to the bathroom, so I quietly got up so as not to wake up mom. I pulled the heavy, blue curtain that crossed the doorway to one side. I heard a crash! It was a trap! Mom had piled all of our toys up on the hem of the curtain. When I had touched the drape, all of our toys had fallen with a CRASH!

Mom came raging and yelling out of her bedroom. She was very mad and beat me for getting out of bed. I spent the rest of the night in the closet tied to the wall. Mom said, "Damn you, Georgie, that's the last straw. You will never sleep in a bed again." She looked like she meant it.

Jill cried that Christmas night also. I think that she was the most sensitive of us children and the most prone to be angry or upset. I believed that it hurt her more when she had to watch me, Peter or Donna being tortured than when she was hurt herself. Maybe Jill was afraid that she would eventually be tortured herself. Who knows? All I know is that Jill cried a lot.

I could tell that Jill cared for us, because often at night she would come into the closet and talk to me while I hung on the wall. If she felt she could get away with it, she would also bring me a drink of water or a piece of bread. Probably the worst part of Jill's average day was when she had to go to the bathroom. Jill always closed her eyes and cried as she sat on the commode so that she didn't have to watch Peter writhing in agony on his place on the pipes. Jill couldn't do anything to help him. He was always bound with wire too heavy for Jill to unwind.

Our days were better than nights, because that winter and spring, Jill and I played outside as much as possible. The yard was my happy place, even when it was cold. It was a much safer place than the house, but the safety was something of an illusion. One day as I listlessly played in the yard, I was too hungry to do much except think about food. It had been a day and a half since I had last eaten. I glanced up and saw mom's angry eyes bore into me. I quickly looked away.

Mom snarled, "Get in here. What the hell are you looking at? Don't give me that look! Get in here. Right this instant."

I rushed into the house. I tried to scurry out of mom's line of sight, but I wasn't quick enough. She threw a half-empty plate of spaghetti at my head. I ducked and the plate crashed against the kitchen wall, breaking into many sharp shards of green glass.

I ran to the bedroom, where my sister Donna was tied in her crib. I hoped that mom was too drunk to come after me. Mom took several minutes to finish her drink. Then she came looking for me. When she found me, she knocked me off my feet with a blow to my face. Then she dragged me by my hair into the kitchen. She pointed to the spaghetti and the broken glass on the wall and floor and snarled, "Look at the mess you made." She lifted me off the floor by my hair and one of my arms and stood me on the table. Mom unbuttoned my jumper and pulled it off over my head. She unlaced my black-and-white saddle oxfords and yanked them and my socks off. Mom grabbed my hair and hauled me back down to the floor. Then she threw me like a bowling ball across the floor. I skidded, tumbled, and spun on my back across the yellow linoleum until I hit the wall at the same spot that was covered with spaghetti. Pasta, glass and blood flew everywhere.

"If this mess isn't cleaned up by the time I get back from the bathroom, you're going to be sorry you were born!"

It was true. I was sorry that I had been born, but I didn't take the time to worry about that now. I knew that mom could always make me sorrier.

I examined the spaghetti quickly and closely. Then I reached into the biggest mass, which didn't seem to have any glass in it. I stuffed as much spaghetti as I could into my mouth. It tasted good, even if it was a bit crunchy from having dirt in it. I dug my hand in again and stuffed some more spaghetti into my mouth. I wiped my lips so mom wouldn't know that I had stolen some food. I then bent down and pulled a sliver of glass out of my leg. Then I furiously set to work, cleaning like my life depended on it.

Long before I was done, mom returned. She was as mad as ever. She stood me up in front of her and scolded me. "I can't believe you're so slow. Look at how filthy you are." I stood there with spaghetti sauce and blood dripping down my right leg. Mom went to the silverware drawer and removed a large stainless-steel serving spoon. She used it to beat my bottom for what seemed like an eternity. Finally she stopped and snarled, "Now get this mess cleaned up!" Mom was smiling now. She went to the refrigerator and poured herself a glass of Kool-Aid and added a couple of shots of vodka.

I finished cleaning up the mess as fast as I could. When I was done, mom said, "Georgianne, get your filthy butt into the bathroom and clean yourself up. Be quick about it!"

When I entered the bathroom, I looked at Peter. He was naked, and his hands were wired over his head. They had turned blue. His waist was also tightly constricted with copper wire, which was twisted around the hot-water pipe. I hardly noticed Peter's condition, though, because that was his usual spot. I jumped into the tub and turned on the water. I hurried as fast as I could. I didn't want her to come and help me, because she would usually turn the water either burning hot or freezing cold. I washed off the spaghetti, glass and blood under the running faucet as quickly as possible. Thank God I finished before mom came to investigate.

I dried myself quickly and rushed over to Peter. He looked so small, thin and hurt. I rubbed some circulation back into his hands and arms. I wished that I could have brought him some spaghetti to eat, but that just wasn't possible. I whispered, "Now you be strong, Peter, and remember that I love you."

Peter was too young to say my name, "Georgianne," so he whimpered, "Uh huh, Gee-Gee."

When I got back to the kitchen, mom forced me to kneel by the refrigerator on the cold linoleum. I was fresh from the shower and still a little damp. The early spring weather in Chicago was still quite cold. I knelt there all afternoon and into the evening. Later I heard screaming and crying coming from the bedroom, and I assumed that something horrible was happening to Jill.

That night dad came in drunk. He looked at my shivering, naked body. I had congealed blood on my thigh from the broken pieces of glass. He said, "Good night, Georgianne." I replied, "Good night, daddy." I knew my daddy loved me and someday he would save me. Someday ... but not today. I spent the entire night kneeling beside the refrigerator. Soon my knees hurt horribly and I didn't know how I was going to make it until morning.

The pain in my knees was killing me, so I started to concentrate all of my attention on some lint behind the refrigerator. I refused to think about the pain in my knees or the cut on my thigh. I refused to think about who might save me or why all of this was happening. I didn't worry about Donna, Jill or Peter. All I did was concentrate on that piece of lint. I was like a cat at a mouse hole. I found that the lint would be stationary until the refrigerator came on, and then it would sway slightly in the warm breeze from the compressor fan. The trick was to pinpoint the exact instant that it started to move. It took all of my concentration to stay that alert. I tried to trace out every tangled little strand as it wove in and out of that ball of fluff. It took a couple of tries before I spotted the lint at the exact instant it started to move. I also liked listening to the compressor, because it soothed me, and the warm air coming off the coils was almost like having a blanket.

As the night wore on, I eased back from my upright position and settled down on my haunches and elbows. This maneuver allowed some relief from the agonizing pain in my knees. I promised myself that I would stay awake enough to hear mom sneaking up on me. I never had dreams or nightmares when I slept. I was so busy surviving that I had no time to hope or to worry. When I slept, I tried to stay alert, but I tried not to think too much.

Hours later I lost my ability to concentrate. I drifted off to sleep. I collapsed into a heap on the floor. In my sleep, I curled up on my side in the fetal position in a desperate attempt to conserve as much heat as possible. Just before dawn, mom crept up on me wielding a large, old-fashioned broom made out of broom corn stitched together with heavy wire to make it flat. She hit me on my bottom as hard as she possibly could. I was dazed, but I instantly realized what was happening and jumped back onto my knees before the next blow fell and smashed me forward into the refrigerator. She hit me one more time as I lay prostrate on the floor.

Mom pulled me up by my hair and screamed, "You filthy, lazy, spoiled brat! How dare you sleep when I told you to stay on your knees!" Mom then put the broom away and got herself a drink. I watched her warily as I knelt there.

Mom smiled sweetly and said, "Good night, Georgie." She put the broom away in my closet and went back to bed.

For the rest of the night, I managed my mind more carefully and stayed on my knees without changing position for several more hours. The morning sun promised me salvation, but I had to wait for what seemed like hours before dad came into the kitchen with a hangover and said, "Good morning, Georgianne."

I replied, "Good morning, daddy."

He went to the sink and turned on the water. "Would you like a glass?"

"Yes, daddy." I paused. "Daddy, my knees hurt so bad. I'm cold."

"I know, Georgianne, but there is nothing I can do that won't make your mother mad."

I drank my water and watched dad as he made himself three eggs and three slices of bacon for breakfast. Dad looked around warily and then gave me two slices of bacon. I wolfed them down as dad rushed out the door and off for work.

I continued kneeling and watching my piece of lint until mom got up. She was neatly dressed and as beautiful as she could be before her morning drink. She got me up and sat me on her lap, where she examined my face closely. My face was unmarked. That was lucky. It meant that I could go out in the yard to play. She gently combed my long hair very carefully for a long time, almost like she was playing with her favorite doll. When she got tired of combing my hair, she carefully and neatly dressed me. I decided to take advantage of her good mood and implored, "Mommy, I am really hungry. Could I have something to eat?"

"Georgianne, you know that you are a bad girl. You made that mess last night and you laid down when you were supposed to be on your knees. I would be a bad mother if I let you eat. You can eat tonight if you're a good girl today."

"Yes, mommy," I meekly said. I knew better than to push the issue and risk making her mad.

Beady, Little Eyes

MOM LIKED TO HAVE a spotless house, and we were required to help her as much as possible. From the time when Jill was four and I was five, we had been washing the dishes every day. We knew that we would get savage beatings if the dishes were not done to mother's satisfaction. Once, while Jill and I were learning to do dishes, mom came in and found a spot on a dinner plate. She determined the spot was my fault, so she made me stand at attention in front of her. She took the plate in both hands and broke it over my head. The blow knocked me completely off my feet and lacerated my head. After that, we were forced to clean up the broken glass. My scalp bled a lot, and the dried blood soon covered my face, except where my tears washed the blood away. I held a dishcloth on my head until the bleeding stopped.

Mom made both Jill and me kneel by the refrigerator that night. Kneeling was better than hanging in the closet. I was relieved but Jill was distraught.

Jill looked at me as we knelt and said, "Georgie, your face is all bloody. You look horrible."

The next day, mom was nice. Jill and I tried to stay out of her way. We went into Jill's room and played with a piece of thread, a large needle, and a jar full of buttons. We spent hours making ourselves necklaces out of the pretty buttons. That night, mom tied me up and hung me in my closet. Peter was tied in his bathroom, and Donna was tied to her crib. Jill was sent to bed.

One Saturday night when the whole family was home, mom bathed Jill and me and curled our hair. She wasn't satisfied with the way we looked, so she dressed and undressed us several times until she was happy. When we were dressed in our prettiest dresses, mom played with us like we were her favorite dolls.

Soon playtime was over. My pretty dress was removed, and I was tied in my closet, with the chamber pot shoved between my legs to collect urine.

Mom said, "I love you, Georgie."

I half-heartedly replied, "I love you too, mommy." Then the door was closed, and the darkness was total.

I remember being so very thirsty that night. My mind raced with frightening thoughts. "Would she come back? Would she beat me while I was tied?" I forced myself to stop thinking these bad, scary thoughts. I concentrated on the little bit of light that leaked in under the closet door. I tried to make out the edge of every board that was near the door. I tried to see as far into the darkness as I could. I traced out the edge of every item in the closet that I could dimly see. I tried to illuminate the closet with the power of my imagination. It worked a little. I even imagined that I could see the boxes in one corner and the broom in the other.

I could hear Donna and Peter crying, and I felt so sorry for them. Donna was too small to talk, so I couldn't tell her how dangerous her crying was. Peter was starting to understand that you would be beaten less if you didn't make any noise, but he still couldn't manage his emotions very well. Sometimes when the pain, hunger or fear got too bad, he would still cry. I hated to hear him cry. I knew from experience that, sooner or later, mommy would beat him into silence. Thankfully, this time my father and mother were gone, so they couldn't hear him sob.

I overheard Jill talking to Donna. "It's okay. Don't be afraid. I'll take care of you." Then I heard her softly sing, "Rock a bye baby in the tree top." It reminded me of Aunt Bea. That was the song that she used to sing.

I talked to Peter through the door. "It's okay, Peter, I'm here. It will be okay. Don't cry, Peter. It will be okay. I'm here. Peter, can you hear me? Peter, be strong. It will be okay. Don't cry. See, I'm not scared, Peter."

I lied about not being scared. I'm not sure that it helped, but telling him that it would be okay made me feel better. It was not easy being a big sister. I felt that I had responsibility for the younger children. When things went bad, I blamed myself.

I squirmed around a little, but I could find no relief for my bound arms. After a while I slumped in my bonds, went numb with pain, and drifted off into a restless, tormented sleep. It wasn't until the wee hours of the morning that my parents came home and went straight to bed.

Being naked and tied against the uninsulated outside wall of the closet meant that my hands soon turned blue from the cold and lack of circulation. I shivered so hard that my body banged against the wall. I was dying a little bit every night. I hoped someone would save me soon.

The next morning I was relieved when mom untied me. I collapsed to the floor. She was agitated, so I crawled out of her way.

"Where in the hell is my vodka?" she screamed. "What have you damn kids done with it?"

I hadn't seen her booze, but she was beside herself with anger and paranoia so she beat me. It seemed to relax her. I think that beating me was her way of calming down. When she finally found her bottle, she started to drink hard and heavy. That was often a very bad sign for us kids. After many drinks, I saw her legs buckle, and she passed out in the middle of the living room floor. I watched her for a very long time. Then I went over to her crumpled body and tried to wake her. She didn't move. I thought that she might be dead. I went to the bedroom to wake dad but he was passed out too.

I got a blanket and pillow off of his bed. I covered mom and then, using both hands, I lifted her head and placed a pillow under it. Then I lay down beside her with my head on her leg. Her body was warm, and I felt warm too. As I lay there, I thought to myself, "I sure hope that mommy is okay."

I think that I loved her at that moment. She seemed so vulnerable and helpless. It is hard to explain how I could love her, but I felt that I was the only person in the house who could give the love and care that mom needed.

Our home was filled with chaos, and everyone was hurting, even mom. Violence was a part of our lives. Every day someone would get hit, and it wasn't always us kids. Sometimes dad would slap mom around, especially if they were really drunk and she started to yell at him.

One night when they were both good and drunk, their moods got black. He called her an ugly whore. She told him that he wasn't much of a man. After that he slapped her very hard on the face. Then dad punched mom. He grabbed her long, auburn hair and threw her onto the floor.

Mom got up and ran into the kitchen and got a knife. "I'll kill you if you touch me again," she spat.

I was very frightened, and I ran and hid, as did the other children.

Thankfully, a few minutes later, they were in each other's arms kissing and making up.

Peter and I weren't sure what to do that night, because we hadn't been tied up. We were confused and lost. Our routine was interrupted. We had nowhere to go. We sat around for quite a while waiting for mom to come back and tie us up. When it became clear she wasn't going to come for us, Jill suggested that we sleep on her bed. After a while, Peter and I got uncomfortable and scared, so we left. Peter went to the bathroom and crawled into the dirty-clothes basket. I went to my closet and lay down on the wooden floor. I closed the door part way. In some strange way, I felt comfortable and safe that night. I had fresh air, and some light filtered into the room from the street light outside.

Dad worked days at the air-conditioner factory. Mom worked nights at the Kool-Aid plant. That meant that dad was up early, and mom usually slept late. I hated it when mom was up and dad was gone. Spending the day with mom was always nerve-wracking. I couldn't wait until she left for work. The best part of my day was when mom placed her metal lunch box on the counter and opened the refrigerator, because that meant she would soon be leaving. Mom seldom fed us during the day, so I was usually very hungry by afternoon.

On a typical day, I could almost taste each item as she placed it in the lunch box. She always started with two pieces of wheat bread smeared with mayonnaise and then piled high with ham, cheese, and lots of lettuce. She closed the sandwich and cut it in half, across the corners. Mom then wrapped her sandwich carefully in waxed paper. She also wrapped a few potato chips in waxed paper and placed them on top of the sandwich. Mom poured her thermos three-fourths full of red Cherry Kool-Aid and then topped it off with vodka, as usual. If mom was running late, she didn't tie me up. That was good.

Mom was so filled with paranoia that it affected everything she did or said. As she rushed out the door, she usually warned something like, "Don't go outside, because the dogs will eat you."

When she told me not to play in the street, she would usually go into gruesome detail about what would happen to me if I were hit by a car. When she told me not to talk to strangers, she went into horrific detail about what a homicidal pedophile would do if he kidnapped me. She told me not to pet strange dogs, because they would tear my stomach open and drag my guts down the street and eat them.

Mom was jumpy and would think she had seen a rat or a snake when, in reality, it was just a shadow. She would scream in real terror at the thought of these awful little imaginary reptiles or vermin. Mom shared her distorted perspective of the world with us. She loved to tell me detailed bedtime stories about the horrid little creatures that lived in dark places such as my closet. Mom particularly delighted in telling me about how the rats had beady, little eyes that glowed in the dark. I was told that a rat would eat a bad little child like me if it were given half a chance.

Then she would tie me in the closet for the night. I soon thought that I saw those beady, little eyes or felt sharp, gnawing teeth on my body. I trembled in stark terror! I believed the outside world was a very scary place.

Comfortable And Adequate

SOMETIMES, WHEN IT WAS SUNNY and warm, Jill, Peter and I were allowed outside to play. We usually played kick-the-can. When we tired of that game, we laid the battered tin soda cans on their sides and stomped on them. The crushed cans wrapped around the soles of our shoes and locked themselves in place. They made great horse's hooves. Peter laughed and ran around, clip-clop, clip-clop. He seemed very happy at that moment. Jill and I were happy too.

After a while, we grew bored with the cans, and we decided to play our favorite game, "happy family." The game was always a lot of fun once we had decided who would be daddy, mommy and child. Peter wanted to be the daddy, but I wanted him to be the baby. He wasn't very pleased but finally agreed. Jill and I both wanted to be the mother, so it took some argument before it was decided that I would be the mommy and Jill would be the daddy. I found a stick and drew a large square on the ground that was to be our house. I drew in a living room, a kitchen, a bedroom for Peter, as well as a bedroom for me. Jill found a Coke bottle that she gave to me as a gift. I decided that this bottle was a crystal vase. It needed a bouquet, so I sent Jill back out for some bright-yellow dandelions.

Jill also found some wooden roof shingles, which we used as plates. Cardboard cottage-cheese cartons became my pans. I whipped up two pretend dishes for our supper. First, we had par-boiled pebbles, then I served stewed mud garnished with sautéed grass. Everyone enjoyed the meal. Most of our days weren't this pleasant. Our real house was usually filled with pain and screams, but for a while on this day, we all lived in our own happy imagination home.

A kindly neighbor heard our frequent screams and became concerned about our welfare. In the early days of March 1953, this Good Samaritan made an anonymous call to the Chicago Child Protective Service to report that she thought Peter and Veronica Burowsky had been beating their children.

The caseworker who received the call opened a file on the Burowskys. She sent them a letter indicating that her agency had become aware that child abuse might have been going on in their home. She asked mom and dad to come into their office to talk. The caseworker also included some brochures on how to be better parents.

When mom received the letter she was upset and scolded, "You kids make too much noise. One of our busybody neighbors doesn't understand how to raise good children. You kids need to learn how to be more quiet."

Mom ran hot water onto a washrag until it was too hot to touch. She then used a wooden spoon to carry the scalding rag to me. Mom then shoved the steaming cloth into my mouth. To keep me from spitting the gag out, she taped it into place. She then gagged and taped Peter the same way, then savagely beat Peter and me with a belt. She wanted us to learn to take a beating without screaming so much, so I did my best not to scream out loud. I screamed plenty in my soul, but very little sound came out through the gag. When she was done, she tied me standing up in my closet. Peter was bound standing in his bathroom.

That night, my brother came up with an ingenious solution to our hopeless situation, and he learned to cope with his world gone mad. Peter took control of his pain, and he taught himself to sing or hum himself to sleep. After that first day, Peter hummed his lullaby every night without fail.

He hummed. Even when his mouth was stuffed with a scalding washrag, he hummed. It is odd that a toddler would sing himself to sleep in the face of torture, but my brother Peter did just that.

I soon discovered that hearing Peter's sweet lullaby was the only thing that allowed me to sleep in my own bonds. His song was my one little ray of hope.

Peter hummed, "Aha, Ah, Aaaah, AAH." The last "AAH" was when Peter and I would breathe. In a way, Peter's lullaby was a work song. Our work was to stay alive. The pacing and stress on the last syllable of his song helped Peter and me to time our labored breathing. It also helped us to calm the terror that sapped our waning strength. His rhythmic singing and breathing calmed us both down. Peter's soft, boyish soprano tones gave his song some aspects of a traditional lullaby, but the main reason I call it a lullaby is because of its effect. Peter's song helped me to stop sobbing, and it had the power to lull me into sleep. Our beatings were horrendous and frequent. From then on, mom was careful to gag us when she played one of her "special games" on us.

In the middle of April, mom received a second letter from the police. The letter said the police had received another anonymous call that reported that Veronica Burowsky was still abusing her children. I really hated it when mom received a letter, because it made her mad. I didn't know how to read, but from her reaction I gathered the neighbors were unhappy with our noise again. Mom became very angry. I begged, "Mom, don't gag me. I will be a good girl and not scream if you don't gag me."

She decided to test me by administering a severe beating on my bare bottom with a wooden spatula. It hurt a lot as it bit into my tender flesh, but I didn't scream.

Peter also promised not to scream, but he wailed the first time he was hit. Mom then gagged him with one of her scalding gags and beat him mercilessly for crying. Peter's cries were muffled, but his large, tear-filled eyes begged her to stop. She didn't notice.

I wrapped my arms around mom's legs and begged, "Mommy he's had enough." I had to bite my tongue to keep myself from yelling at her. When I became a nuisance, she tied me to the bent nails in my closet. It was only then that I realized how much my bottom ached. I listened helplessly to the rest of Peter's beating. I knew that he had been beaten more severely than usual, but hours later, when I heard Peter's lullaby coming softly from the bathroom, I was very relieved. His soft, sweet song gave me the courage to survive that night. Most importantly, I also knew Peter would survive another night.

In the early days of May 1953, mom received a third letter from the police. They had received another anonymous call. The caller reported that little Peter hadn't been seen outdoors for several weeks. A caseworker sent mom a stern letter. She was asked to make an appointment to talk with a caseworker from the police.

When mom received this letter, she was very angry with us. We were again gagged with washrags soaked in scalding water. The gags were then taped into place with black electrical tape. Then she beat Peter and me with a fly swatter. It hardly hurt at all compared to many of the things she had used before.

At this time, the beatings were several per week. The bondage however was every single day. I was so exhausted from never lying down at night for many months.

On May 26, 1953, the police received a fourth anonymous report that the Burowskys had beaten their children yet again. Our caseworker, Miss Vederko, reviewed the case in light of the latest call. She was upset because mom had refused to call and set up an appointment. Miss Vederko took our file to Mr. G. Lewis Penner, her supervisor, for further review. She told him that she wasn't sure if the abuse was real or if the anonymous reports were from a malicious person causing trouble. Mr. Penner said that he wasn't sure either but told Miss Vederko that he would find out what was taking place.

The next day, Mr. Penner picked up the phone and called Officer Carney of the Englewood Police Department (15th District) to request an investigation of the Burowskys. Officer Carney didn't have a policewoman available for this investigation, so he called Ruth Biederman, who was in charge of all of Chicago's policewomen. Mrs. Biederman told Officer Carney that Policewoman Rita Meany, who was normally assigned to the Woodlawn Police Station (7th District), could be temporarily reassigned to the Englewood Police Station (15th District) for this investigation.

Mrs. Meany was well-prepared to handle this investigation. In addition to being a policewoman, she was a registered nurse with a degree in social work and a background in public health. At 10:20 a.m. on Thursday, May 28, 1953, Mrs. Meany pulled into our driveway unannounced. She walked around to the back of our house, where she found Donna and Jill playing in the yard. When the girls saw the police lady they were cautious. Mrs. Meany said, "What dolls you are. Is your mama home?"

Jill looked at the ground and replied, "Yes."

The police officer asked, "What is your name, darling?"

My sister shyly replied, "I'm Jill and she's Donna."

Mrs. Meany wrote that down and then she reached out her hand. Jill took the policewoman's finger and led her to the back stairway.

Jill called out, "Mom, someone's is here to see you."

When mom appeared at the back door, Mrs. Meany introduced herself and produced her badge. Mom graciously invited the police officer in. The two women and the two curious kids stood in the children's bedroom. The beds were all made up, and the house was immaculate, as usual. Officer Meany noticed the crib, which she assumed was for Donna. She also noticed the bunk beds so she asked who slept in them. Mom said, "Jill sleeps in the bottom bunk, and my daughter Georgianne sleeps in the top."

Mrs. Meany apparently didn't know that Peter existed. Mom quickly ushered Officer Meany into the kitchen.

Mrs. Meany noticed that the kitchen was spotless. Mom hurried Officer Meany through the kitchen and into the living room. Mom had reason to move the officer through the kitchen quickly, because I was hanging from nails in the closet on the left of the kitchen and Peter was wired to the pipes in the bathroom on the right. The door to the bathroom was open slightly, and had Officer Meany stepped a few feet closer, she would have seen my battered, naked, and emaciated little brother.

Officer Meany sat on the davenport while mom sat on a chair. The television was still on, so Mrs. Meany had to talk over it. She started out, "You have some beautiful little children."

Mom said, "Jill is a lovely, lively, bright little girl. Have you met my daughter Donna? Say hello to Officer Meany, Donna."

Donna just looked at her shoes, shuffled her feet, and said nothing.

Mrs. Meany said, "What a fine child she is."

Mom replied, "Yes."

Mrs. Meany inquired, "Can I meet Georgianne?"

Mom stammered, "Well, she's in school today. She's a first grader at the Kershaw School."

Mrs. Meany leaned over to Jill and inquired, "Does your mommy ever beat you?"

Jill looked at the floor, shuffled, and slowly said, "No."

"Does your daddy ever beat you?"

Jill quickly answered, "No, daddy is nice."

The police lady talked some more to Jill and Donna, but the girls were shy. They had learned to be wary around people they didn't know. They were afraid to say anything wrong.

Mom said, "Sometimes my husband spanks the kids with his hand, and maybe that was what the neighbors heard. I'm quite amazed and a bit upset to think that anyone would make a report on me, saying that I was neglecting or abusing my children. My husband works from 7:30 until 4, while I work from 4 until midnight, so the kids are never left alone. If we do go out we hire a babysitter."

The two women made small talk about the "Kookla, Fran and Ollie" show that was playing on the television. Then Officer Meany thanked mom for her time. Mom let the officer out the front door this time because she didn't want Officer Meany to go back through the house and maybe hear us moaning.

Mom seemed to be relieved as she made herself a drink and started to get ready for lunch. She opened the door of the bathroom, where Peter was hanging, and unwired him. She then untied me. My brother was semiconscious and had dried blood trailing down his arms from where the bonds had cut into his tender wrists. Mom fed us lunch and told us that things would be getting better soon.

When Officer Meany got back to her desk at the police station she wrote:

Reference: Station Complaint Number #893-398

I went to the Burowsky home where I interviewed the mother Veronica Burowsky (age 28). I also examined Jill (age 5) and Donna (age 18 months). The undersigned finds no reason for complaint. The living facilities are clean, comfortable, and adequate. It appears to be a normal, good-living hardworking family. Mrs. Burowsky denied beating the children but she admitted the father chastised the children occasionally.

Signed: Officer Rita Meany
Dated: May 28, 1953

That night dad untied us and fixed supper that consisted of hamburger, gravy, and corn on the cob. I was amazed that I was eating twice in one day. Dad would only feed us if mom told him it was okay. Even when dad didn't feed us, I found that I could forage for food and he wouldn't say anything. I knew that food came in cans, boxes, and in the refrigerator. I hadn't mastered how to open cans, so I usually went after the boxes of sugar-coated cereal or jars of peanut butter. As a last resort I ate slices of bread or the fresh vegetables in the crisper. My brother Peter would help me eat what I had found. He liked the cereal best, but he would hardly touch the fresh vegetables.

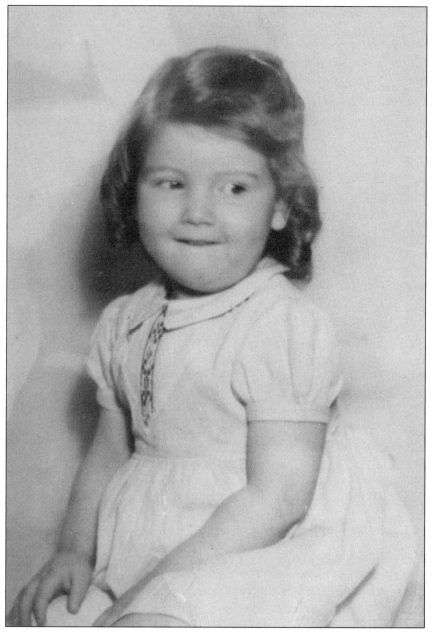

Me at age six, in 1953. Note the dark ligature mark on my wrist.

Chapter Ten

Crying Over Spilled Milk

ON JUNE 19, 1953, Miss Vederko, the caseworker for the Chicago Juvenile Protective Association, called the police and talked to Ruth Biederman, head of the Chicago Policewomen, about the reorganization then going on at the Chicago Juvenile Protective Association.

Mrs. Biederman said that the reorganization was leaving them shorthanded on the south side of Chicago. The two officials decided to close some cases in order to ease the workload. The Burowsky file was then officially closed. This meant that unless something more substantial developed, the police would take no more actions in our case.

The calls continued to come into both the police and the Juvenile Protective Association about our abuse, but from then on they were simply filed. Thankfully, the social workers stopped writing letters to mom. The letters hadn't helped. They had only made mom mad.

On June 19, another event happened—mom's first son, 11-year-old Pug arrived in Chicago. He had been sent to live with us at the insistence of Granddad George's new girlfriend, Bernie. Naturally, Pug did not want to leave granddad's big house and his friends. Pug went to bed early. As he fell asleep he could hear the unmistakable sounds of us children being hurt. Pug hid under the covers until morning. He could tell that his new household was unhappy and dangerous. He hated it in Chicago.

I was so wrapped up in the pain of just trying to survive that I didn't realized that I had a new brother. When Pug got out of bed that first day, he quickly got dressed and went to the bathroom. Pug started to cry when he discovered that his little brother had been wired to the pipes all night.

Earlier in the week, Pug had been the cherished child of the richest man in Plattsburgh. Today, he had awakened in hell. Pug frantically tried to untwist the heavy wires holding his brother, but they wouldn't budge.

Mom saw him and said, "Damn it, Pug, leave Peter alone! I'll take care of him after breakfast."

Pug, crying uncontrollably, left his brother as he had found him and came to the table. Jill and dad joined him for breakfast. A couple of days later, dad and mom got into a fight, and dad threw a heavy glass ashtray at mom. The ashtray missed dad, but it hit the television screen, which exploded into a thousand shards of glass. Dad then stormed out of the apartment. Mom was agitated and, with dad gone, turned her anger toward Peter. She gagged him and slapped him repeatedly in the face with her hand. When Pug intervened, she slapped him in the face for his trouble. Mom snarled, "Pug, DON'T you EVER stick your nose in again when I'm disciplining the kids, unless you want the same thing he's getting! Do you understand me?"

Mom's flashing eyes told Pug that she was dead serious, "Yes, mum," Pug slowly replied. He made every effort to stay out of her way from that point forward.

The television was a necessity for mom, so the broken TV set was taken to the shop the next day, and we had it back within a week.

Two weeks after Pug arrived, dad beat mom while they were both drinking heavily. Mom was so mad that she left Donna bound in her crib for the next 24 hours. Jill was forced to kneel on a broom handle most of the next day. Peter was tied in the bathroom, while I was tied in the closet all night and most of the morning. Pug rushed out of the house after breakfast to be away as soon as possible. He was desperate to have granddad take him back to Plattsburgh along with the rest of us.

Pug had only been here a few weeks, but he knew that something had to be done. He decided to write a letter to granddad in hopes of getting some help for us. My brother had never written a letter before. He figured that it couldn't be all that hard. He knew granddad's address in Miami and his address in Plattsburgh. He wasn't sure whether to send the letter to Florida or New York. He finally decided to send it to Florida, hoping that granddad would still be there.

Pug had to be careful with what he said in his letter, so he sat down on the floor with a spiral notebook and started to write.

Dear Granddad:

   I want to go home. I don't want to stay here any more. Ma always says she hits the kids because of me. Dad never hits the kids. The little boy Peter is all black and blue. He has got a black eye and gets tied up.

Jill is the cause of it all.

Yours Truly
Pug

Pug had searched the house to find a stamp, but none could be found. He determined that he would find the post office and buy one. He planned to go to the store after his paper route to buy an envelope and a stamp. He hoped that it would cost less than the dollar he had saved up. His biggest worry was that the old man wouldn't get the letter before something more serious happened. Unfortunately, time was running out, and Pug's desperate letter was never mailed.

Weekends were our best time, because dad was home and didn't like our screaming, so mom tried not to beat us too much on those days. Monday, July 27, 1953, was a typical workday, and we would be alone with mom all day. I woke up for a few minutes then fell back into a fitful sleep.

Peter was in his usual place, tied to the pipes of the bathroom. I was hopeful when I heard mom and dad's alarm go off early in the morning. I knew that I had made it through another night. Pug was also awake but still in bed.

When dad took his shower, the pipes warmed up, and Peter could feel the warmth in his numb body. It must have been better than the cold pipes he had felt all night.

As dad dried off, he said, "How ya doing, bum?" as he tousled Peter's hair. Then dad nonchalantly got dressed, had breakfast, and left for work.

About noon, mom released us from our bonds. "You kids were so bratty yesterday that you don't deserve any food or television today. I want you to stay in the house. Don't get into anything. Maybe if you're good, you can have some supper, but I doubt it."

Mom took out a bottle of vodka from the cupboard, threw down a big swallow, then cleaned up the kitchen. When she was done, she went back to bed and slept some more. Peter and I were left alone in the kitchen. We hadn't eaten last night, and now we weren't going to eat today either. Since mom was back in bed, I decided that we could sneak a drink of milk. I opened the refrigerator door and very carefully took down the heavy glass jug. I pulled the cardboard disc off the top of the bottle and took a deep swallow of the cool liquid. I handed the jug to Peter, but somehow it slipped from his numb hands and fell to the floor. The jug didn't break, but it made a loud thud and spilled half a quart of milk on the floor. Mom heard the noise and rushed into the kitchen in one of her white-hot rages.

My toy ironing board was folded flat and standing in the corner. Mom grasped it with both hands on the narrow end like a big, flat baseball bat. She chased me around the house until she got close enough to take a swing. The blow connected with my back and knocked me into the coffee table. I rolled over the top of the table and fell between it and the couch.

She then left me and went after Peter. When she hit him, he skidded across the floor. His shoulder crashed into the door with a sickening thud. The blow was so forceful that it broke the toy ironing board in half!

Mom hauled me to the kitchen by my hair and made me kneel on the floor by the refrigerator in the corner. A few moments later, my sobbing little brother joined me.

Mom got herself a cookie. She poured Cherry Kool-Aid into a coffee cup and topped it with vodka. When she finished her snack, she angrily went to work cleaning up her kitchen. By the time she had the kitchen spotless, Peter had fallen over on his side.

Mom yelled, "You little brat! I told you to KNEEL in the corner, not LAY in the corner!" Mom put Peter across her lap and spanked him with her hand. Then we were again forced to kneel in the corner. I was in pain and trembling with fear. Mom went back to finish her nap. Peter was whimpering, but I was afraid to make a noise.

Hours later, mom arose for the day and took a shower. I watched her every move as she dried off, just like a cat watches a mouse. After she got dressed she came into the kitchen to check on us. "Kneel up straight!" she yelled.

I knew the drill, so I slowly lifted my weary body to an upright posture, my arms hung limply at my side. The pain in my knees and back was horrible, and I was badly in need of food, water and sleep. Mom went to the living room and watched television for a while. Peter got up and left. I was amazed. What could he be thinking? Mom would be furious.

I called out after him, "Peter, come back. It will be okay." Peter never replied. He slowed down for a second but then slowly limped off.

After watching the news, mom came back and realized that Peter had disappeared. She searched frantically for him. After about 10 minutes she finally found Peter in the linen closet. He had climbed onto the first shelf, covered himself with towels, and gone to sleep.

Mom screamed, "What the HELL are you doing young man? Messing up every goddamn towel in the house with your FILTHY body."

Mom dragged Peter back to the middle of the kitchen floor and made him kneel. He was weeping, and this made his naked body convulse. Mom went to the trash can and got the broken toy ironing board. She wrenched off one of its wooden legs with her bare hands. That produced a sturdy one-inch-square stick that was about two feet long. Mom admired the creation by slowly turning it over in her hand. Then she held this club tightly in her right hand and slapped it loudly against the palm of her left several times. I trembled in fear.

Mom stood over Peter with her club in both hands high over her head like a baseball batter at the plate. Then she gave Peter a mighty blow on his bare bottom that knocked him flat on his face.

She glared down at Peter. "I ought to tie you up, but I am going to go easy on you. I want you to kneel beside your sister for the rest of the day, and you better not move if you know what is good for you."

Mom, worn out from her exertion, went back to the living room and lay down on the couch to take a nap. I could hear her soap operas playing on the TV. Soon Peter fell over again. He curled up into the fetal position.

I scolded him in a whisper, "Don't you dare lay down, Peter. Mom will beat you if she catches you laying down."

He ignored me. He was just too weak and demoralized to get back up. After a few minutes, I gave up trying to get him back on his knees. I sat my bare bottom down on the cold, yellow linoleum.

I took Peter into my arms and rocked him back and forth. "It will be okay, Peter, I promise. Just don't give up."

He just stared at me with a blank look on his face.

Mom came back into the room. She found us both sitting on the floor. When she went to get her club, she discovered that it had broken in half during the last thrashing, so she ripped another leg off the ironing board and fashioned a new bludgeon.

Mom forced us to stand in the middle of the kitchen. She took careful aim at my bottom. I stood there trembling waiting for the blow to come. She yelled at me for a while, but I didn't listen to what she was saying. My mind was somewhere else.

When the blow came, it knocked me off my feet, and I skidded across the floor on my face. I rolled over just in time to see my brother receive his "punishment." When the blow came, he crumpled on top of me. "Damn," mom said as she examined the broken stick, "look what you made me do."

Exhausted, she sat down, then fixed herself some canned stew and wrote a note for dad explaining how bad we had been. Mom then hurried to pack a lunch. She got dressed for work. Mom tied us up in our usual places and rushed out of the house. I sobbed in the dark closet for the rest of the day.

When dad came home, he read the note and, following it's instructions, untied and fed me some chili and a glass of Kool-Aid. Peter remained tied and didn't get any dinner. Jill and I sat with dad, and we watched television while he drank several shots of vodka and a beer.

About 9 o'clock, dad said, "It's time for me to go to sleep, Jill. You go to bed right now." Jill scampered off, and then dad took me by the hand. "Come with me, Georgie,"

I cried while dad tied me up back in my dark closet. Then dad went to bed. I heard Peter's lullaby coming from the bathroom. He softly sang, "Aah, Ah, Aaaah, AAH...Aah, Ah, Aaaah, AAH...Aah, Ah, Aaaah, AAH." I knew that Peter was okay. He was singing me to sleep, and so I closed my eyes and tried to rest.

A little before one in the morning, Mom arrived home from work. She opened the door to my closet. She had a glass of milk in one hand and some cake in the other. She fed it to me and gave me a long drink. I begged her to untie my hands.

She smiled down at me and said, "Good night, Georgie."

I didn't respond.

Then she repeated, "GOOD NIGHT, Georgie."

I responded, "Good night, mommy."

She smiled again and closed the closet door.

Peter Burowsky, Jr.

Mom kept this framed photo of him on her dresser.

-Chicago Tribune, July 29, 1953-

Gruesome Finger Painting

THE NEXT MORNING, Tuesday, July 28, 1953, was warm and muggy. My big brother Pug was the first to get up, well before dawn. He had to meet his new friend Bob to learn more about his paper route. Pug noticed that Donna was still bound in her crib. She tried to lift her head to look up at her brother. Pug hurried to the bathroom, where Peter was tied to the water pipes. It was hard for Pug not to think about the horror all around him as he took his shower. Peter could undoubtedly feel the warmth of the hot water pipe, and it probably felt good to him. As Pug dried off, he noticed that his brother looked awful. Peter was all black-and-blue, and the little guy was standing in his own waste.

"Are you okay, Peter?" he inquired.

Little Peter mumbled something into his gag.

Pug then wrapped a dry towel around his naked little brother. Then he hurried to get dressed.

The house was quiet after Pug left. A little while later, dad got up to get ready for work. He went into the bathroom to shower and brush his teeth. He could see his namesake in the mirror. Little Peter was hanging on the opposite wall, draped with a towel.

Little Peter watched dad enter the room, and he tried to say something.

Dad couldn't understand him because Peter's mouth was stuffed with a washrag held in place with electrical tape. As dad took his shower, Peter could again feel the water pipe warm up. He was so malnourished that, although it was summer, he had to be cold just like I was. The warmth from the hot water pipes must have been welcome at first. Peter was so run down from the three unusually severe beatings on Monday that he was barely able to moan and squirm to avoid the heat. While dad dried off, he looked at Peter's two little hands and noticed they had turned quite blue from the constricted circulation. Dad unwired Peter's numb arms and let them drop to the boy's side.

Little Peter slumped forward as far as his bonds would allow, but he was still held up by the wires around his waist. Dad cut the tape and removed the gag from Peter's mouth.

Little Peter begged, "Daddy, please let me go. Pleeeeease. I'll be good."

Dad replied, "Bum, you know mom doesn't like to have you up while she's still in bed. You might get hurt."

"Pleeeeease daddy. I won't get into anything," Peter begged.

Dad gave in. "Oh, all right, but I'm late for work."

Dad finished untying Peter and then locked the boy in the bathroom. Then dad made himself some cereal for breakfast and went to work.

Peter did what he usually did when he was locked in the bathroom. He crawled into the dirty-clothes basket, covered himself up, and promptly fell into an uneasy sleep.

When Peter woke up, he had access to "drinking water" in the toilet. In this he was luckier than I. It was often hours or even more than a day between drinks of water for me.

On this day, Peter took some things out from under the sink. He must have known that he would get a beating for doing this. Maybe he didn't care anymore. Maybe he was looking for something to eat. Who knows? When he couldn't find anything worth eating or playing with, he gave up and crawled into the dirty-clothes basket again and went back to sleep.

About 9:30, mom woke up and went into the bathroom. She was surprised to find Peter untied. Her surprise turned to rage when she discovered that Peter had gotten into the cabinet under the sink and taken things out.

She pulled him by the arm into the living room and screamed, "Can't you ever learn not to mess up my house? I don't have time to pick up after you all day. Now you're going to get it."

Peter stammered, "Please, mommy, don't hit me. I'm sorry."

I could hear mother screaming at Peter. Oddly, that lifted my spirits a little, because her screaming meant it was finally morning and maybe she would untie me soon. I was still in great pain from my thrashing the day before. My arms were numb from being tied to the wall all night, and my legs were very shaky. The commotion woke Jill. She ran and hid in the corner behind her bed. Since I was still in my dark closet, Jill would be the only witness to what happened next.

Mom looked around until she found one of the sticks she had used to beat us the day before. She soaked a washrag in scalding hot tap water and stuffed it into Peter's pleading mouth. Then she wrapped tape around his head to hold the gag in place. She held both of his emaciated arms behind his back in one hand and hit him as hard as she could in the face with the stick. The first blow to the face broke his nose.

When she was exhausted, mom put Peter into the bathtub and cleaned him up. She had to hold a compress on his face for quite some time to stop the bleeding. Mom poured herself a vodka and Kool-Aid and took Peter into the living room, where she watched a Bob Hope special about the Korean War armistice called "Give Them This Day."

When Peter calmed down a little bit, she removed his gag. She kissed him and said, "You worthless bum, why can't you mind?"

He said, "I will mommy, I promise."

Mom continued, "I'll take you to the zoo this weekend if you start to mind me better."

"I'll be good, mommy," he whimpered.

She put Peter into Jill's bed, and then she carefully cleaned the blood off the floor and walls before she untied me and took me out of the closet. I was grateful, but I was wary because she seemed to still be angry.

Mom then got out her hairbrush. I knew that this could be a good sign or a bad sign. When mom was in a good mood, she would hold me in her lap and gently brush my hair. I really felt nurtured and loved when mom smoothed my hair and talked lovingly to me. When she was done, my hair would glisten in long, cascading red waves.

That day she told me she intended to braid my hair. I started to weep and beg, because I knew what would happen. When mom was mad, she liked to braid my hair real tight. That amounted to torture.

She held me between her legs so I couldn't get away and started to give me a "hairdo." She divided my hair into three strands with a comb. Then she used all of her might to pull my hair and cross it. She repeated this procedure time after time. Each new braid was pulled tighter than the last. When she was done, my hair was pulled so tight on both sides of my head that I got an instant headache. She tied me back in the closet so that I couldn't loosen my braids. I hoped that this day wouldn't get any worse, but it did.

Late in the morning, mom untied Donna from her crib and gave her a bottle, and then she untied me. We sat down to watch "Love of Life" on television. I fell painfully asleep in her arms.

Peter was holding his head in his hands. He looked like he was in pain. Mom got him a drink of water and an aspirin. Mom poured herself another shot of liquor. She returned to the living room and watched "Search for Tomorrow" while she sipped her drink and brooded.

I continued to sleep fitfully on the couch, my exhaustion having won out over my pain. At noon I hungrily watched as she ate a bowl of soup with crackers. Then she had some cookies washed down with milk. Mom didn't feed any of us, not even Jill. Mom then went to her room to take a nap. Jill, Donna, Peter and I quietly held each other as we sat together on the couch.

Peter mumbled, "I feel really bad, Jill. My head hurts."

Bad wasn't the word for the way he looked. Both of his eyes were black, and his nose was bleeding. Jill and I held him for a while.

He whimpered, "I'm hungry, Gee-Gee." I was hungry too, so I went into the kitchen to find us something to eat. Jill stayed behind to watch television. Peter followed behind me on shaky legs. I pulled a chair over to the sink, climbed on it, and got myself a glass of water. After I drank part of the water, I gave the balance to Peter and he took a few sips.

I moved the chair over to the cupboard and got out the peanut butter and a new loaf of bread. I climbed down and got the grape jelly out of the refrigerator. I struggled to open the sticky jar and to get the peanut butter onto the knife. I dropped a glob of peanut butter onto the bread and tried to spread it around. My efforts managed to tear the bread into shreds. "Oh well," I thought, "it will still taste good."

Just as we were about to eat, mom heard us and came raging into the room. She screamed, "Why can't you kids stay out of trouble, damn it! I was trying to take a nap when I heard you making a mess out of my kitchen. I guess you two brats want another spanking." What mom called a "spanking" would turn out to be two savage beatings, almost unbelievable in their viciousness.

I trembled in fear, transfixed while mom started to run scalding hot water onto a washrag. I decided to make a run for it, but she soon caught me as I tried to crawl behind the couch. She dragged me back to the sink, where the hot water was still running. Mom pried my mouth open and stuffed the scalding rag in and taped my mouth closed. It burned the inside of my mouth and my lips. She searched through the trash until she found the last piece of the ironing board that was still big enough to be used as a club, and she wrenched it free. Mom sat down on a kitchen chair and pulled me across her lap by my braids.

She continued to hold me in place by my hair as she clubbed me with all of her might. The first blow landed on the back of my legs. The next blow hit my bottom. The third savage blow caught me in my lower back and fractured her two-foot long bludgeon. The end of the club clattered to the floor. She continued to beat me with this very short baton until she got tired. Mom pushed me off her lap, and I fell on my face. I was screaming into the gag as I tried to crawl away, but I didn't get far before I collapsed in a heap in front of her.

Mom moved toward Peter, but she had reduced my toy ironing board to kindling by clubbing me with it. She grabbed the last leg of the ironing board. Mom rummaged through the kitchen tool drawer until she found a hammer. Then she took it and left the apartment.

I lay on the floor, but my sister Jill stood at the window and watched as mom went downstairs to the wood pile behind the house.

After a little looking, she found a two by four with some rusty, bent nails stuck in it. With a little bit of work, she removed the nails from the board. Mom straightened out the nails by holding them down on the concrete of the back porch and tapping them with her hammer. Once the nails were straight, she took a tin can from the trash and slid it over the end of the ironing board leg and nailed the empty tin can to the small bat. Mom practiced swinging her new club a few more times.

Mom snarled, "You WILL learn not to mess up my house." I was still gagged so I said nothing. I just cried and tried to think about something else.

Mom continued, "Georgie, you are absolutely no damn good. Maybe a few more days in here without food will teach you to behave." Then she slammed the door.

I slumped forward in my bonds, hovering between semiconsciousness and stark, painful terror. I preferred unconsciousness to the pain, but I knew that I had to suppress the terror to achieve any sort of relief.

Peter was hiding in the bedroom closet. After a short search, mom found him. She gagged Peter with one of her scalding washrags. Peter's eyes were filled with wild terror. Mom smiled. She loved that deer-in-the-headlights look. Peter managed to get away and make a limping run for it. Mom gave chase.

When she caught up to Peter, her first stunning blow broke his right leg, and he collapsed to the floor in pain. He covered his face with his arms in a pitiful attempt to protect himself as much as possible from a blow aimed at his head. His right forearm took the full force of the next blow, and the bones broke. By now, the tin can had collapsed into a crumpled lump of metal. This had the effect of cutting and lacerating his body viciously, as well as concentrating the force of her blows even more. The next blow badly bruised his hip. Then she took careful aim at his good arm, which was still covering his face. She broke his elbow with one swift, brutal stroke. One last blow broke his other leg. Each of the four broken bones from this beating was a life-threatening injury by themselves, as was the broken nose from earlier in the day.

Jill heard a crunching sound as mom hit the back of Peter's head again and again. The sounds made my sister shudder. The sixth time mom hit his head, the stick broke. Blood gushed from his broken nose and lips and ran down his body. When she let him go, he collapsed on the floor unconscious. Mom yanked Peter across the linoleum by one of his arms into the bathroom. He was trailing a red streak of blood across the floor. His toes caused the blood streaks to look like a gruesome finger painting on the linoleum. Jill was horrified as she watched this sight. She felt like screaming but she knew better. She kept the silent scream in her soul. The memory of Peter's little feet being dragged through his own blood across the floor would haunt her forever. Fortunately, I was spared this sight because I was still tied in the closet.

Blood started to slowly seep into Peter's brain through two separate internal hemorrhages. It was at this moment that the hourglass on Peter's life started to trickle down. Emergency medical treatment was his only hope for survival. Mom didn't want to answer any probing questions about Peter's condition, so she didn't even consider taking him to the hospital.

Instead of trying to save her son's life, mom pulled each of Peter's broken arms up high over his head and twisted the heavy copper wire around each of his wrists and around the pipes. The unimaginably intense pain of having his broken limbs bound, again caused Peter to moan in agony.

The water pipes that Peter was tied to went straight up to the ceiling, so that an unconscious toddler would slide all the way down to a heap on the floor. Mom didn't want that, so she bound her son at the waist and at the ankles to force him to stand up on his broken legs all night. Just because Peter's body was dripping blood and he was barely conscious was no reason to change the procedure. Peter was still gagged, which probably restricted his breathing especially through his broken, bleeding nose. Mom then wrapped some tape around Peter's neck and the pipes to hold his head up. My brother moaned one more time when mom finally let him go and his full weight was back on his broken legs and arms and his neck.

A small drop of blood dripped off my lacerated arm and hit my foot. I tried to concentrate on that drop of blood. The more I concentrated on this one tiny red spot, the less I thought about my pain. I knew that focusing was my only salvation from the fear I felt in my heart. I was alone. It was dark. I was frightened. I was in pain. I was concerned for my brother. Of all my concerns, the pain was the worst. I have never felt such intense agony before or since.

Peter was in worse shape. At this point, little Peter's only hope for survival was if dad got home soon, VERY SOON, and took him to the hospital.

Eventually, Pug got home from his paper route.

Mom yelled at Pug, "Where the hell have you been? If you were here watching these damn kids, I wouldn't have to beat them so much."

"I'm sorry, Ronnie," he said. "I'll come home sooner tomorrow."

Chapter Twelve

The Bum Got Up

PETER WAS LOSING his battle to survive. I didn't know exactly what his problem was, but I knew that something was very wrong. Peter didn't sound normal.

Mom was exhausted and exhilarated. She sat down at the kitchen table and wrote a note for dad explaining how he was to torture us in her absence. She neatly folded the note down the middle so that it would stand up. She stood the note up in the center of the kitchen table so that dad would be sure to find it.

Then she yelled at Pug, "Damn it, Pug, you better not get into anything while I'm at work. Don't let Jill or Donna get into anything either. Peter and Georgianne are being punished. Leave them the HELL alone. Do you understand me?"

"Everything will be okay," Pug promised.

Promptly at 3:00 p.m., mom left Pug in charge of the carnage and went to work. Jill was crying too hard to tell Pug about the bloody assault she had just witnessed. For the next one and a half hours, Pug and Jill tried to watch "Atom Squad" followed by "Howdy Doody." Jill mostly cried. Pug was not especially alarmed, because Jill's crying and our bondage were all part of a normal day in the Burowsky household.

When dad got home from a hard day's work at the air conditioner factory, the first thing he did was to go to the refrigerator to get a beer. He noticed the note that mom had left on the kitchen table. He picked it up and read it as he sipped his beer.

Pete:

Well, the Bum got up again this a.m. Same thing. I got him in the bathroom. You can fix him supper if you want and then tie him up again. Same with Georgianne, only NO SUPPER. It depends upon whether she minds Pug or not. Not much else to say. See you tonight.

Love, Vi

Dad placed the note back on the table and went into the living room to watch the news. Around 6, dad made a supper for everyone but me. Dad opened my door and said, "Georgie, you won't be eating tonight because you were very bad today."

Dad untied his son Peter, Jr. and carried him to the table, where the weak boy accepted a sip of water but couldn't eat anything. My brother was unable to even sit up alone, so dad held him in his lap while everyone else ate. After supper, dad took the nearly unconscious Peter to his usual place in the bathroom and tied him back up. It was a sentence of death for my poor brother. His body slumped, and his bound arms slid down the pipe. This caused the noose around his neck to support some of his weight and choke him. This may have been the last pain that Peter ever felt. I certainly hope he didn't feel any more pain.

After Peter was securely tied again, the rest of the family sat down and watched the new Billy the Kid adventure called "The Renegade" on TV. During a commercial, Pug went to the bathroom, where he looked at his poor little brother.

Pug ran back to dad. "I think that little Pete looks really bad."

"Yea, I know. I'll talk to mom about it tomorrow. Hey, get me a beer while you're up."

I was in the dark closet listening as hard as I could for Peter to sing his usual lullaby, but I never heard it. All I could hear over the sound of the television was Peter going, "Ugh, ugh, ugh."

I murmured to Peter, "Are you okay, Pete?" He didn't answer. "Don't be afraid. I'm here for you, Pete. We'll be okay."

Peter still didn't answer me. I couldn't believe there was still no lullaby. A strange kind of fear gripped me. I needed to know that my brother was okay.

At 9, dad changed the channel to WGN-TV so he could watch a gangster movie called "My Death is a Mockery." At 9:30, my father went to the bathroom and found that Peter looked dead and felt cold. He screamed, "Pug, go down the hall and call your mom at work! Tell her to get home right away. Tell her that the bum is sick!"

Dad told Pug, "Go to Mrs. Manley's apartment and call. Don't say anything to Mrs. Manley about what went on here today! Do you understand? Oh, and be careful the nosy Mrs. Manley doesn't listen in on your call!"

"Okay, I'll be careful about what I say!"

Dad emphasized, "Now remember, don't say anything to Mrs. Manley!"

"Okay, I won't forget," Pug replied as he rushed down the hall to the Manley apartment and knocked frantically.

Mrs. Manley came to the door in her bathrobe. "What is it Pug?" she asked.

"Mom has beaten little Peter. He looks really bad. I'm afraid that maybe he's real bad off!" he stammered his eyes full of tears.

"Oh my God, I can't believe this has finally happened!" Mrs. Manley exclaimed.

"Peter wants me to call mom and tell her to come home! Don't tell him that I told you what happened."

"Okay, Pug, I won't tell. Come on in and call your mom."

After Pug finished his call to Ronnie, Mrs. Manley called the police. It was now exactly 10:10 p.m.

When Pug got back to the apartment, he saw that dad had started to unwire little Peter. "Pug, help me. We have to do something."

Pug stammered, "I think that Mrs. Manley might be suspicious."

Dad then realized the police may have been called, so he desperately worked to get Peter unwired from the pipes. When he got Peter freed from the pipes, he laid his son on the floor.

Mrs. Manley hurried down the hall and knocked on the door of our apartment. "Anything I can do to help?" she yelled through the door.

Dad replied in a calm voice, "No thank you. Everything is under control." A few minutes later I heard the sound of a police siren. A squad car that contained officers Spiatto and Ringbloom roared to a stop in front of our house. They were met in the yard by our neighbor, Lillard Johnson, who had been roused by the sirens.

Mr. Johnson pointed out our apartment and said, "I think there is something wrong in the apartment over there."

The officers banged on our door and yelled, "Police. Open Up." Then they crashed through the door. Jill screamed and hid behind the couch.

When the officers discovered Peter's body, they called for a back-up squad car and for the Inhalator Squad of the fire department. The next vehicle to scream into the driveway with sirens wailing was squad car #291 containing officers O'Rourke and Koehler. Then the Inhalator Squad #5 of the Englewood Fire Department showed up with lights flashing and sirens screaming!

Officer O'Rourke discovered me and cut me down off the wall. The commotion got me very frightened. I rushed to Jill and held her very tight. I cautioned her, "Don't scream, they will hear you." That didn't work. The more she screamed, the more frightened I became. When Officer Ringbloom came toward us, Jill screamed and I joined her. We both screamed bloody murder. Officer Ringbloom backed off.

Then policemen Ringbloom, O'Rourke, and Koehler gathered everyone in the living room. Jill and I hid behind the couch. When the police couldn't convince Jill and me to let go of each other, they pried us apart.

Eventually, we kids were taken out into the sad, drizzling rain by the officers and placed into squad cars. Officer Ringbloom sat down on the seat of the car and talked to me. "You are safe now. No one will hurt you again."

I wanted to believe him. I wanted to believe the nightmare was finally over for me.

While I was in the police car, mom pulled up to the house. Police Officer William Nolan put mom into his squad car, and they went to the hospital. Officer Spiatto cuffed dad's hands behind him, led him down the stairs, and placed him in the back seat of his squad car. Dad was taken to the police station jail at 1121 South State Street and formally arrested. Donna and Jill were sent to St. Vincent Catholic Orphanage in Chicago. My 11-year-old brother Pug was temporarily sent to a reform school for lack of a better place to put him.

Officer Ringbloom was crying when he got into the car with me. We cried together as we drove to the jail. The warm rain continued to fall, and it seemed to me like God was crying too.

I think that jail matron Nosko could see that I was exhausted, so she took me into a large, empty cell and gently tucked me into a prison cot. It felt good to have a bed and covers. The jail cot seemed like such a luxury. I never wanted to leave this wonderful place.

My body hurt from the thrashings of the last few days. My head also hurt from the tight braids. The police didn't know that my cute braided hair was actually another form of mom's torture. I certainly wasn't going to take my hair down and make mom really mad.

I was very nervous with all the people around, and I had trouble sleeping without Peter singing me his lullaby. But I finally drifted off to restless sleep.

When little Peter arrived at St. Bernard's Hospital, the sight of his bruised and smashed form appalled the emergency-room nurses. They buzzed for the attending resident, Dr. Fioretti. When he arrived and examined Peter's body, he pronounced Peter dead. His body was frozen in rigor mortis with his hands over his head, just the way dad had left him. Officer Nolan arrested mom.

By midmorning the day after the murder, the authorities realized how badly bruised my body was, and I was sent to St. Bernard's Hospital, where Peter's body was being autopsied.

The police called Granddad George in Florida and told him about the murder. He rushed back to Plattsburgh, New York, where he picked up mom's younger sister Gerry and her husband Melvin. Granddad didn't stop to sleep; he drove all day and night. They arrived in Chicago the next evening and went straight to the jail.

The matron, Ann Nosko, brought mom into the visiting room. Granddad showed no emotion when mom threw her arms around him sobbing. He didn't say anything at first.

Aunt Gerry, crying, embraced her sister. "Why did you do this?"

"Please believe me. God knows I wouldn't murder one of my own children."

After a short visit, the family left and started to take care of the necessary details. They came back the next day, and granddad obtained mom's signature on forms that approved their plan to bury Peter back in Plattsburgh. They then left mom for the night. The media was at the jail in force while her family was talking to mom. The reporters jotted down every word that was said, and everyone was photographed. When the family got up to leave, a reporter asked Aunt Gerry what would happen to us children. She told the press she would take care of us until mom was released from jail.

I wish that had really happened, because Aunt Gerry was a nice lady and she would have been a good mother for us. But something changed her mind, and we were not raised by her. If she knew that she wasn't going to take care of us, I wish that she hadn't told the press that she would. Maybe one of the millions of decent families who were following our case in the media might have opened their arms to us and given Jill and me a good home. We will never know what might have happened.

Crocodile Tears

Members of the press soon discovered that Policewoman Rita Meany had come to our house on May 28, exactly two months before Peter died. They rushed to her office to question her about the report.

All she would tell the press was, "I remember the case for myself, but I don't remember anything for the press."

The press then went to Ruth Biederman, who was in charge of all policewomen, and requested the files about the meeting between Policewoman Meany and our family. At first, Mrs. Biederman stonewalled. "I can't seem to find the report about any visit that we may have made to the home in question."

When Capt. Philip Nulty of the Englewood Police Department was contacted, he apologized. "It appears the three-year old boy was hidden from Mrs. Meany." Eventually, Officer Meany's report was "found" and given to the press. The next day it was plastered on the front pages of newspapers all over the nation. This case was quickly shaping up to be one the police were not going to be real proud of.

It seemed like everyone in the United States was asking how this could have happened. Some of the questions would be answered as soon as the coroner's inquest took place.

Little Peter's former foster parents, Mr. and Mrs. Albert Burnah of Redford, New York, who had tried so hard not to send Peter back to live with mom and dad, had read about the fate of their foster child in the newspaper, and they were devastated. The next day, Friday, they sent a telegram to Warden M. Phillip Scanlan of the County Jail. The message read:

*We are the foster parents of the little Peter Burowsky
STOP
We got him through the Welfare Department at Plattsburgh, New York, when he was two and one-half months*

old and kept him until Sept 15, 1952 STOP
We would like to have the body shipped for burial in
Redford, New York, and will pay all expenses STOP

A reporter visited mom in jail and told her about the telegram. Mom's eyes flashed angrily and she spat out, "I don't know where my boy will be buried, but it won't be by them!"

I spent the first few days after Peter's murder in the hospital. I was later sent to the orphanage with Jill after I was released from the hospital. Several days after that, Officer Rita Meany showed up in a black car to pick up Donna, Jill and me. No one talked as we drove from the orphanage to the Coroner's Inquest. We were all self-absorbed in our own thoughts.

The police took mom to the inquest. As they walked up the steps of the medical examiner's office, a newspaper reporter stuck a microphone into mom's face and asked, "Are you sorry that you killed your son?"

She replied, "I would gladly give my life to have my boy back. I didn't want to hurt him, but I didn't want him to hurt himself. I am willing to take whatever punishment the authorities want to give me."

Before the testimony started, granddad, Aunt Gerry and mom were taken to the basement of the Cook County Morgue to identify Peter's body. He was white and covered with incisions that had been left by the autopsy.

Mom screamed and tried to throw herself onto the table with the body. "I didn't mean for this to happen!" Then mom collapsed, crying hysterically. She had to be half carried into the inquest room by two police officers. She was still wearing the blue cotton uniform issued to her by the Perkins Kool-Aid Products Co. It was wrinkled from her stay in jail. The crepe soles of her tennis shoes were partially melted and stained red by the citric acid and dye from the Kool-Aid.

Policewomen Meany and Biederman brought Jill and me into the courtroom. A nun brought Donna in from somewhere. Pug was brought in by a police officer. He was still wearing the same clothes he had worn the night of the murder. This upset some of the jurors, as it was now six days after the murder. They asked the coroner why a traumatized boy like Pug had been put into reform school for almost a week with no clean clothes. No one seemed to have an answer.

I was very confused about what was going on. Coroner McCarron intimidated us. I was on the verge of tears until he brought out a bag of candy for us to share. Dad was the last family member to arrive. He arrived in handcuffs. When Jill saw him she called out, "Hi, daddy!" Then she turned to Policewoman Biederman. "I didn't get any beatings. I was mother's pet ... but she did." Jill looked toward me. Jill continued, "And Peter's dead; mother hit him."

At 10:30 a.m. sharp, Deputy Coroner Cornelius Dore told the overflow crowd in the upstairs hearing room of the morgue, "This inquest will now come to order. Have the record show that Coroner Walter E. McCarron is conducting this inquest."

Mom was the first witness. Weeping loudly, she slowly shuffled to the stand to testify. Coroner McCarron sternly said, "We want no crocodile tears here, madam."

Deputy Coroner Dore stood up and walked to mom. "You don't have to testify if you don't want to, do you understand?"

Mom managed a feeble, "Yes."

He then asked, "Are you represented by counsel?"

Mom murmured, "No."

Her voice was so soft the coroner had to repeat her answer so the jury could hear her.

Then Sam Papanek, Assistant State Attorney, got up and began his questioning. "What is your name, please?"

Mom whispered, "Veronica Burowsky."

The coroner pointed across the room. "You see those gentlemen over there?" Mom nodded. The coroner continued, "The jury has to hear you, and I want everybody else to hear you so will you speak louder?"

Mom whispered again, still barely audible, "Veronica Burowsky."

The coroner tried several more times to get mom to speak up. He finally gave up, and for the rest of the inquest he repeated all of her answers for everyone to hear.

The coroner asked, "How many children do you have?"

"I have five children." (She really had seven children.)

The state attorney asked, "Now, when you say you saw Philip ... no, pardon me." He looked through his papers ... "When you saw Peter at 4 o'clock Tuesday, what condition was he in?"

"He was badly bruised because I had spanked him ... beat him because he didn't mind." Then she broke down sobbing.

The state attorney continued, "How many times did you beat Peter with the stick?"

"I gave him two. One in the morning and one in the afternoon."

"Just what did you do? Tell the jury what you did to him.... Go ahead."

Mom stammered, "I-I-I struck and I-I-I spanked him w-w-with ... (her answer trailed off into hysteria.)"

Papanek gently asked, "Why did you punish Peter?"

Mom, wiping tears from her eyes, whispered, "Peter was always in mischief."

Papanek inquired, "What kind of mischief do you mean?"

Mom softly replied, "He was always pulling bottles out of the medicine cabinet. He would take towels out of the linen closet. I caught him taking food out of the refrigerator, tearing all the food up. Sometimes he would break the dishes and the girl's dolls ..."

The coroner interrupted, "In other words, he was just a healthy boy?"

Mom whispered, "Yes."

The coroner continued, "You, as a mother, shouldn't have things within his reach, that's your responsibility, not his."

Then the state attorney resumed the questioning. "Did you ever beat the other kids with anything except your hand?"

Mom defensively replied, "No. When I beat Peter with that stick that was the first and only time."

"Do you recognize this stick?" the state attorney asked as he exhibited a broken baton about a foot long and an inch square. It had spots of blood on it.

Mom said, "It's part of Georgianne's ironing board that I used to beat Peter."

Papanek asked, "How did the stick get broken?"

"I broke it."

"Why did you break it?"

Mom stammered, "So I-I-I could hit Peter with it."

Papanek showed the exhibit to mom and asked, "This stick was broken on both ends. It was also cracked in the middle. Did you break it over Peter's body?"

Mom looked down at the floor. "I don't know."

Papanek asked, "In between beatings, where did you put Peter?"

"I bound his hands and feet and put him in the bathroom."

Papanek asked incredulously, "Why did you do that?"

Coroner Walter McCarron holding the leg from the ironing board that was splintered over Peter and me. Officer Rita Meany is standing in the background. She had checked our home while Peter and I were tied in separate torture chambers. She didn't find us, so she reported our home to be abuse-free.

-Chicago Sun Times, July 31, 1953-

Mom replied matter-of-factly, "I did that to keep him out of mischief. He never would mind. He was always unruly."

The coroner interrupted, "You know, I have children too, and I know how a normal child acts. You should thank God that a little child is well and healthy, so that he could get around and play. You should have been grateful."

Mom meekly replied, "Yes."

The coroner continued, "You were blessed with healthy children, and you were hardly worthy of the blessing."

Then the state attorney resumed his questioning. "What parts of his body did you beat?"

Mom said, "His shoulder mostly ... all over I guess."

The state attorney asked, puzzled, "The face too?"

Mom quickly answered, "Yes, but-but I didn't mean to hit him in the face. He turned an ... (she became hysterical.)" When she calmed down, mom finished her answer. "I didn't mean to kill him. I'm so sorry. I want my baby back. I meant to spank him easy." Then she became hysterical again.

The coroner soothed, "Take it easy. You should have thought of those things before."

The state attorney quietly resumed questioning. "Why did you beat Peter so often?"

"He was getting worse and worse. I figured that if I spanked him hard enough with a stick, he'd mind me."

State Attorney Papanek asked, "Did he say anything when you beat him?

"He never said anything except that he'd be a good boy."

"How many times did you punish him on Monday?"

Mom answered, "I took his television privileges away from him. I tied him up twice Monday because he refused to stay in a corner. I spanked him three times and didn't give him his dinner."

Papanek asked, "And on Tuesday?"

Mom: "I gave him two spankings and bound him in the bathroom like yesterday before I went to work. I-I-I can't believe he's dead."

Coroner McCarron examined the bloody, broken stick and hurled it down on the evidence table with a resounding "crack!" The courtroom murmured.

State Attorney Sam Papanek continued, "How did you learn that your son was dead?"

Mom started to weep again. "I got a call from Pug, and I found firemen trying to revive my son."

Papanek: "Did your husband condone your treatment of your kids?"

Mom firmly replied, "I alone am responsible. I don't want him to get into trouble over this. In the seven years we've been married, I controlled him. He did only what I told him to do. When he tied up Peter, he was only doing what I had instructed."

The coroner asked, "You have had a chance to do some meditating."

"Yes I have."

The coroner commented, "Well, you have to live with yourself."

Then State Attorney Papanek resumed questioning: "How did you discipline your other kids?"

"I would spank them."

The state attorney asked, "Do you mean beat them with a stick?"

Mom defiantly said, "No. I just spanked them with my hand."

Papanek asked, "Did you use any other form of punishment?"

"I make them kneel in the corner."

"How long?"

"A few hours."

The state attorney asked, "Did you ever deprive them of food as a punishment?"

"Yes, sometimes I wouldn't let them eat supper."

The state attorney asked, "What was the longest they would go without food and water?"

"Never for more than 24 hours."

The audience started murmuring at this answer.

The state attorney asked, "Now, getting back to Georgianne, you struck her also?"

"I just spanked her when she wouldn't mind."

The state attorney asked, "Did you ever tie up your kids?"

Mom said, "No. Just that one time."

Papanek asked, "You didn't tie her hands and feet, or anything?"

I was listening to mom's testimony very carefully. I couldn't believe my mom had the nerve to answer "no" to that question. Her answer made me mad. I hoped that no one believed her.

The state attorney asked, "You never tied her at any time?"

I was outraged when mom replied, "No, not that I can remember."

The coroner asked incredulously, "Not that you can remember?"

"That's right."

Papanek pointed at me and asked, "Did you ever tie her hands and feet?"

Mom said, "I don't think so."

The coroner looking at mom and said, "Sit right there." Then he turned to Mrs. Meany. "Bring that little girl to the stand, please," and he pointed at me.

I began to cry.

Chapter Fourteen

Quite A Hero

Mrs. Meany got up and came over to me. She took my hand and led me up to the table where Coroner McCarron and my mother were both sitting.

The corner picked me up and sat me down in front of him on the table. I was watching mom, not him. I was trying to figure out what was happening and what I should do. He said, "My how pretty you are. Would you like some candy?" He retrieved some hard candy from his desk. Then we talked for a while about truth.

After my talk about the truth with the coroner, the state attorney gently asked me, "How old are you Georgianne?"

I held up one hand. "I'm six."

"Do you know why you were beaten?"

I shrugged. "Because I'm bad?"

"What did you do bad?"

I meekly answered, " 'Cause I tell lies."

"Do you think you are bad?"

I nodded.

The state attorney held my hand. "How did you get those marks on your wrists?"

I took a long time to answer, because mom wouldn't approve of my not agreeing with her story, and she was only an arm's length away. Finally, I closed my eyes and replied, "She tied me up with rope and cloth, real tight."

Papanek asked, "Would you go to bed with your hands tied?"

I continued, "I don't go to bed. I stand up all night, and we don't go to bed."

Papanek, not believing what he had just heard, asked again, "You mean, you stay there all night? You have to stand all night, hands tied?"

I meekly replied, "Yes."

Papanek asked, "You can't go to bed?"

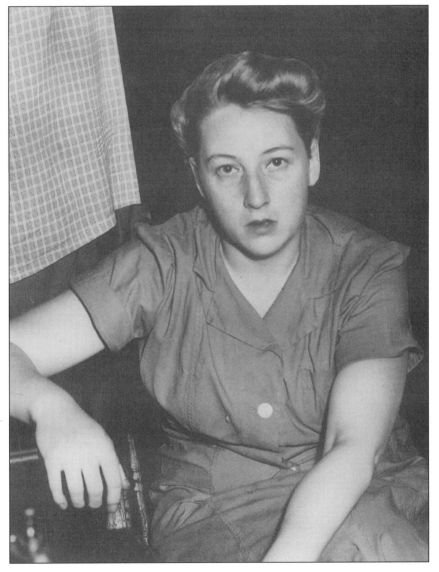

Mom glared at me while I contradicted her testimony.

-Chicago American, July 30, 1953-

"After midnight, when mom comes home, we can't be in bed."

Papanek asked, "Did your mom tie you up the day Peter died?"

I watched mom's expression as I replied, "She put me in a closet, and my hands and feet were tied so I had to stand."

The state attorney asked, "Do you remember about your little brother getting a beating the other day?"

"No," I lied. I was getting nervous with mom glaring at me.

Papanek continued, "With a stick?"

"No," I lied again. This was making me very nervous.

Papanek touched the scabbed-over, tender spot on the back of my head, and I winced. "Where did you get that big bump on your head?"

"I fell off a swing, "I lied again.

"Did your father beat you?"

"Father never beat us," I replied confidently.

"Did he tie you?"

I carefully responded, "Sometimes he untied us for supper, and then tied us up again after supper."

Papanek asked, "Did your mom ever hit you with a stick?"

I closed my eyes again so I wouldn't have to look at mom. "My mother spanked me with a stick because I wet my pants. She hit me with a stick lots of times."

Papanek asked, "Where did she beat you?"

"In the kitchen, living room, bath ..."

He interrupted, "What part of your body?"

I pointed at my bottom.

The coroner interjected, "I would like for you to show the jury your bruises."

Mrs. Meany came over and picked me up. She stood me on the table, lifted up my dress, and pulled my panties down, exposing my badly bruised bottom. A gasp of disgust rose from the audience, and many flashbulbs went off. They frightened me, and I began to weep.

The coroner handed me some more candy. "You are excused little girl."

I concentrated on my candy as Policewoman Meany pulled my panties up and placed me on the floor.

The coroner asked, "Do you have any questions, Mr. State Attorney?"

Mr. Papanek replied, "Of this woman, yes." Then turning to my mom, "Those bruises don't look like they were caused by your hand as you earlier testified."

Mom said, "I guess that I struck both my son and daughter with the stick."

Papanek asked, "Why did you beat Georgianne with the same piece of wood the same day?"

Mom said, "Because she messed her pants."

Papanek picked up the stick and asked, "Is that blood on this stick?"

Mom said, "Yes."

The state attorney asked, "Where did you hit him to get blood on the stick?"

Mom said, "In the face, I guess."

Papanek asked, "You hit him in the face with a stick?"

"I didn't mean to. W-when I went to hit him, he turned around and got it right in the face."

State Attorney Papanek asked, "What kind of a mother are you?"

Mom made no response.

The coroner said, "Madam, you are excused."

The coroner then called my dad up to testify. I hoped the coroner and State Attorney Papanek wouldn't be too hard on my dad, because he usually untied me. Dad was my hero.

Dad was solemn as he walked up to the stand. The state attorney began, "Why didn't you call the police about your wife?"

Dad said, "I didn't want any trouble."

Papanek asked, "Where was young Peter when Mrs. Meany came to investigate?"

Dad said, "He was tied up in the bathroom."

Papanek asked, "Have you ever hit anyone in your home?"

Dad said, "I beat the boy sometimes but never with a club. The last occasion was with a ruler to punish the child for getting into the peanut butter. I beat Veronica twice for beating the kids. I had threatened to leave Veronica because of the beatings she gave the children. I never saw my wife beat Peter, and the only beatings I learned about were those administered on Monday and yesterday. I came home about 4:30 yesterday afternoon and read the note that my wife had left. I untied him, and I gave him a drink of water. When I saw him punished like that, I didn't know what to do. I have had my trouble with my kids. I have had more trouble with this kid than I think anyone has ever had."

Papanek asked, "Didn't you see the boy had been beaten and had bruises?"

Dad said, "Yes, the boy bruises easily."

"Is that right? Go on."

"After supper, I made him stand again while I tied him to the pipes, and he made a noise. He continued making a noise in his throat I guess, or a rattling like his teeth were chattering. Then I tied him by his wrists to the hot-water pipe in the bathroom. I used a piece of rope. I heard him whimpering and mumbling about 9 o'-clock. At 9:30, when I didn't hear anything, I untied him, and I started to try to revive him."

Papanek asked, "Why didn't you call the police or an ambu-

Dad holding his head in his hands while Jill, I and Pug look on curiously. Dad would testify that he was afraid that his wife would hurt him if he didn't help her torture the children.

-Chicago Tribune, July 30, 1953-

lance?"

Dad said, "I told Pug to run to the neighbors and call mom and the police."

Papanek picked up the note that mom had left for dad on the kitchen table and asked, "In this note, what does 'The Bum' mean?"

"That was Peter's nickname."

Papanek asked, "How long have these beatings been going on?"

Dad replied, "She has been beating them ever since we moved to Chicago."

Papanek asked, "Did the neighbors complain about the violence going on in your home?"

"I don't know. I don't bother neighbors, and I don't want them to bother me."

Papanek asked, "Has your wife ever beaten you?"

Dad said, "Yes."

Papanek asked, "What did she use? Did she use a stick?"

Dad replied, "My wife has beaten me with a glass ashtray, and then she ran out of the house. I don't remember anything after that. I got scars all over my goddamn body."

Papanek asked, "Would you say that you were in such fear of your wife that you were afraid not to tie your son up in the bathroom?"

"Yes."

Papanek asked, "You're quite a hero aren't you?"

Dad looked down, but he made no response.

The next person called to testify was the Director of Policewomen, Ruth Biederman.

Papanek asked, "Tell us what you have learned about this case?"

Policewoman Biederman: "Georgianne has been horribly beaten, and the child's legs and buttocks were blue, black, and yellow from bruises new and old. Her cheeks were battered and bruised, and her wrists bore red ligature marks. The little girl told me that Peter had been tied to pipes in the bathroom. Jill appears to be unmarked. Jill said that she had not been beaten because she was "mommy's pet."

Papanek then called Policewoman Rita Meany to the stand and began, "Have you ever had occasion to go to the Burowsky home?"

"I went to the Burowsky home on the 28th of May to investigate Mrs. Burowsky's treatment of the children, because neighbors had turned in complaints to the police."

Papanek asked, "Did you examine Peter Burowsky, Jr.?"

"I didn't know that he existed until this week. Mrs. Burowsky didn't mention the boy."

Papanek asked, "Did you see the other kids?"

Meany: "Yes, I talked to Jill, five years old, and Donna, 18 months old. I saw no negligence either in the home or on the part of the mother. The kitchen was like anybody's kitchen. The living room was quiet and comfortable. I'm a registered nurse, and the children did not look physically abused to me. Mrs. Bur ..."

The coroner interrupted, "Don't you think you could have talked to someone to verify her stories? I don't think you made a complete investigation."

Papanek scolded the coroner. "I don't think that's a proper question. The Commissioner of Police pointed out that Veronica registered her daughter with the clinic at the Chicago Board of Health. This was only one of a number of indications to Officer Meany there was no neglect. The worst that we can say about Rita is she might have been fooled. That's the worst we can say about her."

I Guess I Was Angry

THEN STATE ATTORNEY PAPANEK called Doctor C. A. Fioretti from St. Bernard's Hospital to the stand and asked, "What are your qualifications in this case?"

Dr. Fioretti: "I have 13 years' experience as a staff surgeon at St. Bernard's Hospital, where Peter's body was first taken."

Papanek said, "Dr. Fioretti, what was the condition of the boy's body when it arrived at the hospital?"

Dr. Fioretti gravely replied, "I've never seen a child so abused or mutilated. The cause of death could have been shock, skull fracture, or a concussion from the beatings. Malnutrition or suffocation are both also possibilities."

I was interested in hearing what the doctor had to say so I listened intently, but he was using words too big for me to understand. Most of what he said sounded like "blah, blah, blah" to me. I only had a little grasp on exactly what was going on. Heck, at that point, I didn't even really understand that I would never see Peter again.

The doctor continued, "I found rope marks on the boy's neck, stomach, ankles and wrists. The marks on the neck were consistent with the type produced by rope, which may have been used to suspend Peter. He had rope burns entirely around his neck; rope burns around both wrists and around both ankles. He also had rope burns around his waist."

Dr. Fioretti droned on, "The boy had multiple lacerations from head to foot. He also had a broken nose, black eyes, and skin burns. He had a hemorrhage of the left side of the face. Some of the multiple abrasions, which covered the boy from head to foot, were old. Some of the bruises were new. He had a large healed abrasion to his face."

Well, such big words certainly sounded bad, but I had no idea what he was talking about. So I looked around the room at all the people and at my mom and dad. They both seemed to be upset. Dad had his head in his hands, and he was crying. I couldn't believe that dad was crying. I had never seen that before. I nudged my sister and pointed at dad.

Jill said, "Dad is crying 'cause mom killed Peter. Did you know mom killed Peter?"

"Yeah, I know. They told me," I replied.

The police lady whispered, "Shush. You aren't supposed to talk here."

Jill said, "I saw it all. I saw mommy nail the can on the stick and hit Peter. Georgie, they said that I would have to tell the judge what happened. I'm scared. What if mom finds out I told? She might kill me too." Jill's blond hair shook and fell down over her tear-filled blue eyes. Her slender frame trembled.

"I'm scared too," I said, and I started to cry also.

I was surprised and touched by her fear. Jill was a very slender, little five-year-old girl. When she cried she looked a lot like little Peter to me. For some reason, mom had seldom beat Jill. I was surprised that Jill was more frightened of mom than I was.

I held Jill's small, cold hand in my trembling hand and whispered, "I feel sick." The doctor continued, "Peter couldn't have eaten very much ever. My autopsy showed that his stomach was completely empty. Peter's body weight was 24 pounds. This is less than the weight of an average one-year-old child. Peter should have weighed at least 40 pounds. In fact, his weight was so low that it didn't even show on my chart as a possibility for a child of his age."

I was confused, but I listened as the doctor continued his testimony. "Peter was apt to die from malnutrition at any time. However, he didn't die of malnutrition. He died that night of cerebral lacerations and trauma. Peter also showed old, partially healed scars on his face, nose, lips, left forehead, and right temple. The old scars continued down his torso, arms, and legs and covered most of his body. Both thighs had large abrasions both front and back. His left elbow had large, new bruises, as did his right wrist."

The doctor held up his arm and pointed to his wrist before continuing. "There were bloody marks on both of his wrists and on both ankles, which were consistent with ligature abrasions."

I looked down at my own scarred wrists. I squirmed on the hard wooden bench. I was bored, and every part of my bruised body hurt.

The doctor took a deep breath and continued, "A possible cause of death was the fresh indications that Peter had been strangled with a garrote of some sort. Peter had taken a blow to the mouth, which cut his upper lip, and another blow, which broke and lacerated his nose. A fresh, jagged cut to his forehead was quite prominent. The back of Peter's head showed six separate blows with a club of some sort, such as this chair leg." The doctor held up the broken and bloody stick.

Dr Fioretti continued, "Those head blows were the direct causes of his death. The boy also suffered leg and arm fractures. Of course, the little boy might have strangled from the noose around his throat. I believe that he was forced to stand on those broken legs while being hung from his broken arms. If his broken arms and legs failed to support his weight, he would have strangled."

Dr Fioretti continued, "The healed and partially healed wounds indicate that the torture had been going on for many months. It was just a matter of time before he died. I guess if I have to pick just one cause of death, I think that I would say that Peter died of traumatic cerebral lacerations. You know, the real mystery is not what killed him last Tuesday, but what was keeping that little boy alive."

Police Lt. Thomas Cacy was then called to testify.

Papanek asked, "What was your relationship to this case on the night of the 28th?"

"I was the acting captain at the 15th Police District. I had Policemen Harold Ringbloom and Ernest Spiatto search the home. They found six nails driven in a wallboard in the broom closet. The nails were about three feet from the floor. The nails were bent as though they had been tugged out of shape. The closet was splotched with bloodstains, and the girl had been standing in her own waste. The detectives found the beatings were administered with a stick from a child's broken ironing board. Pieces of rope, tape and cloth tied together were discovered in the apartment, along with the legs from an ironing board, which Mrs. Burowsky admitted thrashing Peter with. Peter's hair was matted, indicating that he had attempted to slip the tape that bound him over his head."

The state attorney excused the lieutenant, and he called a few more people, but they didn't add much to what was already known. The coroner read several documents into the record that showed that Veronica had her children removed three years earlier in Plattsburgh for child abuse. They also showed that Granddad George asked the welfare officials to take Veronica's children because she was beating them. According to the records, the welfare officials refused to permanently remove us because of insufficient evidence. That concluded the inquest, and the case was then given to the jury for their judgment.

After only 20 minutes of deliberation, the Coroner's Jury returned and handed the decision to the coroner. The coroner read the verdict out loud. "We have found that Peter Burowsky, Jr. came to his death because of traumatic cerebral lacerations due to external violence caused when the deceased was brutally assaulted, battered, abused, and otherwise criminally mortified by one Veronica Burowsky. Said violence was participated in and condoned by the father, Peter Burowsky. We urge that custody for the three other Burowsky children be given to an institution for their future betterment in the light of becoming good citizens."

The 50 spectators applauded as the verdict was read. Veteran morgue employees were surprised at the applause, and they later told the press that they didn't remember ever hearing applause at a verdict from a coroner's jury before.

The coroner then ordered that the case be sent to the Grand Jury with a recommendation of a murder indictment. He also ordered that Mr. and Mrs. Burowsky would go to the Psychopathic Hospital to be given psychiatric examinations.

Coroner Walter E. McCarron then talked to the press. "This is the most dastardly thing I ever heard of. I recommend that the juvenile authorities should be more careful in the future and go further in their investigations. They should go into the community and interview neighbors. I understand that we get anonymous calls from some 'crackpots,' but generally there is some basis for the calls. If this complaint had been followed up further, maybe this tragic thing would not have happened."

Then the coroner was struck with emotion and began to weep. He regained his composure and continued, "I also recommend that both the mother and father be confined to the Psychopathic Hospital or given psychiatric attention, because this is one of the worst things I have ever seen and heard of. Please believe me, and I further hope I never see another one. This inquest is closed."

Mom and dad had been sitting silently in the inquest room during the jury's deliberations and the reading of the verdict. When they were taken out to a patrol wagon for the trip to the state attorney's office, they leaped into each other's arms, where they embraced and passionately kissed. The bailiff and a deputy forcefully pried them apart. Mom and dad were then taken back to jail.

Mom, sitting in her cell alone, wrote a letter to her husband, who was occupying a single cell in a tier in the men's section on the other side of the same building. The letter said in part:

> *Dear Peter,*
>
>   *Forgive me for what I did to the children and what I have done to you. I would like to have Little Peter's body shipped back to Plattsburgh, New York for burial in my parents plot.*
> *Love V*

When mom was asked about her son by the press that night, she became almost sluggish. "I would welcome a psychiatric examination. Maybe they can find out why I did these horrible things. I don't know myself. I spanked my children like any other mother would spank them. I don't remember anything about the 'accident.' I guess I was angry. I don't know. Peter was my husband's favorite child. He was his only son, you see. We did spoil him more than the others; maybe that's why he never minded me. My husband is taking it terribly, but he's not mad at me. He knows I didn't mean to kill Peter."

The next day, First Assistant State Attorney Richard B. Austin said, "Murder indictments will be sought when the August Grand Jury is impaneled. The husband either aided or abetted his wife in this crime. Both are equally guilty. They beat, tortured, strangled, and hung that child."

A few days after the grand jury met, Aunt Gerry and granddad came to the children's home to visit Jill and me. As they left, Aunt Gerry said to us, "We will be back in a few days to take you back to New York, where you will be safe." I believed her, and I sure hoped that they would hurry back.

On Monday the Grand Jury convened before Chief Justice Joseph A. Grader. Both dad and mom pleaded not guilty. The Illinois State Prosecuting Attorney Gutknecht asked the judge for psychiatric examinations of both of them. Judge Grader agreed and ordered mom and dad examined by Dr. William H. Haines, head of the Cook County Behavior Clinic. He was asked to report at the next hearing.

Granddad went to family court and met with Judge Thomas Hluczynski. The judge told him that he had every right to take the boy back to Plattsburgh because he had already legally adopted Pug. The judge also ruled that, "A court must determine what is to be done with the other three youngsters." Peter's body was released to granddad for burial.

On Tuesday a true bill charging murder was voted on and passed by the Cook County Grand Jury for the fatal beating of little Peter. After the decision, granddad told the press waiting outside the courtroom, "I'll stand by my daughter because I believe she's a sick woman. I have begun proceedings to obtain custody of Georgianne, Jill and Donna, so that I can raise them in a safe environment."

I was in the orphanage the next day, when a nun came in with the paper and read to me what granddad had said. I was happy to go to live with granddad. When we got back to Plattsburgh, granddad kept Pug. However, instead of taking Donna, Jill and me into his home, he put us in his Lincoln Towne Car and drove us to the Clinton County Welfare Department.

Granddad sat down next to Jill and me and said, "I have to leave now, but you girls are going to be all right. When you are settled in your new home, I will come to see you."

I grabbed granddad's leg and screamed, "Please don't leave me. Please, granddad, I'm afraid."

Granddad took me in his arms and said, "Georgianne, I can't keep you girls. Jill, Donna and you will be together in a nice home. It has to be this way. Once you are settled, I promise I will come and see you. Now be a good girl and take care of your sister."

He sat me on the chair next to a sobbing Jill and walked out the door. Jill and I held each other's hand and cried. I was very sad when I learned that granddad didn't want me. I hoped that one of my other relatives would take us in, but no one came forward. Everyone was now gone. Mom and dad were gone. Granddad was gone. Aunt Gerry was gone. Donna went to a nice family and was adopted. Peter was dead and buried. I never got to say goodbye. My family was now reduced to just Jill and me. As it turned out, it would take me 45 years to find Peter's grave and my siblings.

After granddad left, a social worker came in and asked me some questions. She took notes as I spoke. "How old are you, Georgianne?"

I held up both hands and replied, "I'm six."

She wrote that down and continued, "What grade are you in?"

I said, "I don't remember going to school." The welfare lady went to the sink to get a glass of water.

When she turned on the tap, I screamed, "Please don't burn me

I'll be good."

She rushed back and comforted me. "I won't burn you. You are safe now. There, there. It's okay now."

I started to cry, "I want my daddy."

"Your mommy and daddy are in jail; they can't hurt you now."

I begged, "I want my daddy. When is granddad coming to pick me up?"

"Your granddad isn't coming to pick you up; you are going back to live with the Duquettes. You remember them don't you?"

I responded, "No, I want my granddad"

Chapter Sixteen

I'm A Little Tea Pot

WHEN SHE SAID, "DUQUETTES," I didn't know who she was talking about. The social-service lady put us in her county car and drove us to our new home. When we arrived, I knew right away where I was. I was so happy to see Aunt Bea, I could hardly wait for the car to stop. Aunt Bea held me and we both cried with joy. Jill was introduced to Aunt Bea.

I was not the same girl who had left this house only one year ago. For one thing, I wouldn't go near anything that might be hot. This included the stove, the bathtub, hot food, and the washing machine. Aunt Bea did the laundry on Mondays, and I watched her from a distance, with fear in my soul, but she never came after me with that hot water. After she finished washing, Aunt Bea would hang the clean sheets on the clothesline. I loved the way the clean, white sheets waved in the wind and how wonderful those sheets smelled when I went to bed at night.

Aunt Bea would hold me for hours and sing to me. She had to be so gentle with me. My head was full of sores from the "punishment braids" mom would put my hair in. My body was black and blue, and I had cuts on my wrist from the ropes. I was a very frightened girl. The slightest noise would startle me. I hated bathing because I had been scalded so often at my mom's home. Aunt Bea softly touched my face and held me in her arms while she gently brushed my long, red hair. She curled my hair into gentle ringlets on the side of my head so that the angry wounds on the back of my head would have a chance to heal.

Aunt Bea knew how I felt, but she couldn't abide a filthy child forever. She would gently coax me to take a bath. I would make my feelings known by folding my arms across my chest and pouting, "I don't want to take a bath. Please don't make me." When Aunt Bea would insist, I would stick my lower lip out in a big pout and say, "No. I don't want to take a bath. Not ever."

I couldn't stand being in a room that was dark. Aunt Bea would leave the closet light on for me so that the bedroom was not dark. I wet the bed almost every night. Aunt Bea would find the bed wet in the morning, and I would start crying immediately, fearing that I was going to be punished.

Aunt Bea would say, "Oh my, we better get these in the wash right away."

She didn't yell at me or sound angry at all. "Can I help?" I asked with tears rolling down my face.

"Sure, honey, I could use some help from my big girl today." She hugged me, and together we took the sheets off all the beds and started to do the laundry. I would like to say that I never wet the bed after that, but the truth is I wet the bed for quite a while. Each time, Aunt Bea handled it the same way. Soon I noticed that I wasn't wetting the bed very much anymore, and eventually I wasn't wetting the bed at all. When the bed-wetting completely stopped, Aunt Bea made a chocolate cake for Jill and me to eat with our lunch. We asked her what the special occasion was.

She said, "Oh I just thought we should celebrate how grown up my two girls are." Then she looked at me and gave me a wink. I felt like such a big girl at that moment. I had passed a big milestone. I was proud.

When Uncle Doody came home from the mill in the evening, he went to the barn to take care of our two cows, which furnished us with fresh milk, cream and butter. Then he came into the kitchen for dinner. After supper, Jill and I would watch television in the living room with our pajamas on, while Aunt Bea and Uncle Doody would sit at the kitchen table and have a beer—not a lot of beers, just one bottle each—while they discussed their day. He and Aunt Bea were gentle, and they spoke softly to each other.

Every day was filled with tenderness, and I never heard an angry word between them. While they talked, Aunt Bea would smoke an unfiltered Pall Mall Red, while Uncle Doody would slowly puff on a Lucky Strike. Whenever they were together, he often put his arm around her. After the violence I lived with at my birth parents' house, this was such a change. Jill and I knew that as soon as their cigarettes, beer, and soft conservation were done, it would be time for us to be tucked into bed. Unlike many children who hate to go to bed, I considered a bed to be a luxury, and I was eager to crawl under the sheets. To me they always smelled like the sunshine that had dried them. Those same hands that had worked hard all day gently tucked us in at night. Aunt Bea would then read us a book while we fell asleep.

Jill and I loved our new life. I, however, had a problem. When I was at Aunt Bea's house before, I had her all to myself. Now I had to share her with my sister, and I wasn't all that eager to share. When I didn't get all the attention, I would throw a fit and pout. This behavior was growing into a rather large problem.

Aunt Bea and Uncle Doody went to town and brought back a special book just for me. I was so happy; I had won and got a special present that I didn't have to share. The book, however, did not come out until the next time I threw one of my fits, then Uncle Doody smiled broadly and said, "Why the long face, Georgie. I'll bet that you would like for Bea to read the 'Pouty Teddy Bear Book' to you." I was so excited. We sat on the couch, and they read my special story to me. When they were done, I thought the bear sounded a lot like me, but I dismissed that thought and just enjoyed the time I had just spent with Aunt Bea.

Soon, however, it dawned on me that every time I pouted and threw a fit, I got to hear this story. I soon hated this book. It had been read to me several times. As Aunt Bea read, she would point out how silly the little teddy looked with the big pout. Aunt Bea would put a big pout on her face, and I would soon quit pouting and start giggling. I got to the point where I would happily do almost anything if it meant that I didn't have to hear "The Pouty Teddy Bear Book" again.

One Sunday morning we got up early. Aunt Bea had Jill and me put on identical white dresses that had short, puffy sleeves and delicate lace around the collar. We also had bobby socks and black patent leather shoes to wear. Aunt Bea then put little white bonnets on our heads. They had little blue ribbons that she gently tied with a bow under our chins. Getting dressed up gave me mixed feelings. I enjoyed looking pretty, and it was especially nice to have a dress just like my sister. I was uneasy, however, because I remembered the many times when my mother had dressed me up only to take my pretty clothes off and hang me on the wall when she was finished playing with me.

We all got into the car and drove to the Morrisonville Catholic Church. When we got out of the car, we talked to some of the parishioners. They commented on how attractive Jill and I looked in our identical outfits. We then went into the church for the service. The building was a massive gothic building made of gray stone. Each of its 12 windows had beautiful stained glass that I was told depicted the Stations of the Cross. It all seemed so serene and beautiful, but something was unsettling to me.

As I sat in the church in the midst of all this beauty and tranquility, my attention was drawn to a statue of a tortured man. I was told that the statue was called a crucifix, but the concept was somewhat beyond me. I was haunted by a sense of fear, because I had seen crucifixes before. A crucifix hung on the wall of every home I had ever been in, but this was the first time that I had really studied it. My stomach churned as I stared at the statue. The half-naked man had his arms stretched out and was nailed to a cross. He had blood trickling down his hands and wrists and a pained look on his face. I choked up as I remembered the hundreds of times that I had hung naked on the wall of the closet by my outstretched arms. I couldn't help but feel empathy for the pain of the man on the cross. The statue opposite the tormented man was of a mother holding a child. I couldn't help but think that she would soon tie her baby to the wall, just the way my mother had.

I listened to a man who wore a beautiful robe as he droned on for some time about Jesus. He often spoke in Latin, so I couldn't understand what he was talking about, but the message of the statue was unmistakably plain to me. Fear gripped my soul, and the color drained from my face as I glanced toward Aunt Bea. I just knew that I would soon be hanging in a dark closet again. I couldn't understand WHY, but I knew it was just a matter of time before the horror would resume.

Aunt Bea calmed my fears when we got home. She assured me that no one was going to hang me anywhere. I learned why the man was on the cross and what he stood for. I came to understand that Christ had suffered and died for us all. I had questions in my heart. I wanted to know whose sins did Peter and I suffer for, and who did Peter die for.

We had been returned to Aunt Bea just in time for Jill and me to start the first grade together. For the most part, I got along well at school, but I was quite shy. I had some trouble concentrating on lessons. Sometimes the kids teased me about my name. They loved to sing, "Georgie Porgy pudding and pie; kissed the boys and made them cry." I soon realized that Georgie was a laughable name for a girl to have.

That fall I was cast as the teapot in the school play. My role was to sing the "Teapot Song." My teacher tried to take special care of me. She made my teapot costume herself. She wanted my song to go well. I was frightened, but I looked sweet as I put all my heart into the performance. I began, "I'm a little teapot short and stout." I put my hand on my hip and continued, "This is my handle." My other little hand waved high in the air as I finished the song, "And this is my spout."

I was beginning to love it here at school, and I loved Aunt Bea even more. At Aunt Bea's, our lives were carefree. We could spend all of our time playing and exploring our world without fear. Jill was braver than I. She was always climbing trees and doing other things that I was afraid to do. One day, Jill was climbing the apple tree in the front yard when she slipped and fell. I was very frightened for her and I ran to get Aunt Bea. When we got back to her, we found the hem of her skirt had caught on a branch as she fell. Jill was hanging, suspended upside down in the tree a few inches from the ground.

Aunt Bea's dog, Lady, kept turning her head to the side to get a more normal look at the crying little girl. Aunt Bea and I both laughed and laughed. After a while, Aunt Bea finally helped Jill get down. Thankfully, nothing was hurt except for her pride. We thought it was funnier than Jill did. We couldn't help laughing at her predicament. Jill scowled back at us, but soon she was laughing as well.

Aunt Bea's dog was my constant companion when I was outside. Lady loved to chase squirrels. Thankfully, she never caught any. When we got home from school, Lady would always be there to greet us in hopes that I would play fetch-the-stick with her. I was very close to Lady, while my sister Jill became close to Uncle Doody's horse, Bessie. We weren't allowed to ride Bessie but were allowed to play with her. I loved to feed Bessie oats and carrots, but I was afraid that she might bite me, so I laid the carrots on the ground for her to find. Jill was bolder. She went right up and fed Bessie from her hand. Jill liked to pretend she was a horse, and she would gallop around the field for hours talking to Bessie in horse talk. I really think they could understand each other.

Life was good. Jill and I were happy. We were children again. We had learned to laugh, play and love.

Just Too Sick

JILL AND I LIKED to play marbles on the sloping root-cellar door at the sunny back side of the house. We'd throw the marbles onto the top of the door, watch them roll down, and catch them before they hit the ground. Then we'd laugh with glee each time we repeated the process. Occasionally, we played with the neighborhood kids. That was fun too. We also often played school or house.

During the Labor Day weekend of 1953, Susan Brown and her sister came over to play with us. The Browns were our next-door neighbors. Susan was a happy girl about Jill's age. She was full of life and adventure. The four of us played marbles on the cellar door for a while. We then played house in the front yard with a small table and a plastic tea set. After a while I suggested we play my favorite game, pretend school. I always wanted to be the teacher, but Aunt Bea encouraged me to let the other girls teach for a while. After a while, Susan got tired of playing school and said she missed her mother, who was across the road visiting a friend.

Susan suddenly stopped playing and darted out into the road. A car struck her, right in front of our eyes. I can still see her body bouncing between the tire and the fender before it landed lifelessly in the ditch just past our house. The next day, we went to her wake. It was held in the living room of the Brown's home. Her body was in a small, white coffin on the coffee table. The mortician had done his best, but you could still see the damage that the car had done to her face. When I saw her in the coffin, I wondered if that was how Peter had looked when he was killed. Jill and I cried and cried. Aunt Bea tried to comfort us, but we were upset about the death of our new friend for quite a while.

That summer, sometimes Aunt Bea took us to the wild strawberry patch beside the house. She would put the strawberries into a bucket to make jam with them. Jill and I would race to see who could eat the most strawberries. I loved picking strawberries because we could eat as many as we wanted, and Aunt Bea wouldn't even get mad if we stomped on some of them in our eagerness.

Every day, Aunt Bea would take milk from the cow and run it through the milk separator. When she had enough cream, she would pour it into the wooden churn. Then she would pump the paddle up and down for over an hour. Sometimes we would ask if we could help. We would churn away until our little arms got tired. That was about two minutes. Then Aunt Bea would take over again. When the churning was done, she would add some salt until it tasted just right.

We would then help her smear large gobs of this fresh, yellow butter and Aunt Bea's homemade strawberry jam onto slices of her fresh-from-the-oven bread. The bread was warm and steaming, and the fresh butter and jam was far better than the store-bought kind. It tasted heavenly.

Most of my memories at Aunt Bea's were happy, but not all of them were pleasant. I was very frightened of the busy county road in front of Aunt Bea's house. I hadn't recovered from the tragedy of seeing my friend Susan killed, when another child from the neighborhood was killed by a car. I didn't see that accident, but I heard that the 11-year-old boy was hit while riding his bicycle. I really hated going to another wake, because it reminded me of my brother so much. I remember how distraught the neighbor boy's mother was.

Granddad came over to visit one day shortly after the boy's funeral. The best part of his visit was that he brought toys and clothes for us. We enjoyed his visit, and the dolls he brought were great fun to play with. Jill and I each had our own shelf for our growing collection of toys. I kept a special place of honor on my shelf for granddad's presents.

In March of 1954, I caught whooping cough. I was deathly ill and couldn't sleep at night. The burning sensation in my throat and lungs was terrible. I was only seven years old, but I thought that I was going to die. Aunt Bea was very worried about me. Her loving and tender touch helped a lot. She gave me over-the-counter medicine to help my cough, and she introduced me to the best remedy of all, cold, pale-yellow Canada Dry ginger ale. This was very good stuff, and the bubbles in it made my throat feel a little better, but my cough didn't get any better. When my coughing was at its worst, Uncle Doody would tease me, "There goes that hound chasing the rabbits again."

He was cute, but I was too sick to laugh. The next day, Aunt Bea called the doctor, and he came to the house to treat me. I had seen many doctors and other official people recently, but that was in a courtroom or a doctor's office. To me, having a doctor come to the house was odd. That was a pretty neat thing to me. He gave me some pills, and pretty soon I was better and back to playing and being my old self again. Everything Aunt Bea did, she did with love. In short, I was like her child and she was like a real mother. It was a truly wonderful experience.

A few weeks later, Aunt Bea told me about seeing this story in the Plattsburgh newspaper, and I asked her to read it to me. I felt sorry for dad when he said the police were mean to him. Aunt Bea cut the clipping out for me, and I kept it.

Burowsky Says, "Police Forced Confession."
Chicago, April 27 (AP)...*A small 35-year-old man testified today that police threatened him with a gun to make him "confess" that he and his wife beat to death their three-year old son. Peter Burowsky and his wife, Veronica, 28, were charged with murder. A pre-trial hearing before Judge John T. Dempsey of Criminal Court seeks to determine whether alleged confessions by the parents can be admitted into evidence. Their son, Peter Jr., was found fatally beaten in the Burowsky bathroom last July. Burowsky took the stand and identified Police Lt. Thomas Cacy as the officer he said threatened him with a gun.*

Earlier, Burowsky declared an officer with a pistol in the station said:

"I'd like to see you run so I could give you one in the back."

Two police detectives testified they heard no threats against Burowsky. Two other officers gave similar testimony Monday.

That clipping was the only news about dad or mom that I would ever keep. I just knew that dad would get out of jail and come for me. When a new article would appear in the *Plattsburgh Press*, Aunt Bea would sit down with me and read it. These were sad times, but Aunt Bea's tender words of comfort made it easier for me.

On May 1, 1954, during the selection of a jury, Peter and Veronica decided to plead guilty to involuntary manslaughter rather than risk continuing with the murder trial. The pleas of guilty to the lesser charge came after Assistant State Attorney Frank E. McDonald told the court that he would seek to send the couple to the electric chair unless they took his plea bargain. When a deal was reached, Judge John T. Dempsey sentenced both Veronica and Peter to ambiguous terms of one to 14 years in jail.

Later that month, Aunt Bea sat me down and read the newspaper accounts of dad's parole hearing to me. She said that the Judge had set May 21 for a hearing on an application for probation for dad. Dad asked if he would be able to be released for time already served. He told the court that he was planning to take care of his remaining children if he could only get out of jail early. Assistant Prosecutor McDonald told Judge Dempsey that he would not oppose probation for dad, because the evidence showed that he was a mere passive participant in the murder. The judge said the evidence showed that Mr. Burowsky had threatened to call the police unless Veronica stopped thrashing little Peter. He also said that Mr. Burowsky had never struck the child.

Dad's landlady and his neighbors were in support of his desire to be released on probation. They all attested that dad was a good father to little Peter and the four other children.

Peter Burowsky was released that day and given five years probation. Dad decided to return to Plattsburgh to work for his father-in-law, George Trombley, at the Lido bar.

On May 22, 1954, Aunt Bea picked up the newspaper and said, "Look here in the paper. This is a story about your dad. It says here that he is being released early."

I said, "I like daddy 'cause he untied me and fed me. I want to see my daddy, but I don't want to leave here."

"I don't want you girls to leave me, but we have to do whatever the court says." Aunt Bea replied.

Life with Aunt Bea was wonderful for the next couple of weeks. Our days were filled with play, laughter, and lots of love, and our nights were full of peace and rest.

Then one day, a somber Aunt Bea sat down with us at the kitchen table. She looked so sad that I thought maybe I had done something that had made her unhappy. She held Jill's and my hands and said, "I need to talk to you both."

"Did I do something wrong?" I asked with a shaky voice. I glanced over at Jill, our eyes welling with tears.

"Oh no, honey, neither of you girls have done anything wrong.

Uncle Doody and I love you both very much. I'm sad because I'm afraid that I am unable to take care of you anymore."

I screamed, "No, Aunt Bea. Don't make us go back to mother. I'll try harder to be very good. You'll see. I can be s-o-o-o good, you won't hardly know we are here. We promise. Don't we Jill?"

Jill nodded as the tears ran down her face.

I gripped Jill's hand as Aunt Bea softly said, "You don't have to go back to your mom. I am sick and I need an operation and that is why I can't take care of you girls any more. I love you both very much, but I am not well enough to take care of two little girls."

I spoke up, "You don't look sick."

"I know I don't look sick right now. The part of me that is sick is inside. I need an operation to make it better. It will take me a long time to get well after my surgery. Uncle Doody and I need to do what's right for both of you girls." Tears rolled down Aunt Bea's face.

I cried even harder and stammered, "I-I-I can help you. I'm a big girl. I can help you take care of Jill. Please let me try."

Aunt Bea took me in her arms and said, "I know you're a big girl and that is why I know you will be strong and understand that, if I could, I would never let you girls leave. You are going to a wonderful new home. They have other children there to play with, and you will have a lot of fun in your new home."

I clung to Aunt Bea sobbing and said, "I don't need other kids to play with. All I need is Jill and you and Uncle Doody."

She stroked my hair, held me, and softly said, "Georgie, you will always be in my heart no matter where you are. You girls are very special to me, but right now I have to do what is best. The best thing I can do is let another family take you. Georgie, be a big girl for me and take care of your sister. Give this new home a chance. I'm just too sick to take care of two small girls."

Jill and I both hugged Aunt Bea, and all three of us cried and cried. I wiped the tears from Aunt Bea's face and said, "I can be good, Aunt Bea. You'll see. I am a big girl and I'll take care of Jill."

Aunt Bea shook her head and continued crying. I tried another approach, "Maybe, when you're all better, we can come back."

"Maybe you can, Georgie. Maybe you can."

The next day, I helped Jill pack our clothes in a brown paper bag. It was a very sad day. Jill and I cried a lot and so did Aunt Bea and Uncle Doody. I went over and sat beside Jill on her bed and held her in my arms. I tried to comfort her by saying, "Don't worry, Jill. Daddy is out of jail now, and he will come to rescue us soon."

She replied, "I don't want daddy. I want to stay here."

I replied, "Well, we can't stay here. You love daddy, don't you?"

She said, "I guess so."

I concluded, "Well daddy loves us. He told the judge he was coming to get us. Everything will be okay."

Jill just looked at me without replying. We sat on the bed for a while until the car came for us from the Clinton County Welfare Office. Jill and I fought the social worker as she put us into her car. After we drove away, I implored the social worker, "Are you sure these new people won't hurt us?"

She said "Georgianne, these people are a wonderful Catholic family who love little children. You couldn't hope to have a better foster family and, besides, they want to keep you together with your sister. Won't that be wonderful?"

I said, "I never ever want to be away from Jill.

Jill piped in, "I'll never leave you, Georgianne." She turned to the social worker, "Georgianne needs me to protect her and love her, and I need her more than anything."

I asked again, "Are you sure these people won't hit us? When will daddy come to get us?"

The lady said, "I don't know. Maybe soon."

Jill said, "If we can't stay here, I want to go with daddy."

"Me too," I piped in.

The social worker replied, "You will be going to a wonderful place. You'll like it at your new home."

The Bravest Thing

AS WE DROVE down the road toward our new home, Jill and I were very unhappy and filled with fear.

The social worker said, "The Yelles are wonderful people who would never hurt little girls like you. Trust me, they are a wonderful couple. They have four daughters of their own."

Sometimes people mix up "Altoona" with "Altona" because their names are similar, but the similarities end there. Altoona is a large city in central New York. The hamlet of Altona, where we were sent, was a wide spot in the road within a stone's throw of Canada.

I looked out the window of the car and saw a clean babbling brook on the edge of Altona that flowed into a small, picturesque reservoir. Next to this lake was a large park with many picnic tables. Altona was so small that almost all of the homes in this little town were on Main Street. Altona only had two businesses—a gas station and a grocery store.

Our car pulled up to the Yelle family home, which was a large two-story house next door to the grocery store. We got out of the car and were introduced to Mrs. Yelle. She explained that her husband couldn't be here to meet us because he was at work delivering milk for the nearby dairy.

Mrs. Yelle then said, "I hope you will be happy here."

Mrs. Yelle was a homemaker who had four lovely daughters of her own. I met them all later that day when they got home from school. The youngest child was about my age. I hoped that we would be good playmates.

My first night at the Yelle's home, I was given a new pair of blue pajamas and shown my bed. I wet the bed that night.

In the morning when Mrs. Yelle came into the room that Jill and I shared, she discovered my situation.

She started to yell at me, "This is the last time that you're going to get away with soiling your bedclothes, young lady! Just because you were spoiled at your other home doesn't mean that I'll put up with this behavior! You're big enough to use the bathroom in the middle of the night if you need to! The next time you make a mess, you'll get a spanking! Do You Understand Me?"

I was very upset and stammered, "P-P-Please don't hit me! It will n-n-never happen again! I p-p-promise. I am t-t-trying as hard as I can!"

"You're not trying hard enough! This better not happen again! OR ELSE! Now get cleaned up!"

I was so scared. Just thinking of the threat of a spanking caused me to start crying. Jill tried to comfort me. "It's okay, Georgie. I will help you and take care of you. Don't worry, it will be okay."

That night I nervously put on clean pajamas and got into my bed. I didn't use the warm blankets this time. I wanted to be cold, because I was desperately trying to stay awake all night. That way I would know when I had to go to the bathroom. I felt in my heart that the mattress, pajamas and covers were just a trick to get me to let my guard down and go to sleep.

I spent the night kneeling in my bed crying. By staying awake I managed to make it through that night, but I was both physically and emotionally exhausted.

The next night, I again tried to stay awake all night, uncovered and on my knees, but the bed was just too comfortable. I was so worn out that my eyes grew heavy with sleep, and I nodded off. When I woke in the morning, I was stunned to find that I had soiled my pajamas. Mrs. Yelle came in and found my predicament. She shouted, "I can't believe that you're such a baby that you wet your bed after I warned you! What the hell is wrong with you, Georgie? Why can't you act your age? You are not going to be spoiled here like you were at Bea's house. I'm going to go get Mr. Yelle and he's going to tan your hide."

"Please give me another chance. It will never happen again," I begged.

She snarled, "It's too late, little lady. You were warned yesterday! Now you're going to learn the hard way! You are going to get the beating you deserve!"

Mrs. Yelle angrily turned on her heels and left. A minute later, Mr. Yelle came in and threatened, "Look here, little miss, you aren't going to get away with your tricks here! You're going to do some growing up today, and I am going to see to it!" My bottom was completely healed, but my mind was back at the house where my mother had beaten me so often. I prayed that he would kill me with the first blow. I began to struggle as he pulled my wet pajama bottoms down, but to no avail. He threw the soiled garment to the floor. I screamed as he pulled me to him. He used his left hand on my neck to bend me over his lap. I couldn't get away and I couldn't struggle. All I could do was to cry and stare at the floor as I waited for the blows to fall. Mr. Yelle, using his hand, gave me three hard spanks on my bare bottom. Then he grabbed my hand and released my legs. I stood up, but I couldn't run as he scolded me, "Well, I hope that you have learned your lesson. This had better not ever happen again.

He then released my hand, and I ran over to Jill and hugged her. After Mr. Yelle walked out of the room, I collapsed on the floor. Jill lay down beside me and held me in her arms. Most of that day, Jill comforted me and tried to persuade me that the Yelles weren't nearly as bad as mom had been. I was not convinced. A crib was brought into the room, and I was told that this was my new bed. I was seven years old and much too big for a crib. But Mr. Yelle said, "If you wet the bed like a baby, you will sleep in a baby's bed."

That night I again knelt uncovered in my crib. I made it through the night without wetting my bed, but the night after that I was again a complete wreck. When Mrs. Yelle woke me in the morning, she discovered that I was wet. I started to sob as she spoke. "Well you just can't learn anything, can you? I think you're just too lazy to get up and go to the bathroom! Well your laziness isn't going to fly in this house!"

I could feel myself falling apart as she left to go get Mr. Yelle. Jill exclaimed, "Quick, Georgie, switch pajamas with me!"

I couldn't believe what I was hearing. "Thank you," I sighed.

I quickly pulled off my wet pajama bottoms as Jill took off her dry ones. Then we switched clothes, and I started to climb back into my crib. Mr. Yelle arrived wearing a T-shirt and boxer shorts. He looked at me and ordered, "Come here, Georgianne. I'm tired of your childish behavior! It's time for your spanking!"

Jill piped up. "It wasn't Georgianne, it was me." She lifted the edge of her pajama top and turned around to show that, indeed, her pajama bottoms were wet, not mine.

I was so thankful that she was offering to take a thrashing for me! I had never seen a braver thing done. I loved Jill so much!

Mr. Yelle was confused at first, until he noticed that Jill's top and the soiled pajama bottoms didn't match. He went over to my crib and discovered that my sheets were wet, not hers. "Well, Georgianne, your little trick didn't work did it?"

I ran into the closet and closed the door behind me. I held onto the doorknob with a death grip and braced my feet. I could hear the muffled sound of Mr. Yelles voice. "Now, come here this instant, or it will be worse." He grabbed the doorknob and pulled. My feet slid across the floor as the door opened.

He grabbed me and stripped Jill's pajama bottoms off me. Before he could bend me over, Jill wrapped herself around his leg like an octopus and shouted, "Leave my sister alone!" Then she bit him on the calf.

"Damn!" he exclaimed as he tried to kick Jill out of the way. My little sister wouldn't let go, and try as he might, he couldn't shake her loose. He pulled her hair, and when she didn't stop biting him, Mr. Yelle punched her on the side of the head, knocking her to the floor.

Jill's teeth had broken the skin on his leg, and he was fighting mad. Jill tried to crawl under the bed, but Mr. Yelle caught her foot. I couldn't let him hurt my hero, so I started swinging my little fists against his back, and the war was on.

We were soon overpowered. Mrs. Yelle came upstairs with her husband's heavy belt. Mrs. Yelle pulled Jill's pajama bottoms off, and then they forced us both to bend over Jill's bed. Mrs. Yelle held us down while Mr. Yelle gave us both a beating on our bare bottoms with the belt. After the beating, we held each other and cried, but no one heard us or cared. As tears rolled down our faces, we dressed in our day clothes.

Mrs. Yelle came and got us and said, "I want you girls to march downstairs and sit on the kitchen chairs that are against the wall. If you move I will give you a beating that you will never forget."

We quietly went down to the kitchen and sat on the hard, wooden chairs. The chairs had thin, blue plastic cushions, but after a couple of hours they became very uncomfortable. I just stared at the empty kitchen and cried. We sat there all day and all evening. Then we were sent to bed.

My mind soon developed a friend to help me get through the night without wetting the bed. I dreamed about a frog that was sitting on a small hill of sand about a foot tall. It was hard to tell if the frog was awake or asleep. Suddenly, the frog leaned to the side and tumbled down the hill. I was startled awake. I found my eyes wide open, and I was breathing hard. I always woke up scared, but I also realized when I woke up that I needed to go to the bathroom. I would go down the hall to the bathroom and then would go back to bed. I never wet the bed again. My frog always seemed to wake me up in time.

The next day, we went back to sitting on the chairs. Jill and I continued sitting on those chairs for the rest of the week and then the week after that. All in all, our life here wasn't a good life. Sitting in a chair all day, every day, was horrible, but at least we weren't wired to a wall listening to someone being beaten to death. Both Jill and I had lots of time to think and talk as we sat there on those kitchen chairs. We never played with the Yelle children, nor did we participate in any family activity.

Mr. and Mrs. Yelle and their kids loved to watch television by the hour. We would have preferred to spend our evenings playing games and watching television in the warm living room like the Yelle children did, but this was never allowed. Jill and I were only allowed to watch one-half hour of television per week. I convinced Jill that we should pick "Bonanza," on Sunday night, as our show. When Sunday evening came around, Mrs. Yelle allowed Jill and I to get off our chairs in the kitchen and go into the living room with the family.

I was thrilled when the Bonanza map started to burn. I watched intently as the Cartwright sons discovered a squatter on Bonanza land. Mr. Rossi and his family thought that the Cartwright land was open for homesteading. He had already planted a field with grapevines. He intended to harvest the grapes and make them into wine. Ben informed him that the land was part of the Cartwright ranch. A commercial came on, and Mrs. Yelle informed us, "Georgianne. Jill. Your half-hour of television is up. Go back to the kitchen and sit on your chairs until bedtime."

"Pleeeeease let us finish watching 'Bonanza' first," I begged.

Mrs. Yelle declared, "Too much television is bad for little girls."

"Pleeeeease let us finish the show," I begged.

She screamed, "Listen to me and get back to your chairs right now before I get mad!"

We were so frightened we scurried back to the kitchen to sit on our chairs for the rest of the evening.

Jill had gotten to the kitchen first and had taken the better chair—the one where you could hear the program fairly well, and if you were brave enough, you could even stand near the chair and look around the corner to see the television. Jill soon got out of her chair and crept over to the corner and was watching the end of "Bonanza." I was outraged. I impulsively called out, "Mrs. Yelle, Jill is out of her chair!"

Mrs. Yelle came in and put Jill across her knee. "You kids are spoiled rotten, but you're going to learn to mind one way or the other!" Then she gave Jill a hard spanking with her hand.

I was stunned and guilt-ridden. I trembled in my chair and cried as hard as Jill did. I thought, "How could I put her in danger over a TV show?"

The next week was uneventful. We just spent all of our waking time in the kitchen staring at the wall and sitting on those hard, wooden chairs with the thin, blue plastic cushions. On Sunday when "Bonanza" came back on, we chose to watch the last half this time. My theory was that we could figure out the beginning of the show based on its ending, which we were about to see. It was more satisfying for us to see the part of the program where the problems were solved, rather than the part where the problems were being created.

Mrs. Yelle came into the kitchen and said, "Okay girls, 'Bonanza' is half over. You may come into the living room and watch the last half. I don't understand you girls. Why don't you pick a half-hour show? That way you could watch the whole thing."

I felt like saying, "Why don't you let us watch as much television as we want, like your own kids do?" I didn't want to talk back to her and miss my television for the week, so I kept my mouth shut. She didn't understand that it was a matter of principle for me. I would prefer to go half an hour in a direction that I had chosen than to be forced to take an easier path not of my choosing. By god, I would watch half of what I wanted.

When Jill and I entered the room, Speedy Alka-Seltzer was singing, "Relief is just a swallow away." I sat down on the couch and was relieved by how comfortable it felt compared to the hard chairs. After the commercial, the glowing wonder of "Bonanza" came flickering on the screen in living color. Someone had trapped Ben Cartwright and another man in a large hole in the ground for some reason that we had missed. They had been in the hole about a month when Ben explained to his kidnapper that a captor who is full of hate is more trapped in the situation than the person who he detains.

The bad man apparently didn't like what he said, because he lit a stick of dynamite and threw it into his homemade dungeon. The other man in confinement wouldn't let Ben throw the dynamite back out. He just wanted to die. Fortunately for them, the dynamite didn't go off. When their captor went for more supplies, he had an accident and broke his leg. Hoss Cartwright came along and saved the bad man's life. He was so grateful to Hoss that he told him where he was holding Ben and the other man captive. The show ended with Ben patting his tormentor on the shoulder and forgiving him.

Our last half of "Bonanza" was over, and we were sent back to the kitchen for the rest of the evening. Jill and I talked and talked about the part of the show that we had missed. We tried to figure out why the man was so angry, but we couldn't figure it out.

I learned a lot that evening from Ben. He showed me not to give up. He also never allowed himself to become angry and vindictive. I wished that I had the strength of Ben Cartwright, because I really needed it.

The weeks stretched into months, the months into years, and we were still sitting on those chairs. The only exception was when we went to school and when we stayed outdoors playing. We stayed outside as much as possible, but the rain, snow, cold or darkness would eventually drive us indoors to sit on our chairs.

Chapter Nineteen

Candy From A Baby

MRS. YELLE WAS IN THE KITCHEN often, where she made pies, cakes, roasts and steaks. She appeared to be a wonderful cook. I say "appeared," because unfortunately, Jill and I didn't eat any of those delicious foods. Mrs. Yelle fed Jill and me cereal for breakfast and peanut butter sandwiches without jelly for both lunch and supper.

Night after night, we would sit on our chairs against the wall of the kitchen and watch the family gather around a huge feast. It looked delicious and smelled like heaven. My mouth watered as I watched them savor the roast beef with gravy, steaming ears of corn, and baked potatoes in little foil wraps.

I would eat my one peanut butter sandwich and die inside, not because I was hungry for food, but because I was hungry for love. After supper, Jill and I would be ordered to wash the dishes. One of the Yelle girls was a picky eater, who oftentimes left a scrap of meat on her plate. I would snatch it up and savor its juices. Although my stomach was full, my heart was empty. After we finished the dishes we were sent back to sitting on our hard kitchen chairs until bedtime, while the Yelle children would play or watch television.

February 1, 1955, was my eighth birthday. I remembered the happy celebration Jill and I had had at Aunt Bea's house. I told Mrs. Yelle that today was my birthday.

She said, "Congratulations, Georgianne, have a happy birthday." That was it. I received no presents and was extended no special privileges, such as regular family food or television. I received no cake with candles, party hats, or party. I never mentioned one of my birthdays again to a foster parent. I spent most of that day siting with Jill on our chairs in the kitchen. I noticed Jill was working on a project, but she wouldn't tell me what it was. When she finished she proudly showed me her handiwork. It was a piece of notebook paper that said:

TO GeORGie
HAPLY BIRtHDAy TO yoU
HUGS aND KISSÉI OOOOO XXXXX
FROM Jill OOOOO XXXXX

I was very touched by her effort.

By that spring, we either outgrew or wore out the beautiful clothing that Aunt Bea had always dressed us in. We were given hand-me-downs from the Yelle children. A few of the kids at school would make fun of my ragged clothes. Jill especially hated her worn-out, ugly brown shoes. I hated not having black buckle-up overshoes like the Yelle children did. The winters on the border of Canada were quite severe, and my toes were often nearly frozen by the time I arrived at school.

I was very happy when spring came, because it meant that my toes wouldn't freeze on the way to school. It also meant that it would be warm enough to stay outside and play, rather than sit on those hated kitchen chairs all evening.

On the 31st of March, 1955, Jill turned seven years old. The weather was nice, so we played outside all day. I baked her a birthday mud pie. I used seven twigs for candles and fresh green grass for frosting. I wrapped things that I found in the yard with newspaper and gave them to her. She enjoyed unwrapping them almost as much as if they had been real presents. Then I sang the "Happy Birthday" song to her.

I loved Jill so much. We were inseparable. I felt that it would have been impossible for me to survive without her.

Just before Easter, Granddad George came to visit us. He was laden down with two Easter baskets full of candy. He also had Easter dresses and patent-leather shoes for us. We were thrilled to see him! It meant we had a real family, a family who loved us and remembered us on Easter. When he was getting ready to leave, he gave the Easter baskets to Mrs. Yelle to keep for us. He then came over and gave each of us a quarter to buy whatever we wanted. We never saw the candy from the Easter baskets. They were given to the Yelle children. The new dresses were also given to the Yelle girls, as were our patent-leather shoes.

The Yelles didn't know about the quarters, and naturally we didn't say anything. The next day, Jill and I went to the store that was next door to our house on Main Street. We bought penny candy with our quarters. Back then a quarter would buy a lot of penny candy. We hid our candy when we got back home so that we wouldn't have to "share" them with our "sisters." It was the first we had received in a very long time, and it was all the sweeter because it came from granddad.

Later in the spring, Jill and I decided to have a memorial service for Peter. Aunt Bea had explained what Peter's death meant, but we felt that a little memorial to him was the least we could do.

I found a drab, gray cobblestone about the size and shape of a saucer. Jill wrote "Peter" on it with a red crayon. We then stood the small stone on its edge and pushed it into the soft ground so that it would stand up. We mounded up a little earth in front of the "tombstone" and laid an oval of closely spaced pebbles to mark the outlines of Peter's pretend miniature resting place. We gathered wild flowers, mostly bright-yellow dandelions and blue lupines, to make into bouquets and laid them on the mock grave. Jill and I both said a few words and then we began to cry.

Our memorial gave us a chance to say goodbye to Peter and to honor him. I knew that I could have been the one who died. I should have been the one to die. I owed my life to Peter.

Every day seemed to be the same as the last day. We sat on our hard chairs. We ate peanut butter sandwiches. On Sunday we watched half of "Bonanza."

Late in the summer of 1956, our Clinton County Social worker came around on her routine visit. She took Jill and me over to the store to get some ice cream. Then we went down to the park by the lake to eat it. The social worker said, "How are things going with you girls. Are you happy?"

I replied, "Things are fine. I'm happy."

The nice lady pressed on. "Are you sure things are okay? You look sad. You can trust me. You can tell me anything."

She seemed sincere, and I believed that I could trust her. Besides, we were away from the Yelles, and I felt brave.

I looked at Jill. She could tell what I was thinking. Jill just shrugged. That left the decision up to me. Maybe if our social worker knew how bad things were, she would send us back to Aunt Bea's. I looked at Jill again and raised my eyebrows. She nodded slightly and shrugged.

I then opened up to our trusted social worker and told her everything. I talked on and on about the spankings, the two years of sitting on the chairs, and the peanut butter sandwiches every day. Jill added how much she hated the ragged hand-me-down clothes and our 30 minutes of television a week.

I told her, "Jill and I aren't like real children to the Yelles. They show their love to their own children but not to us."

Jill added, "If they are having a bad day, they yell at us. When Mrs. Yelle was mad at her husband, she yells at us instead of him. The Yelle children blame us for stuff that they do, and Mrs. Yelle always believes them."

The social worker said, "You poor dears. I'll take care of it. Don't worry about anything." With those words she took us home, spoke briefly with Mrs. Yelle, and drove away.

Fear gripped Jill and me. We grabbed each other's hands, and all the color drained from our faces. We slowly walked out the back door hoping no one would notice us. We rushed to our favorite spot under a tree in the back yard. As Jill and I looked at each other, we both seemed to have the same question. "How could she leave us here?"

Jill asked me, "What do you think Mrs. Yelle will do to us?"

With fear in my voice I replied, "I don't know." I hugged Jill and said, "Whatever she does, it won't be nice."

We sat together the rest of the day in silence and fear, just waiting for the beating we knew we would get. When we were called into the house for dinner, we walked on very shaky legs. We took our usual positions on the hard, blue chairs. We were given our usual peanut butter dinner. After dinner we were ordered to clean the kitchen. The rest of the family retired to the living room to watch television. Jill and I looked at each other and went about our chores in silence. After the kitchen was clean, we sat on our chairs some more, and then we went to bed. Nothing was said to us. I was scared that any minute we were going to get the thrashing of our lives. We got ready for bed in silence. I think we were both so scared that we didn't dare speak or make any noise. I slipped silently into bed with my own thoughts and fears. I couldn't sleep, so I climbed into bed with Jill.

The next day when Jill and I came downstairs, there at the foot of the stairs were two paper bags containing our clothes. Our social worker pulled up in a car. Within seconds, another county car pulled up with another social worker. They both got out and came to the door together. Mrs. Yelle opened the door for them. I was quite surprised to see two social workers back so soon. Mrs. Yelle handed each of the social workers a paper bag full of our clothing. She then turned toward us with a wicked smirk on her face and led Jill to one worker and me to the other. Mrs. Yelle then sweetly said, "I understand you girls don't like it here. Well maybe you will like your new homes better."

We were led out the door and toward the two different cars. Jill and I realized what was happening and rushed to each other screaming. We looked at the social workers in horror. They were going to take us to separate houses!!!!!!!!!

I screamed frantically, "You can't separate us. Jill is all I have. We trusted you. You asked us to be honest with you. We would have never told you anything if we knew we would be separated."

We clung to each other crying uncontrollably. The two social workers pulled us apart. They carried us screaming and calling out to each other over to the cars. Jill was forced into one car, and they shoved me into the other. The two cars drove off in different directions. I waved at her and she waved back. My tears would not stop, and my heart was breaking as I looked out the back window of the car. I was straining to see the only family I had left. Jill was looking out her back window and crying.

As I looked at this woman driving the car, I knew that I would never trust the social workers or the welfare department again. They had managed to rip my entire family from me, and they called it "doing what was in the best interest of the child." The social service people may have had good intentions in everything they did, but to me, they had already ruined my childhood, killed my brother, and caused me to be separated from my other siblings. Now they had removed Jill, the last precious fragment of my family. From that point on, I refused to talk to any representative of social services. I was nine years old and Jill was eight. We would both be grandmothers before we found each other again.

Do You Like Kittens?

HALF AN HOUR LATER, my car arrived at the office of social services in downtown Plattsburgh. I was taken to a psychiatrist for an evaluation. He wrote in my file that I had a primary behavior disorder, a habit disorder, enuresis, neurotic disorders, and fears. The plain English translation of this jargon was that I was frightened, upset, nervous, and I wet the bed. This diagnosis was correct, except for the bed-wetting, which had already been beaten out of me at the Yelle's home.

The psychiatrist felt the probable cause of my symptoms was my abusive and deprived background. He also cited instability caused by numerous foster placements as a contributing factor. His recommendation was that I needed psychotherapy. I never did receive any therapy. After my session with the "shrink," I was again ushered into the social worker's car, my mind still in a fog. So much had happened to me that day. I didn't want to talk to her or have anything to do with anyone connected to the social services, but I had to know a few things.

"Will Jill be at the new place?" I asked.

"No, Jill is going to another nice family, where she will be happy."

"I want to go where Jill is going," I insisted.

"Georgie, it is very hard to place children together. We tried, but no one wants two little girls right now. We were lucky to find good people who will take one little girl. The place you are going to is a big dairy farm with many animals—dogs, chickens, horses, cows, baby calves and cats—everything a little girl should love."

"Do you like kittens?" she asked.

"No, I like Jill," I defiantly replied.

We left Plattsburgh and drove into the country. We sat in silence for about five minutes. To the many casual tourists from far away New York City, driving in the verdant countryside west of Plattsburgh, New York, was paradise. We turned right, at a large sign advertising the Beartown Ski Area, which was located at the end of the road. I noticed a cute one-room little red schoolhouse on the corner.

We topped a small hill, to where a red barn with white trim stood on the left-hand side of the road. It was solid and in good repair. Next to the barn was a tall, gray wooden silo. We pulled into a large driveway between a large two-story farmhouse and a small one-story bungalow. Both of these houses had glassed-in porches.

The social worker said, "Well, this will be your new home. Your new parents are named Bill and Margaret Rivers. They are great people who love children very much."

I heard the social worker talking, but my mind was on other things. I felt scared and I didn't want to be here.

The social worker got out of the car and took my hand. She wiped the tears from my eyes and said, "Will you try to get off to a good start with these nice people?"

I replied, "I will do as good as I can." I looked up at her and asked, "Will these people be nice to me?"

"Oh yes. They are very nice people. They have a little girl about your age and four foster children."

I took a deep breath, sighed with relief, and allowed myself to hope that they would treat me okay. We went over to a man working in a nearby field, and the social worker introduced me to Bill Rivers. He was a small man with a sunburned face and neck from being out in the weather so much. His cap was pushed way up on his head, so that it wasn't shading any sun from his face. He took off his cap and wiped his brow with a handkerchief. Then he shook my hand. I could see that he wore the cap to cover his large, bald head. His nose was the longest and thinnest I had ever seen. I tried not to stare, but that wasn't easy. I was fascinated by the size of it.

Bill Rivers took us into the house and introduced us to his wife, Margaret. She was a stocky, tough-looking woman a little taller than her husband. She had short, black hair that was curled in the front but not in the back. She smiled as she spoke to me, but her face and eyes didn't register any warmth or friendliness. Margaret's facial features seemed hard and masculine to me. I was scared of her. She seemed so glad to have me living with her that I began to relax just a little. I was afraid to trust.

We stood on the shiny hardwood floors in the living room, and I looked around at my new home as we talked. Everything was so neat and clean that it didn't look like a room that was used very much. My new mom took my hand and showed me around the rest of the ground floor. I noticed that none of the rooms looked lived in. Everything was so clean. Mrs. Rivers showed us her warm, cozy kitchen, which had a wood-burning cook stove blazing away under a pot of coffee. I had never seen a wood-stove, and I was quite curious and fascinated by how it worked.

Mrs. Rivers introduced me to her daughter, Susie, who was five years old. Susie was not particularly attractive. She was a little chubby, and she had heavy features a lot like her mother, except she had long, black hair that fell in ringlets. If not for these curls, I could have easily mistaken Susie for a boy

Mrs. Rivers turned to her daughter and said, "Susie, take Georgianne upstairs and show her where to put her clothes."

We quickly climbed the polished hardwood stairs, and Susie pointed to a large room off to the right with three twin beds. The room, like the rest of the house, was very neat and clean. She said, "This is my room, but I don't sleep here very often 'cause it's too cold." She pointed at the bed on the left and said, "This is Margaret's bed." Then Susie nodded toward another neatly made twin bed and said, "This is yours." She pointed across the hall and said, "I sleep in mom and dad's room over there." Susie opened a dresser drawer and said, "You can put your stuff here." I quickly unpacked my paper bag, and we went back downstairs.

As Susie and I entered the kitchen, where Mrs. Rivers was having coffee with the social worker, I overheard the social worker telling Ma Rivers that I had asked her if they would be nice. I hadn't asked the social worker this question so she could repeat it now. The social worker soon left, and I turned to Mrs. Rivers and asked, "What should I call you?"

She said, "Well, you can call us Margaret and Bill, or Ma and Pa Rivers, or Mr. and Mrs. Rivers, whichever you choose."

Eager to please them and even more eager to feel that I belonged, I said, "I'd like to call you ma and pa if that's okay with you."

They smiled and nodded. Ma Rivers said, "That's just fine." I felt like I had started on the right foot.

Ma Rivers took me outside and introduced me to a young man named Billy Light. He was much older than I. Although his age was not given to me, I guessed him to be 16 or 17 years old. He was tall and strong-looking, and his skin was browned by the sun. He had dark hair and a mustache. We then went around to the back of the house, where a young woman was hanging up clothes. Ma said, "Georgianne, I would like for you to meet Billy's sister, Joan."

Joan told me that she and Billy had been on this farm for many years. I couldn't help but stare at Joan. She was a very beautiful young woman. She had the whitest teeth I had ever seen. Joan told me that she was about to finish high school and that she was engaged to a marine. Later she showed me a small, framed picture of him in his uniform. Joan said that her fiancé was stationed far away but that he was due back in about a year. Although they were nearly grown up, it turned out that they were welfare kids, just like I was.

Joan introduced me to Margaret Franks, who was a thin, cute, outgoing girl about the age of my little sister Jill. Margaret had light-brown hair and a beautiful tan. She wore cheap horned-rimmed glasses on her small, oval-shaped face. They immediately drew your attention to her big, brown eyes. I thought that she was a really pretty girl, but her clothes looked old and ragged. Margaret was wearing worn-out jeans, a torn cotton blouse, and scuffed tennis shoes with big holes in them. Margaret told me that she and her brother had been on the farm for about three years. She said that her parents were both alcoholics who couldn't take care of her and Kenny.

I told her that my parents were alcoholics too. I hoped that this connection would mean that we would be instant friends.

I then met Margaret's brother, Kenny, who was only about seven. He had brown hair and eyes like his sister. He did not have the delicate oval face his sister had, but he had the same brown skin tone. He was not as tiny as Margaret, although he was younger than she. Kenny was short and solidly built. He kept his eyes downcast as he said that he was just starting first grade. I got the impression that he was bashful.

Ma Rivers then took me over to the tiny house that was next to our big two-story white farmhouse. A little old lady was sitting at a small kitchen table that was covered with a neat, clean, white tablecloth. Ma Rivers said, "Georgianne, I would like for you to meet my mother-in-law, Grandma Rivers."

The old woman gently cupped my left hand in her left hand and patted it with her right hand. Her touch was surprisingly gentle and her voice soft as she said, "My, what a precious little girl you are. I hope you will be happy here, Georgianne." I noticed that Grandma

Rivers' hands were gnarled and wrinkled where time and the weather had toughened them. Her face was very furrowed and leathery. She had short, white hair that was mostly covered with a hairnet. She was diminutive and looked like she had seen many years of hard work. After we left grandma's house, I spent the rest of the day walking around the farm looking at my new home and thinking about Jill. I cried quite a lot. I sure hoped that Jill would be okay.

That night when Margaret and I went to our room, I was very nervous. I timidly asked her, "What are my new foster mother and father like?"

Margaret said, "This farm is a very bad place, where you will be worked very hard every day. They will hit you often."

I hoped that she was exaggerating how bad it was. I asked, "Is it okay if I leave the closet light on with the door open a crack?"

She said, "Sure, no problem."

I went on to tell her that I had spent my childhood hanging in a dark closet and that I was deathly afraid of the dark. I then told her about my poor, dead brother Peter and about my sister Jill, who had been taken away. Margaret didn't ask me any questions nor offer any more information about her natural family. She tried to change the subject several times and seemed to be agitated. I could tell that I was upsetting her and that she was not interested in pursuing this discussion. I stopped telling her my story.

Over the next few weeks, I learned that Kenny and Margaret would never talk about the past. Joan and Billy Light were so much older than I that I never even considered talking to them. The Light children went about their lives as if I wasn't even there.

At first, life on the farm was okay. I was with a real family, and we ate at the same table. I had all the food I wanted to eat and a nice warm bed to sleep in. I missed Jill tremendously. About once a week I would have the same frog-on-the-hill nightmare. When he fell over, I would be startled awake in a cold sweat. I wasn't allowed to keep the light on in the closet. Ma Rivers said, "There is nothing in the dark that is going to get you." I continued to fear the darkness and the return of the frog.

I don't know exactly how or when things started to change, but little by little, everything got worse. At first I thought it was fun to go to the barn with pa and help with the evening milking. I just watched pa and played with the cats and their kittens. It reminded me of helping Uncle Doody when he went to the barn.

I was in awe about how the milking machines worked and how they got the milk out of the cow. I learned that all the cows had names. These names were written on boards above each stanchion. Each cow always went to the same stanchion every day. The cow would then be locked into her personal stanchion to receive her grain and be milked. Ma Rivers would squat and use her hard, practiced hands to get the cow's milk started. The barn cats knew to come around and try to catch this first squirt of warm milk while it was still in the air.

This looked like fun, so I asked ma to let me try to milk the cow. I tried but I couldn't get any milk to come out, so ma had to do it. After the milk started to flow, pa cleaned the teats and hooked up the milking machine. Then he turned on the vacuum, and the milk began to flow. When the milker was full, pa poured it into a pail that he took to the milk house and poured into a milk can that had a filtered strainer. This separated the milk from any dirt that may have fallen in. When this milk can was filled, pa lifted it into a large tank of very cold water. Later in the morning, a big truck would come and take the cans of milk to the milk plant.

The Human Gate

IT ALL STARTED AS FUN, but after a few days of watching, ma told me that I would be getting up at 5 o'clock in the morning to work from then on. The next morning, pa called, "George, it's time to get up."

Everyone on the farm called me "Georgie" or "George." My true name, "Georgianne," was rarely used. Somehow I went from being a little girl named Georgianne to being a hard working farmhand named George. The whole process was done so smoothly that I never knew what hit me.

Everyone had chores to do. The oldest girl, Joan, mostly did the housework and the cooking. Her brother, Billy, worked with pa in the barn. Although Kenny was only a small first-grader, he could handle a shovel, so he had to clean the cow manure out of the barn's gutters. Kenny's big sister, Margaret, worked with Joan in the house. I was expected to do barn chores, like washing the milkers. I also had to keep my room clean and help Joan with the dishes. Ma Rivers did both cooking and barn work. She needed help and I was it.

Ma took me to the barn and showed me how to wash the entire heavy milking equipment. She used very hot water mixed with an antiseptic solution. I still had a lot of fear of being scalded, but I tried to do what ma wanted. I didn't want her to be disappointed in me, but I was very frightened.

The only person who didn't have any chores was ma's only natural child, Susie. She usually spent the day playing with her many toys. Sometimes Susie would get bored, and ma would take her to play with her cousins, who lived in the nearby farmhouse. The two families were very close. This was partly because they lived at the farm next to ours, but mostly because ma's brother had married pa's sister. I never got to go play with Susie's cousins or play with anyone for that matter. I was here to work.

One day, ma dropped Susie off at her cousin's home then took me to the store to get a few things. Ma had never taken me to the store before, because we grew most of our own food. What little groceries we needed to buy, ma usually had delivered.

When we got to the store, ma gave me my 10-cent per-week allowance. I was thrilled to have a little spending money. I spent my allowance on penny candy, mostly root beer barrels, bubble gum balls and Tootsie Roll Pops. When I got home, I shared my bounty with Margaret and Kenny but not with Susie.

My chores soon became routine. One job was to gather eggs twice a day. Ma would reach into the hens' nests with such ease, and she expected me to do the same. I dreaded this. I was very timid about touching the eggs, especially if the chicken was still sitting on her nest. I was afraid the chicken would bite me, and they did. Another reason I didn't like gathering the eggs was that there were chicken droppings on them and in the nest, and I wasn't too thrilled to get that on my hands.

On the first day, I gingerly picked up an egg with my fingertips. The chicken flapped her wings and tried to peck me. I was scared! My delicate grip slipped. I dropped the egg. It broke and dripped on my shoes.

"Damn you," ma screamed, "this farm is our livelihood and the source of our meals. I expect you to treat the farm and what it produces with the utmost respect. I think that you need a lesson in responsibility."

Ma grabbed me and gave me several swats on my butt. After she spanked me, she said, "Now take this handful of eggs to grandma and be quick about it."

I rushed to grandma's house with tears streaming down my face. She noticed that I was crying and asked me, "What's wrong, Georgianne?"

I was crying so hard I couldn't respond. Grandma gently took my hand in hers and patted it saying, "Shush, little one, it's okay. Grandma is here."

I looked into her soft eyes and told her what had happened in the chicken coop. Grandma cupped my chin in her hand and said, "Listen to me, Georgie, the chickens are more afraid of you than you are of them. When you collect the eggs, just reach under the chicken with authority. Be quick and confident. That way the chickens will know that you are in charge and will not peck at you."

I looked up at her and said, "Really, that is all I have to do?"

She smiled and said softly, "That's all you have to do. Now let's dry those eyes and show me that pretty smile of yours."

I hugged grandma and smiled at her and was rewarded with a smile back. Her words touched my heart with their gentleness, and then she gave me a hug. She was warm and soft. She was tiny, but her heart was huge. To me she was a beautiful woman.

Grandma's house only had one bedroom, a small kitchen, and a glassed-in porch full of flowers. She had running water but didn't have an indoor bathroom, so she had to use a "honey pot," which was in the corner of her bedroom. Pa had built a box around it, which made it a little higher than a normal toilet. That way it was high enough for her to get onto from her walker. It was my job to empty the honey pot every morning. I didn't mind this job or any other job I did for Grandma Rivers. Every chance I got, I spent time with grandma.

I had never known a grandmother's love before, and our bond became very close. This did not please Ma Rivers, and she soon started to limit how much time I could spend with grandma. Whenever I wanted to go there, ma would always find some chore for me to do. I found myself sneaking to grandma's house whenever ma was gone. That meant that I would have to hurry back to the house to rush and finish the chores that ma always gave me to have done before she returned. Grandma Rivers was a wonderful woman and soon became my dearest and only real friend on the farm.

Most of the farmers in our region had fences around their fields. Each field also needed a gate to allow access for machinery, livestock and people. These barriers were important, because many times one field might be full of corn, while the next field might have grazing cows. If not for walls, they would get into the corn and ruin the crop. They might also eat too much at one time, and this could cause the cows to founder and die.

Pa had rustic stone fences between his fields. They were about four feet tall and about four feet wide at the base. The fences tapered until they were only one stone wide at the top. At first, I wasn't much of a farm hand, so I was often given the job of being a human gate. I spent a lot of my time standing out in the sun at the gaps in the fields. The cows could see over the low stone wall. They undoubtedly thought the corn looked tasty. My job was to shoo the cows away from the fields of corn. If I let my mind wander for an instant,

I would have a cow in my field of corn. When I left my post and tried to chase the cow back into the field, all of the other cows would head for the cornfield. Soon I would have several cows in the corn. Ma gave me a severe beating for this mistake. I was more diligent after that and tried not to ever let a cow get past me ever again.

By my second month on the farm, Ma Rivers started hitting me on a regular basis. I was usually punished for chores not done, not done properly, or not done fast enough. One day I was hit when I didn't finish a chore as fast as she expected. The next hour I was hit because she found a spot on something I had cleaned. It seemed like putting swats on my bottom had become Ma Rivers' favorite sport. I was looking forward to the end of summer and the end of all-day summer chores.

When I would go to bed at night, my heart would be heavy with such sadness and hopelessness that I started to hum Peter's special song. Even with him gone all these years, he could still bring me comfort when I hummed his lullaby

Ma said, "The one-room little red house at the beginning of the road will be your school. There is only one teacher for kindergarten through eighth grades, so I don't want you acting up and giving Mrs. Bombard any trouble.

"Wow. How can one teacher teach so many different grades?" I asked.

"You will soon see how it all works," she replied.

I was excited the next morning when Ma told me she was going to take us to Burlington, Vermont, on the ferry to get our school clothes. This would be quite an adventure for me, and I relished it.

I was amazed when our car drove right onto the big blue-and-white ferryboat. Ma parked right under the captain's bridge.

"Can I get out of the car, ma?" I asked with excitement.

"Okay, but stay close to the car."

"This was so neat," I thought to myself. The wind blew my hair and was cold against my face. The whole experience was so new and wonderful to me that I didn't notice the cold breeze off the lake.

I ran to the end of the boat and watched as the gate closed. Two large concrete blocks were held high in the air from towers. The captain seemed to have a great job with a great view. When he blew his whistle, a man on the shore pulled a lever and the two blocks of concrete slowly came down. This raised the car ramp and we were afloat.

I was afloat for the very first time. I was thrilled as the wondrous boat took us across beautiful Lake Champlain. This was all very exciting and a little scary to me. The ferry traveled about five miles from Plattsburgh, New York, to Grand Island, Vermont. We then drove off the ferry and onto the highway. The broad, tree-covered island was about six miles across. When we got to the far side of Grand Island, we took the narrow causeway to the mainland of Vermont. From there it was a short drive south to the clothing store in Burlington.

Upon arriving, I was in awe of the big, bright, clean, wonderful clothing store. I ran toward the children's clothing. By the time I had taken my second step, ma had grabbed me. Her stern voice warned, "We all stay together, and I'll pick out what we are going to buy."

All in all, the day turned out to be okay. Ma Rivers bought me some socks and underwear. Then we got jeans and plain cotton blouses to wear around the house and barn. I was more excited about the two nice dresses, two skirts, and two sweaters that she bought for me to wear to school and church. I just loved my new school clothes. They were not hand-me-downs like I had to wear at the Yelle's home.

We then went to the shoe department, where ma bought me a cheap pair of tennis barn shoes and a nice pair of brown school loafers. I was very excited when she bought me a new pair of black overshoes to keep my feet dry. That meant that there would be no more walking to school in the cold snow without overshoes. I could hardly wait to go to school.

When school finally started, I was very nervous there would be so many kids there. I hoped that they would like me. I didn't really know what I was supposed to do. While I was getting dressed, I glanced in the mirror and thought to myself, "I look very pretty today." I glanced out the second-story window of my room and could see the bus. It was at the neighbor's home picking up Susie's cousins. It would be at our home in a couple of minutes. The butterflies in my tummy were fluttering with excitement as I rode with Kenny, Margaret and Susie for the short trip to the one-room schoolhouse at the end of our road.

We drove half a mile south. Then we turned left and drove another half mile into the sun. Finally we turned south again and drove another half mile. Susie said, "Georgie, this is all my farm. All the way to school we never leave my farm."

I was impressed with how big our farm was. In fact, the Rivers' farm was so large that in the nine years that I lived there I never did see all of it.

As I entered the schoolhouse, I said to Kenny, "These desks are weird. They're all connected together."

Kenny replied, "Yeah, I guess."

As my eyes took everything in, I noticed a big wood-stove sitting toward the back of the room. To the right of the stove was a room where we hung up our coats. I could see another door, so I gingerly opened it up and went inside. To my surprise, I saw two holes on what appeared to be a platform, and as I looked closer, I saw that this was actually the toilet. "Yuck," I thought to myself. "I can't believe this is the bathroom. It's as bad as Grandma Rivers' honey pot." I saw big bags of a white chalky stuff sitting on the floor in the privy, but I didn't know what this was used for. I quickly closed the door and went into the room where the other children had begun to gather.

We were all assigned seats according to our grade. I sat with the third graders. There only seemed to be four of us. My eyes and mind tried to take in all of my new surroundings. As I saw each grade start to take shape, I realized the older woman directing everyone to his or her place was our teacher. She seemed quite old to me, but when you're nine, everyone seems old. She appeared to be even older than Ma Rivers, so to me, she was definitely an old lady. Her name was Mrs. Bombard. I could tell she was very smart, because she would teach the third graders one lesson, then go to the first graders and teach them an entirely different one.

Later that first day, as I was doing my lessons, I had to go to the bathroom, and I remembered the two holes that I saw earlier. I tried to wait but finally I knew the time had come for me to raise my hand and get permission to go to the bathroom. As I sat on the toilet, I thought the whole school could hear what I was doing. As I walked back to my desk I looked straight ahead and pretended that everything was normal. Finally, after lunch and recess, we were assigned chores to do. The older boys were in charge of keeping the firewood box filled. Some of us girls took turns cleaning the blackboard and erasers.

After school, I was surprised to see ma and Joan pull up in ma's shiny, new, green Chevrolet. Ma told Susie to go play on the playground for a few minutes with her cousins. Then she turned to Joan.

"Here are the keys. Get the cleaning supplies out of the trunk. It turned out that Ma Rivers had contracted with the school for us to clean the building and the grounds every night. Kenny and Margaret started to clean the playground while Joan and I went to work sweeping and scrubbing the floors. After we got started, ma loaded Susie and her cousins in the car and took them for ice cream. Joan and I then mopped the floors and scrubbed the blackboards. Joan showed me what the bag of white stuff in the bathrooms was for. She said that it was called quicklime, and it was used to keep the smell down.

With four of us working, we were finished in no time, and then we took the mile-and-a-half walk back to the farm. Just as we were walking up the last hill, ma and the girls came whizzing past us and pulled into the drive. Kenny and I went straight to the barn for the evening milking, while Joan and Margaret started supper. Cleaning the school was part of our day from then on.

Chapter Twenty-Two

A Doll Of My Own

A FEW MONTHS into the school year, I got the chicken pox. Ma told me not to scratch because I would get a scar. I still had part of my chores to do, but they were not too bad, just helping in the kitchen with the dishes. I didn't have to do any barn chores. Everyone's main concern seemed to be that Susie not catch my chicken pox. No one seemed worried about Kenny or Margaret. Mrs. Bombard, our schoolteacher, knew how concerned ma was, so she offered to have Susie come and stay with her so she wouldn't get sick. "Gosh," I thought, "We can't let precious little Susie come down with the chicken pox."

The next morning, as if my prayer was answered, Susie was covered with little red spots. She actually had them worse than I did. She scratched them all the time.

Ma Rivers nursed me back to health. Her level of care was totally different and much less-loving than when I had whooping cough back at Aunt Bea's.

Susie was whiney and acted like such a baby. We both had medication to put on the bumps to keep us from itching, but Susie had to have socks put on her hands to keep her from opening the sores. By this time, I felt sorry and guilty for wishing the chicken pox on her. In a couple of weeks, we were much better.

Since I had come to this farm, ma and pa had taken me to Mass every Sunday. We went to the big, beautiful, gothic Morrisonville Catholic Church. It was the same church that I went to with Aunt Bea. The Rivers were considered to be pillars of the community, and I was expected to be at Mass, scrubbed and reverent, every Sunday. They were so nice and polite at church that they didn't seem like the same people. Everyone at church knew ma and pa, and the congregation and priest always greeted them warmly.

I could see Aunt Bea and Uncle Doody across the chapel, and I wanted so badly to tell them "hi" and let them know how happy I was to see them, but I was not allowed to have any contact with them.

I liked church a lot. Church was a comforting place for me. Soon the weather started to get cold, and everything was covered in a thick blanket of snow. Everyone at school was looking forward to Christmas, even me. The day before Christmas, Granddad George came to visit me. Granddad had a large wrapped present with him that was put under the tree by ma. On Christmas morning, I was eager to open my presents, but I took my time because I only had two packages, and I wanted my joy to last as long as possible. Susie was giddy as she opened toy after toy.

I knew what to expect from ma, because Margaret had already told me that foster kids always got clothes. Clothing was the traditional present for us. Sure enough, little Margaret was right. I got work pants and a green flannel work shirt from them.

I saved granddad's present for last, and I opened it very slowly. It turned out to be bride doll. I was unbelievably thrilled to have a real present, especially a doll of my very own. I called my doll "Jill," after my sister. I was very happy; I played with my doll all day. When I got out of bed the next day, my doll was gone. I asked ma where my doll was, and she said, "You don't need a doll. You are here to work, not play." Tears silently ran down my cheeks. My heart was broken. Peter's lullaby put me to sleep again that night.

My first Lent was introduced to me two weeks after my birthday. Unfortunately, Ma Rivers chose what everyone was to give up. She decided every year that the foster kids had to give up television and sweets for Lent. Everyone else gave up gum. I never remember ever seeing Susie chewing gum in all the years that I lived on the farm. Everyone except Margaret, Kenny and me ate dessert every night of the 40 days of Lent. They would retire to the living room for a night of television viewing and sweet snacks.

I knew from going to church what Lent was all about. What I had trouble with was, that if this was such a holy thing to do, why wasn't everyone giving up something important. Even as a child, I could see a big difference between the Rivers family giving up gum and the welfare children giving up television and sweets. It could cause a person like me to reflect negatively on the season and on "the church." I didn't think I could lose anything else, but this caused me to lose my faith in God. As a child, I felt that even God didn't like foster children. Nothing was left for me. Losing God was the last thing I had left to give.

After Lent came the joy of Easter day. We all had baskets full of candy and chocolate bunnies to find on Easter morning. We never knew where the Easter Bunny would hide the goodies. After the barn chores were done, we ran around looking for a basket with our name on it. Squeals of laughter and excitement would be heard throughout the house as, one by one, we each found our baskets of goodies.

We could all eat just one thing, and then it was time to get ready for church. This was a wonderful time, because I had a beautiful new dress, a new hat, and black patent-leather shoes to put on. My excitement continued as I dressed in the new clothes that had been hanging in my closet. The clothes had been there for many days just waiting for me to wear them on this special morning. The warm sun of spring had lifted everyone's spirits, and flowers were starting to bloom. The church was filled with Easter lilies. The priest was dressed for the season in his white vestments (after many weeks of wearing purple). Everyone was happy at church, and I felt that I looked beautiful.

For the first time in 40 days, I did not see one iota of difference between any of us. We all wore new clothes and we all had lighter hearts. I looked forward to Easter, because I would be able to have dessert and watch television again

That spring, I found a bicycle in the back of pa's tool shed. It had belonged to Joan, the girl who was getting married. With some begging, I got pa to let me use the bike. It was rusty, and the tires were flat. Pa showed me how to fill the tires with air. I loved to ride to the top of the hill behind the house. Then I would turn around and pretend that I was a police officer on a motorcycle. I would shout into my pretend microphone, "Officer number 22 in pursuit, over and out!" Then, wailing like a siren, I would race at top speed back to the barn. My playtime with my bike was a very special time. I could enter a fantasy world of play and forget about the work and loneliness.

On a typical day, I was up at 5 a.m. I dressed in my work clothes and went to the barn to work. When the barn chores were done, I helped fix breakfast. After breakfast, Margaret and I would hurry to do the dishes. Then we would rush upstairs and change out of our work clothes and into our school clothes.

It was my job to lay out clothes for Susie and ma. Susie was very particular about her clothes and would send me back upstairs time after time for different outfits. Although Susie was not what you would call a dainty child, she was always dressed in pretty dresses. I guess that the one thing that made Susie unattractive in my eyes was her personality. To me she seemed very spoiled. She was very bossy and rude to us foster kids. I seldom fought with Susie about this, because ma would always take her side, and it was easier to make trip after trip upstairs than to get a beating.

Every morning, I would watch ma gently brush Susie's hair as I did my chores. Ma would carefully roll each strand around her finger and make ringlets that would fall beautifully past Susie's shoulders. I watched this ritual with envy. I longed for the gentleness of Aunt Bea. It was just like the way Ma Rivers treated Susie.

Margaret and I didn't have much time to think while we did our chores. We knew that if we didn't get everything done before the bus came, we would have to walk to school. The school was a little over a mile and a half from the house, and walking would make us very late. I missed the bus once and had to walk to school. This made me late. I loved school and I hated to be late. I somehow learned to get my barn chores, house chores, helping Susie, and getting myself ready on time.

Each day after class, I cleaned the school building. After I got home, I would change into my barn clothes. After several hours in the barn, I had to clean myself up and help with supper. Then I went back to the barn to do my evening chores. By the time I got back to the house, it was time for bed. Weekends were worse, because that's when we did the heavy cleaning and the heavy farm maintenance. I soon learned that if I had any homework, it was better to try and get it done at school, because I didn't have much time at home.

I don't remember exactly when Joan got married, but I believe that it was shortly after my 10th birthday. Joan was a major work force in our home, and when she married, there was a lot of her work that needed to be done by someone else. Joan had done much of the gardening as well as the cooking and cleaning. Margaret and I had to do Joan's work, as well as our own.

In the spring, we helped with the planting. Our biggest crop for the house was potatoes. Once the potato plants were full-grown, I was given a soup can with gasoline in it. There were rows and rows of potato plants. On many of these plants were small orange bugs that had to be picked off and put into this can of gas. I hated insects.

I couldn't believe that I actually had to touch those nasty bugs. I tried in vain to find ways to put the bugs in the can without touching them, but this did not always work. Sometimes if I tapped the leaf, they would fall into the can, but most of the time I would have to make myself touch them. I learned that I could get them on a small stick and into the can without touching them. This was slow and resulted in my getting yelled at a lot. I kept trying to make the stick work and soon got pretty good at it, but the whole thing still made me cringe. It was a horrible job, and I was always glad when it was over.

Just as summer started, ma, who loved to sew, was busy making all of us girls pretty, new dresses to wear to the Franklin County Fair, in the nearby town of Malone, New York. Margaret, Susie and I all had identical homemade dresses. People who saw us at the fair thought that we were sisters. Pa loved to spend this day betting on the harness races, so we didn't see much of him. Naturally, I wanted to ride on all the carnival rides, but I only got two tickets. Susie got so many ride tickets that her string of tickets hung to the ground, and I watched jealously as she went from each joyous experience to the next wondrous thrill. The only good part of Susie's bounty of rides was that I didn't have to be with her most of the day.

All of the foster kids had to walk around with Ma Rivers all day. I actually enjoyed this. I got to look at all of the wonderful things the people in Franklin County were doing and making. I loved the fair. The wonderful, exotic exhibits of plants, animals and crafts really impressed me.

In the months before the fair, I had saved some of my 10-cents-per-week allowance money. I had 35 cents saved up, and the money was burning a hole in my pocket. I decided to blow it all on that swirling, sticky, pink cotton candy. After the fair, we didn't get any more time off until fall. Summer was hay-baling time. Or as pa would say, "Lets make hay while the sun shines."

There seemed to be an endless supply of bales of hay to stack. We put up thousands of bales. Ton after ton of hay went into our barn. My hands were raw during the summer from all my work in the hay fields. I didn't have hands of a little girl; I had hands of a man. They had cuts on them from the hay, and my nails were short and ragged. I no longer had smooth, soft hands like the other girls.

I believed that Peter could hear me when I spoke to him, so I took comfort from the belief that my little brother Peter was safe. He was living in Heaven with the other angels. These thoughts sometimes made me cry, because I wanted to be safe and happy too. Sometimes I went to bed feeling so lost and alone that I would cry and talk to my brother Peter. My heart ached, and I thought surely it would break. I felt that I was totally alone, with no hope for a bright tomorrow. When I talked to Peter, I would ask him, "Why did you die, Peter? I wish I had died and that you had lived."

I would hate myself for these selfish thoughts, because I knew that Peter had suffered enough. He didn't deserve the life I was living. In times of need, I would hum the gift that my brother gave me, "Aaah, Aaah, Aaah, AAAH," and for a precious little while I wouldn't be alone anymore.

I eventually made it through the summer and was overjoyed to be going into the fourth grade. I was told that my picturesque, little one-room school was being closed, and I was going to be bused to the brand-new consolidated school on the edge of Plattsburgh. I felt lucky to have spent some time in the little, red one-room school. Mrs. Bombard had been kind and fair to me the whole year that I went to her school.

I hadn't seen the new school yet, but I had heard that it was huge. Ma Rivers had taken a job as a cook at the new school. Ma explained to Margaret and me that when she started cooking at the school, we would have to work harder at home on the housework.

On the first day of school, I did my morning chores quickly. I had a light heart, because I would soon be back in school and away from this hell, at least for part of the day. Kenny, Margaret and I stood at the end of the drive eagerly awaiting the school bus. Ma and Susie came out of the kitchen door and climbed into ma's brand-new Chevrolet. When they pulled out of the drive, Susie smirked at us through the side window of the car. Her smile seemed to say, "I'm special." It made me want to stick my tongue out at her, but of course I didn't. I watched them drive out of sight. A few minutes later, our bus showed up, and we were taken to the very same school. Ma and Susie were there, and Susie had already started playing with her schoolmates. Susie rode with ma, and the rest of us kids rode the bus from then on. I soon made friends on the bus. Since Susie almost never rode the bus, she missed out on all of our socializing. After a while, I was glad that I didn't have her with me, tattling to ma about everything I did.

I found that school was a great equalizer. I worked hard in school, and the praise I got from the teachers was all the reward I needed.

I had a little trouble at first when a whole new batch of kids discovered that my name was George. They sang the "Georgie Porgy" song to welcome me and see what I was made of. A little teasing couldn't get to me. I was made of stronger stuff than that. Some of the kids had beautiful names like Debbie, Carol and Nancy. I didn't let the hurt show on my face; the kids soon gave up on teasing me about my name.

In the fall, the maple leaves on our mountain turned into a riot of color. Then they gently fell from the trees to the forest floor. Fall didn't last long and quickly turned into the bitter cold of an Adirondack mountain winter.

Aunt Bea Duquette
(June 8, 1913 - April 18, 2000)

from an oil on canvas portrait by Jeanne Fowler

About Painting

In order to shed some light on the reality of child abuse, it was natural for me to do a series of paintings about my past. Unfortunately, I discovered that it was remarkably difficult for me to spend the hundreds of hours of work and study that it would take to do an honest portrait of my beautiful but evil birth mother. I eventually came to terms with my misgivings by an odd bit of logic. Mom decorated her home by using her children, including me, as gruesome, horrific wall hangings. Now it was time for her to be immortalized in wall hangings. I hope that these images can help bring awareness to the problem of child abuse.

Peter's sad lullabies eased my pain as we both hung on the wall. His death saved my life.

"Peter and Me," oil on canvas, 1996, by Jeanne Fowler.

Mom used the broken pieces of my toy ironing board to beat Peter. Then before she left the house, Mom hung us both back on our walls and wrote a note to Dad, telling him how to continue our torture that evening.

"Mom killing Peter," oil on canvas, 1998, by Jeanne Fowler.

During the inquest, they sat me right in front of my tormentor and questioned me about the abuse she inflicted on me.

"Coroner Questioning Me," oil on canvas, 1998, by Jeanne Fowler.

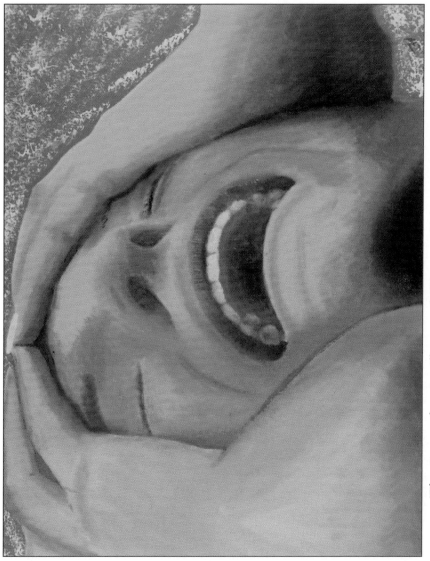

When it seems the pain will never end. When you think you can't take it any more!

"Screaming Face," oil on canvas, by Jeanne Fowler.

Turning 18 meant for the first time I was free ...

"Freedom!" oil on canvas, by Jeanne Fowler.

Behind The Eight Ball

MOST OF THE YEAR, no one drove down Bear Town Road, but in the winter it was packed with cars heading toward the Bear Town ski area. It was about a mile away from our barn. The ski area didn't belong to pa, but it did belong to Uncle Norris.

Pa had an open invitation from his sister for all of us to ski free, but pa never accepted this kind offer. He had no use for such frivolous things as skiing or skiers. Uncle Norris' ski area might as well have been a million miles away. As I went about my winter chores, I often watched the people go by on their way to the ski area. These happy, laughing skiers in their bright clothing seemed to be from a different world than mine.

As Christmas grew near, ma took Kenny, Margaret and me to the welfare office for a Christmas party. It was held in a big, empty conference room. There were many foster kids there, and I was amazed to see that they looked just like any other kids. I always thought people could tell us foster kids from other kids. Foster parents sure treated foster kids differently than they treated their natural children. Santa Claus showed up and had presents for everyone. There were two bags full of toys, one for girls and one for boys. Margaret got a coloring book and crayons, while Kenny got some toy soldiers. I eventually made my way toward the front to take my own present out of the sack. I was excited about the paper-doll book that I got. It had two paper dolls and several pages of clothes. The next week after the welfare party, we had our family Christmas. I got my usual pajamas and school clothes from pa and ma. Susie got a bike, a playhouse, a doll, and a lot of other toys. Oh yeah, I also got a sore throat.

During the previous winter, I had been plagued with many sore throats. This winter was no different. On January 19, 1958, the doctor said that my tonsils and adenoids had to be removed. He told me that everything would be okay and that I would get a lot of ice cream after my tonsils were out. I tried to be a big girl, but this was very scary to me. I really didn't know what to expect as I was wheeled down a hall and into a large room and placed in a tall bed with a very big light over it. The nurse came in wearing a mask and put something over my nose. I smelled this awful odor, but before I could protest, everything went black and I went to sleep.

When I woke up, my throat hurt more than it did when I was sick. The nurse told me, "Relax. Everything is going to be all right."

I saw her smile, and then I remembered the ice cream. I tried to talk, but my voice was a soft, horse whisper. "When can I have my ice cream?"

The nurse patted me gently on my hand and replied, "Soon, Georgie. Real soon. You just sleep for now, and when we get you back to your room you can have that ice cream."

When I got back to my room, she brought me a bowl of vanilla ice cream and a glass of Canada Dry ginger ale. The ginger ale brought back memories of Aunt Bea. I smiled just remembering her.

Life at the hospital was fun, because everyone was kind to me. I had no chores to do, and I got to watch all the television that I wanted. I never wanted to leave. While I was in the hospital, ma treated me very nicely. Soon the fun was over, and it was time to go home. The first few days at home were great, because I got to eat ice cream and I could do my schoolwork in bed. Ma Rivers even treated me nicely for a while. I enjoyed the special attention I received for as long as it lasted. As soon as I got well, it was back to work.

In February, again my birthday wasn't celebrated or acknowledged in any way. I had really hoped for a cake. Ma had decorated several cakes for church functions over the last couple of years. She had also baked spectacular cakes for pa's birthday. When Susie's birthday had come around last year, ma had decorated a special white birthday cake for her. It had wonderful red roses made from cream frostings all around the base and birthday wishes written in green frosting on the top. Ma let me have a slice of Susie's cake. It tasted very good, but the fact that she never made cakes for us left me empty inside on my own birthday.

Most of my time was spent on chores. On top of house chores and farm chores, there were punishment chores. When Ma Rivers would get mad at me because the house was not spotless, she would go to my room in a fury. She would grab everything in the room and throw it forcefully to the floor. Every stocking, blanket, blouse, knickknack, skirt, dresser drawer, pair of panties, pillow, and school paper ended up in this pile. In some ways this was worse than a beating, because it showed me that nothing was truly mine. I knew that my work was valuable, but I felt like I personally was not. Everything that I was or had could be violated with impunity. I cried quietly while I cleaned up the punishment mess that ma made out of my stuff. I would never let Ma Rivers have the pleasure of seeing how bad it made me feel.

One day, a cute pony showed up on the farm. It was a gift to Susie from her maternal grandma. He was a dusty-black Shetland with a long mane and big, brown eyes. Susie named her new pet, "Smoky." He was just as cute as he could be. Kenny, Margaret, Susie and I were very excited.

I jumped up and down and shouted, "When do I get to ride, when do I get to ride?" Pa quickly burst my bubble of excitement when he said, "This is Susie's pony, and she's the only one that is going to ride Smoky."

Ma added, "You're too fat to ride anyway." I was stunned and suddenly ashamed of being too fat.

I stepped back a couple of steps and defensively said, "I am not too fat to ride. I'm the same size as Susie."

Ma Rivers shouted, "No one rides this pony but Susie. Is that clear?"

Pa put Susie on the pony's back, then as we looked on, led Smoky around the yard. Soon the beaming Susie was riding by herself. She shouted, "Look at me. Look at me."

I just gritted my teeth as I seethed with anger at the sight of her happy face. When Susie got done riding Smoky, pa told Kenny and me to put the pony into the barn and rub him down. While we worked, I looked at Kenny and said, "Yes, everything is very clear now. We are too 'fat' to ride but not too 'fat' to feed, water, and rub down the pony."

Kenny responded, "Yeah, that's what this damn farm needs, another hay burner to take care of."

After a couple of weeks, Susie lost interest in Smoky. After that, the pony was never ridden again by anyone, but for years, Kenny still had to feed Smoky along with the other livestock.

It seemed like anytime something nice took place, ma would have to erase the joy by being as cruel as she could be. If she couldn't get to me with violence, she would try to break me by messing with my mind. Ma Rivers knew how I felt about my birth mother, and she would take every opportunity to rub it in. "You're lucky a good Christian family like ours took a worthless welfare kid like you in off the street. You're going to grow up to be worthless just like your mother. I can see you in a few years abandoning or killing your bastard children just like she did."

I would think, "No, you're the one who is just like my mother." But I never said anything.

Susie was actually a fairly nice girl at heart. Even though she was lazy and ordered me around a lot, I knew she was the way she was because of her upbringing. Unfortunately, I eventually got to the point where I couldn't see her good points. I just hated her. We all felt that Susie was not "one of us;" she was a part of the Rivers' family. We were more like the tractors, cows or fences. My main reason for being on the farm was to work. The other reason was to be a punching bag for ma. She beat me often and viciously and for little or no reason. She usually used a large, heavy belt, or if she was really in a mood to do some damage, she used the rubber hose from the barn.

One Sunday morning before church, I was a little bit hungry so I grabbed a cookie from the cookie jar. I knew that I wasn't allowed to eat cookies without permission, but stealing food was an old survival strategy for me. When I was with my birth mother, I either had to steal food or starve. At any rate, I didn't worry too much about stealing a cookie. I just enjoyed my snitched treat. I then put on my Sunday hat and off I went to church for Mass.

After the church services we went home. Ma Rivers counted the cookies and discovered that one was missing. The only people who could have a cookie when they wanted one were ma, pa and Susie. Ma checked with pa and Susie, and they said they didn't eat a cookie. That meant that one of us must have stolen from the cookie jar.

Ma lined up the three of us to get to the bottom of the crime. No one would admit to stealing a cookie, so ma went and got Susie's fortune-telling "Eight Ball" toy. This toy was about the size of an apple, but it was painted black. It had a large, white spot with a black "8" painted on it. It was filled with water and words. Ma handed me the 8-ball, then she asked it if I had stolen the cookie. She made me turn that little ball upside down and look at the window in the bottom. Slowly the answer appeared. It said, "NO WAY." I was thrilled because it looked like I would get away scot free. Then she did the same thing to Kenny. When he turned the ball over and the answer floated to the top, it said, "YOU'RE IN LUCK." He was happy too.

Unfortunately, Margaret wasn't so lucky, because her answer came up, "YES." Naturally, she protested that she didn't steal the cookie. It was no use. Ma went and got pa's heavy leather belt. She used it to give Margaret a terrible thrashing. The girl wouldn't stand still and take her beating quietly like Kenny and I took our beatings. She ran. She screamed. Margaret fought back against the injustice by kicking and scratching as hard as she could. Ma seemed determined to break Margaret's will no matter how much violence it took. Margaret's struggling made ma swing the belt even harder. They landed time after time with a sickening SMACK.

I felt unbelievably guilty for stealing a cookie and letting Margaret take my thrashing, but I got my share of the beatings and I didn't want to volunteer for an extra one. I was sure Margaret never trusted Kenny or me after that. She undoubtedly knew that one of us had let her take a beating that should have been our own. I could see that Margaret's defiance made the beatings she received even more severe than the ones I received.

Sparkling Snow

MA NEVER GOOFED OFF. She was a hard worker and a wonderful cook when she had the time. Most of the day-to-day cooking was the responsibility of Margaret and me. Meals on the farm consisted of low-cost, filling foods. I became fairly proficient at cooking these foods over the years. After meals, we were expected to do the dishes and clean the kitchen. My life seemed to be an endless round of chores.

Doing the supper dishes for seven hungry farm hands usually took Margaret and me about half an hour. Therefore, I was surprised when ma got up from the table one day and said, "You have 15 minutes to do the dishes, or else!" Ma then left the kitchen and went out to the barn.

We worked as furiously as we could, but it just wasn't fast enough. Just as we were almost done, ma walked in the back door carrying the heavy rubber milking-machine hose. It was about the size of a garden hose, but it was much thicker and heavier.

Ma told me to stand still. I did my best to stand in one spot while ma proceeded to beat me. As the heavy blows fell, I buried my face in my hands and kept my elbow tight to my side. Most of the blows fell on my bottom, back, or on the back of my legs, but ma would hit any target that presented itself as I squirmed around. After my thrashing was over, I stood in the middle of the kitchen floor sobbing.

Ma shouted, "Okay, Margaret, it's your turn." I quickly moved over to the corner of the kitchen so that I wouldn't receive any more blows. As the first blow whistled through the air, Margaret vainly tried to catch it in mid air. I winced as I heard the sickening crunch and then Margaret's scream as she took the full impact on her delicate fingers. The next blow landed on her left arm, while the third landed on her desperately grasping fingers again. After that, Margaret gave up trying to grab the rubber hose. She dashed out into the snow-covered yard with ma in close pursuit. I went to the kitchen window over the sink and rubbed the fog off the small pane. Through my tears, I watched as a well-placed blow to the back of Margaret's legs brought her to her knees in the cold, fluffy snow. The next blow to her back put Margaret on her face in a snowdrift. Margaret was dressed in shirt sleeves. She desperately dug her way into the snow bank with her bare hands. Ma's furious blows threw a cloud of sparkling snow crystals into the air. Margaret screamed in pain and exclaimed, "DAMN YOU! You BITCH!" Margaret continued to curse for a couple of more massive blows. Then she quit cursing and only screamed in agony.

Eventually, the heavy thuds of the rubber hose thankfully stopped.

Later that night, Margaret staggered into the room, disheveled and dripping wet from the melting snow. I asked, "Are you alright?"

She spat back, "I hate that bitch."

I held my finger up to my mouth. "Shush, not so loud.

Margaret sobbed loudly, "Someday I'm going to whack her, but good."

I buried my head under the pillow and murmured Peter's lullaby, "Aaah, Aaah, Aaah, AAAH," to drown out Margaret's sobs. I finally drifted off to sleep.

I was forced to work extra hard the next day. I was in great pain. Margaret was in worse shape, but she had to work hard also. We had to sleep on our stomachs for several nights after that thrashing, because the bruises on our bottoms, backs and legs were so tender.

When school ended, I knew the dreaded haying season would soon start. In the middle of June, pa and the boys started to mow the green fields of hay. A large tractor-drawn rake was used to gather all the loose grass into windrows to start the drying process. This step was vital, because wet hay could generate enough heat to spontaneously combust and burn the barn down. After the hay was thoroughly dry, pa would bale it. Then the backbreaking job of loading hay onto the wagon and taking it to the barn would begin.

Sometimes when I would roll a bale of hay, a snake would slither off through the field, scaring me half to death. Worse yet, one day I rolled a bale over and confronted the angry, weaving head of a snake that was tightly trapped in the bale, unable to escape. This scared me and caused me to scream and run. After that, I was leery of every bale, because I expected a snake to jump out. Ma yelled at me, "Keep working and stop being such a baby. Now get busy and don't make me tell you again!"

When I turned a bale over, sometimes the action would release swarming bees and result in me receiving many stings. I would go crying, running, and screaming across the field. Ma would tell me that I was just fine and tell me to get back to work.

Thankfully, much of the time my job was to stay on the wagon and place the hay. I eventually got to where I could lift the hay bales three layers up, but then someone else would have to lift the hay higher. Moving hay bales was very hard on me. The bales weighed at least 40 pounds. Each bale was a foot and a half square and three feet tall. When stood on end, that was nearly as tall as I was.

I continued to grow through the years, and as I got stronger, my workload got heavier. Pa showed me how to put the bale up on my knee first. Then by using my arms, back, and legs, I could just manage to push the bale up high enough that Ma Rivers could sink one of her hay hooks into it. The two of us together would then wrestle the bale onto the bed of the wagon. Ma would then place the bale onto the growing stack.

I was careful not to get in her way when she was swinging one of her hooks. I also had to be careful not to get run over by the wagon, because usually the wagon didn't stop. It just continued to roll slowly while we loaded it.

One day several weeks into the haying season, I found myself riding back to the barn on top of a load of hay. Margaret, Kenny and I were 20 feet in the air on top of seven tiers of intricately interlaced hay bales. The wagon was full, so I had nothing to do until we reached the barn. I lay back and stared at the clouds in the sky, wishing they would come over and shield me from the sun. As we took the 20-minute ride to the barn, we rounded the corner of the house, and the wagon brushed past our two apple trees. The apples were small and green, but they looked inviting and they practically fell into my hand as we passed.

I greedily picked as many of the little, green apples as I could. I didn't even have to sit up. By the time the wagon made its way to the road, I had bitten into one of my little prizes. I quickly spit out the mouthful of green, sour-tasting fruit. "Yuck, this is not good," I thought. I knew how apples were supposed to taste, and I couldn't believe my prize from the tree tasted so bad. For some reason, I took another bite. This time I did not spit out my morsel. Instead, I made a horrible face as I let the sour juices just sit in my mouth. The taste was bitter, but as I slowly started to chew, I realized the taste was not all that bad. It took some getting use to, but I was determined to enjoy that apple and then the next one. We reached the barn before I could finish the second apple, so I threw it into the barnyard and went about unloading the hay wagon.

I couldn't get my mind off the apples and their unique taste. The next load of hay gave me the opportunity to get another handful. I quickly ate two more apples before reaching the barn. This time my taste buds actually welcomed the sour flavor, and I found that the apples tasted quite good. By the third wagonload, I wasn't quite as eager to eat apples. My stomach was churning, so when we got to the barn I said to ma, "I don't feel very good. I need to go to the house!"

Without waiting for a reply, I raced to the house. By the time I got to the bathroom, I was ready to spew in every direction. I didn't know whether to sit on the toilet or kneel next to it. I was out of time, so I sat on the commode and heaved into a wastebasket held between my knees. Boy was I sick! My face started to sweat, and I felt both cold and hot at the same time. When I got back to the barn, the wagon was nearly half unloaded. Ma gave me that "I'm not too happy with you look." I started talking real fast, telling her that the apples made me sick and I needed to stay in the house for the rest of the day.

She coldly replied, "You are just paying for being such a pig and eating all those green apples. Maybe now you have learned your lesson. Get on the wagon and finish your work. You'll live."

I did live, and I sure learned a valuable lesson. Thankfully, we were working near the house that afternoon, because I had to rush inside a couple of more times. I was dehydrated and weak by the end of the day, but most important to ma, I finished my work in the hay fields.

Most evenings in the summer, I was too exhausted to do anything except fall painfully into bed, but sometimes after the chores were done, ma would let us go swimming at the ski area pond while there was still enough light.

Uncle Norris' ski area was on the northern edge of our farm. No one was at the ski area in the summertime, so we could play there whenever Ma Rivers would let us. There was a wonderful cold pond at the bottom of the hill, where I taught myself to swim. In the middle of the swimming hole, there was a rather deep spot where we couldn't touch the bottom with our feet.

One day, Kenny was splashing around and had gotten to that deep spot by mistake. All of a sudden, he started thrashing his arms and screamed, "I can't feel the bottom!"

His scream caused all of us to stop playing. Without thinking, I swam over to him and grabbed his hair. I started to make my way back to shallow water swimming with one arm. Kenny was thrashing so much, I lost my grip on his hair.

"I can help you," I shouted. "Let me help."

Kenny was terrified and kept thrashing around. I grabbed his hair one more time and, with one arm, started to make my way to shallow water again. As soon as Kenny's feet touched the bottom, he calmed down. Margaret rushed over to us and hugged her brother and me. Kenny didn't say, "thank you," but I knew from his eyes that I had done a good thing.

Unfortunately, bringing in the hay was not just a one-time job in the summer. The first cut was painful enough, but in the latter part of summer, when the sun was even hotter, we did a second cut. Since I had been lifting hay bales all summer, I was in better shape by the time the second cut came along, but I dreaded the sun and the work.

When early autumn came and we cut the hay in the fields farther back, I was not so quick to grab the apples off the tree again. Kenny and Margaret grabbed them, and I reminded them of how sick I got when I did this earlier that summer. They both laughed at me.

Margaret said, "Everyone knows not to eat apples in the spring." Then she took a big bite. Between chews she continued to speak. "Silly, this is the time of year you can eat apples." I was hesitant, but Kenny and Margaret didn't get sick, so on the second trip, I grabbed an apple and bit into it. Unlike the first time I had eaten an apple off this tree, I found it sweet and juicy.

Treat You Like A Girl

I WAS A VERY FAIR-SKINNED REDHEAD, so the hot summer sun was merciless on my body. I would burn and blister badly during haying season. I once burned from the sun so badly that I suffered from both heat stroke and a nosebleed. When I collapsed, pa took me into the shade and gave me plenty of cold water to drink and a much-needed rest. I drank up pa's kindness and concern more than the water he gave me. As soon as I was cooled down, it was back to work again. Before the day was over, my sunburn turned into water blisters on my arms and shoulders.

While ma and pa wore hats and long sleeved shirts when they were in the hay fields, they never gave these items to us.

We had to move the heavy bales of hay by working our hands under the baling twine. The hay cut the back of my hands to shreds, while the twine left friction blisters on my palms. The hay pricked the blisters and broke them open as I continued to work. Sweat and dirt soon got into the raw burns. It was then that I remembered how to concentrate on other things. This made some of the pain go away, like it had done back in Chicago.

I thought about a nice, chilly shower when the day was over, or how good the cool sheets would feel when I went to bed that night. The next thing I knew, the pain was not so bad, and my day in the field was quickly over.

One night, ma decided that we were going to have salt pork and potatoes for dinner, so I was sent to the basement to get the food. I found the potatoes and placed a dozen of them into a basket. Then I went to the large pork barrel to get the meat. In addition to the meat, the barrel was filled with a salt-brine mixture. We had placed chunks of raw meat into the pork barrel during the last winter. These chunks could sit in the brine for months before they were ready to eat. My hands were covered with small cuts and scratches from the hay. The salt solution was cold and gritty as I reached down into the barrel, fishing for a chunk of pork. The salt permeated my open sores and caused incredible pain so intense that my first reaction was to pull my hand out. This, of course, didn't solve the problem, because I still had to come upstairs with a piece of salt pork or else. So into the brine went my hand and arm again. I grabbed the meat and raced upstairs and gave the food to ma.

I rushed to the bathroom and quickly rinsed my arm off so that the pain would go away. I came back and started to peel potatoes while ma sliced the salt pork and fried it. Salt pork tastes a lot like bacon, only it is sliced thicker. I hated the pain that it caused me, but I loved the food.

Pa never raised hogs, so we always traded another farmer for our pork, or we would get a hog at the auction. It didn't come all wrapped nice and neat and ready to put into the freezer. We butchered the pig ourselves, and the hog carcass would be taken to the package plant, where pa would have them make it into ham, sausage, bacon, chops, and everything else. He brought it back home for us to wrap. The beef and chickens that we ate came from our farm, so we had plenty of meat. We never had a shortage. The good cuts of meat were packaged and placed into the freezer.

We saved the pig's head for headcheese and the blood for Grandma Rivers' long, fat rolls of blood sausage. I don't know how she made it, but I know it was awful stuff, and I wouldn't have touched it if I hadn't been forced to. Ma would cut it into slices and fry it. It had a horrible smell and an even worse taste. I knew I would have to eat it, but it gagged me when I did. The only good thing was that this sausage didn't last long. The story was the same for the heart, tongue, and liver of the beef. I had to eat them whether I liked them or not.

When it came time to eat these things, there was no such thing as, "I don't like it." When food was prepared, foster kids ate it. Of course if you were Susie and you didn't like something, you didn't have to eat it. But as for us, you ate it because you were forced to.

Soon, the long hot summer was over, and it was time for the potatoes to be picked. This wasn't a particularly strenuous job, but it was a very tiring and dirty one. We stored the potatoes on the dirt-floor cellar of the house. After a few months of being in that cool, damp environment, they would grow sprouts. This was the only time of the year that we were able to earn extra money.

Kenny, Margaret and I would have to go down and sprout the potatoes. This was a dirty, grimy job. The potatoes were crawling with bugs and spiders. Sometimes I would grab a potato, and it would be rotten, and the slimy goo would get all over my hands. As I sprouted each potato, I would put it in a bushel basket. When the basket was full, I would empty it in a different corner of the basement. Another bushel basket slowly filled with the rotten potatoes and sprouts. Nothing ever went to waste on the farm. These rejects would be fed to the chickens. My hands became black with the dirt. My back hurt from the hours I would be in the dimly lit, cold, damp basement hunched over that pile of spuds.

That year, for the first and only time, ma sent Susie to help us. Susie didn't like the work. After a few minutes, she got tired of cleaning sprouts and went out to play.

For each bushel I removed the sprouts from, I would earn a penny, and there were many bushels of potatoes. I would usually make about 25 cents extra for sprouting the potatoes. This 25-cent "bonus" would raise my pay to almost five and half dollars per year.

My summer work week was over 80 hours long. We had tons of hay to bring in, and we needed two silos full of corn to feed the cows through the long northern winter. We had planted a garden in the spring, including a field of potatoes, in order to feed our large family, and these crops needed attention all summer. Besides our summer chores, we had the year-round chores of milking the cows, washing the milking machines, and gathering the eggs. I also had housework and cooking.

Our picturesque farm was half covered by a large, rocky hill. It was the terminal moraine of a prehistoric glacier. The glacier had covered all of Canada and part of our farm. The glacier had left many rocks in our fields that had to be removed. Our farm had many miles of dry-laid stone walls between our fields. These walls had been stacked by generations of farmers who had gathered the stones that the plow turned up. Over the years, I would add tens of thousands of rocks to these walls. The walls were a little taller than I was and wider than a kitchen table at the base.

One day after school, mom gave me an old, beat-up gallon galvanized bucket and sent me out to the stone walls around the southeast pasture, with instructions to pick raspberries until the bucket was full. It was rather hard at first, because the raspberry bushes had sharp thorns, but once I got the hang of it, I soon had the bucket half full. Wild bees liked to build hives in the many cavities of stone walls. The bees didn't like me climbing on their home. I angered them, and they stung me many times. I dropped the bucket and ran back to the house screaming. Ma was not sympathetic to my plight. She was angry that I hadn't picked the raspberries as I had been instructed. She grabbed me by the hair and threw me against the wall. She started yelling, "When I give you a job to do, I mean for you to do it. Do you hear me?"

I was surprised by the attack. The pain from my pulled hair caused me to wail. Through my sobs I replied, "Yes." As I slowly got up off the floor, I rushed out the door and back to the stone wall for more berries. I gave the bees a wide berth this time, and I cried and picked raspberries until after dark, when I finally had my bucket full. Raspberry picking was a yearly chore, and the bees stung me every single year.

That spring, I was given the job of doing the family laundry. The laundry was done with an old wringer machine. The machine was in the basement. I had to fill the washer with a hose. I added the clothes and some soap flakes. I turned on the motor, and the agitator would pump up and down until the clothes were clean. Then I ran the clothes through the wringer. The jeans were by far the hardest items to get through. The whole process scared me. I rinsed the clothes in a large, galvanized tub that took two of us to dump. I carried the clothes up the stairs to the clothesline in the back yard.

After several years of this drudgery, we got an automatic washer and dryer. Ma liked the washer just fine, because the spin cycle was an obvious improvement over running the clothes through the dangerous wringer. Ma didn't let me use the dryer very often. She saved it mostly for our dress clothes. Everything else went on the line, like it always had. I had to iron the clothes after I took them off the line and put all the dry laundry away. I discovered that I hated washing and ironing the family's clothes. The only good part of laundry was that I could do it alone.

The number-one rule I had for my self-protection was not to get close to anyone, including my foster brothers and sisters. I had loved and lost all of my natural siblings, and it had hurt terribly. If I got too close to Kenny or Margaret, I would start to feel their agony like I had felt Peter's. Frankly, I just couldn't stand the thought of losing another sister or brother. Kenny, Margaret and I all received our own beatings. The pain that I received from the physical abuse was quite enough without worrying about their torture as well. I tried not to know how much they were being beaten. I was too tortured by my own demons to try to help them fight theirs. To a substantial degree, we were just acquaintances, like one factory worker would be friendly with a co-worker. We never really loved each other like a family. We all knew at some level that love could be a very expensive emotion when you were being abused. Bad things were bound to happen to Kenny, Margaret and me in the future, just as they had in the past. The less you cared about those bad things, the less they hurt you. Kenny and Margaret still had each other, and they loved each other very much. It was very touching, but I wasn't about to get emotionally attached to anyone.

Caring about other people could get you into trouble. I remember one time when Kenny knew that ma was giving Margaret and me impossible time limits for doing the dishes. Ma set the limits just so she would have an excuse to beat us with the rubber hose. In order to protect his sister, Kenny pitched in to help do the dishes one night. When ma came into the house with her rubber hose, she found all of the dishes done. She was furious with Kenny for spoiling her fun. She immediately went to get pa. He stormed into the house shouting, "So, you want to do girl's work, do you? Well, if you want to act like a girl, I'll treat you like a girl!" Pa dragged Kenny into our room by his hair. Pa went through our closet and picked out Margaret's best blue church dress, which was covered with yellow and white flowers. The dress had a square-cut neck opening that was edged with white lace. It also had white lace around the hem.

Then pa forced the crying, young Kenny to put his sister's dress on and hauled him back downstairs. Pa and Billy made fun of the humiliated Kenny all that evening. After that, Kenny never helped us with the dishes again. This meant that we could never meet our time limits. The beatings continued with increasing frequency and ferocity.

I only had two avenues of refuge—one was to sing Peter's lullaby at night, and the other was school.

I'm sure I was the only kid in school that disliked weekends and holidays. I was happiest in school. The teachers were wonderful, and they praised me and gave me good grades for my hard work. This was the only place where what I did was noticed and appreciated. I always loved it when report cards came out, because my grades were always better than Susie's. I reveled in my superiority and gloated to myself. No one cared about what I had accomplished except me, but that was enough. Spring turned into summer and soon school was out. Summer was the worst time of the year.

Ducking Donuts

MORE BIRTHDAYS CAME and went unnoticed. The summer after I turned 13, Mother Nature played a scary trick on me. I woke one morning to find blood on my sheets and pajamas. I thought that I was dying, so I jumped out of bed, with fear gripping my stomach. I examined my arms and legs to see where the blood had come from and discovered that it had come from my private parts. I quickly rolled my soiled clothes and bedding together, put them in the laundry, then stuffed my underwear with toilet paper to keep them clean. I had no idea what was happening, and I spent the next three days in fear that someone would find out. I knew that I must have done something to cause this bleeding, but I had no idea what. When the bleeding stopped, I relaxed, knowing that whatever had happened was over.

The next month, the same thing happened, only this time ma discovered the soiled sheets before I could hide them. "What happened here?" she asked.

I could hardly talk. My mouth was dry with fear as I lamely lied, "I had a nose bleed in the night, and I guess I laid in it."

I could tell that ma did not believe this story. She told me to come with her. With legs shaking and fear dragging my steps, I tried to prepare myself for a thrashing for something over which I had no control. I had no idea what I had done to soil the sheets, but I knew ma would never believe me. She took me into the bathroom and handed me a white elastic belt with some hooks on it. She held up a sanitary napkin, showed me how to attach it to the belt, and explained how it went in my underwear. She ominously told me, "This means you're a woman now, and you have to do your work better."

Now I knew why I was bleeding. God had found out that I hadn't worked hard enough, and this was his way of punishing me. I was relieved that I hadn't received a beating from ma. I had no intention of bleeding again. I could show God what a hard worker I could be.

I set about working harder and better than I had ever worked before. I even looked for jobs I could do before I was told they needed to be done. Not only was I physically working harder, but also mentally. I was drained from the knowledge that if I slacked at all, the bleeding would start again. I was exhausted most of the time. I was happy when I had gone three weeks with no bleeding. I knew that God was rewarding me for working hard, because the bleeding had not reoccurred.

The next week, my worst fear became reality. The blood was back. I slipped into the bathroom and got one of the sanitary napkins and prayed that no one would discover that I was lazy and the bleeding was back. I felt that I had worked as hard as I could. I was confused that this could happen again. I was so scared. Now Ma Rivers would know that I hadn't done my best work. The strange thing was that ma never said anything to me. I didn't get a beating for not working hard enough, but from then on, I worked with a will to survive, month after month. I went at my work like I was killing snakes, but every month, I would start to bleed again. I thought that I might bleed to death. I was so frightened, even Peter's lullaby could hardly sooth me.

It wasn't until years later, when I was married, that I learned about my monthly cycle. I was surprised to learn that the shame and fear I had for all those years was so unnecessary, because this scary bleeding was a normal process that all women go through, whether they worked hard or not.

Every day when I had finished my work, I would go and sit on the porch with Grandma Rivers and drink a cold glass of iced tea. Sometimes I would help grandma cook her supper. Other times I would just go over to grandma's house to cry and tell her about what was happening to me. Grandma Rivers knew how badly her daughter-in-law was treating me. She would hold me in her arms as she rocked on the porch. She stroked my hair and said, "Georgie, I love you."

Grandma Rivers had worked hard all of her life. She was very old and suffered from arthritis. Her disfigured, gnarled hands could hardly move, but she still somehow managed to sew. Grandma would spend most of the day sitting in her rocking chair watching television and sewing quilts. I was enthralled with how beautiful the quilts were. When our clothes wore out, she would cut them up and make beautiful patchwork quilts from the pieces. When I outgrew my favorite blue dress, she sewed it into a special quilt. While she was alive, grandma would never give away this quilt like she did the others. She proclaimed to me, "This is my favorite blanket, because it's got part of you in it, Georgie." I always felt she liked me better than she liked her own granddaughter, Susie.

The blissful serenity I knew on grandma's porch was routinely pierced by the sound of ma's voice calling me to do some god-forsaken chore. If I didn't answer, she would come looking for me. One of the first places she looked was grandma's house. Ma came screaming through the door, "Didn't you hear me calling for you? You get over here. You're in for it now."

"I'm sorry, I didn't hear you."

Ma slapped my face and hustled me out the door. She roughly pushed me toward the house. "When I call for you, I want you here now! Do you understand?" With each word, her fist would jab me in the back.

"Now move," she screamed.

As tears silently fell from my eyes, my legs would move as fast as they could toward the house. The cold punch of ma's fist replaced the warmth of grandma's hug. As we entered our kitchen, Ma Rivers threatened, "Now get started on supper before I get the hose out again."

While I peeled the potatoes, I noticed that ma was getting out her donut-making supplies. Ma was a wonderful cook, and we often had delicious desserts. Pa particularly loved the homemade donuts that Ma Rivers frequently made for the family. I both loved and hated the times that she made donuts. Ma would take the donuts out of the bubbling deep-fat fryer, and when they cooled, she would cover them with frosting or sugar glazing for the "real" family.

We weren't allowed to eat the warm, frosted donuts or the cold ones for that matter. We were required to stand next to the stove and hold out our cupped hands. Then ma would take a donut straight out of the boiling grease and drop it into our outstretched hands as fast as she could. The object of ma's "donut game" was to not drop the scalding food. If I dropped the donut, I would lose the only chance I had to eat one of the delicious treats. I juggled the donut in my hands as fast as I could in a vain attempt to keep my hands from burning. The hot grease dripped onto my hands, where it would leave deep blisters on my skin. But I didn't drop my burning prize.

So after the donut cooled down, I was allowed to eat it. The pain in my hands was temporarily eased by the sweet flavor of the home-made pastry. I savored it, chewing each bite as slowly as possible, en-joying every second of the treat my pain had earned. As soon as I fin-ished eating, I rushed to the sink to soak my blistered hands in cold water while I watched Kenny and Margaret receive their scalding desserts.

One day, pa left to go into town to run some errands, and ma started to fix lunch. She reached to the back of the refrigerator to get something and discovered a horrible mess. I knew that I was in trou-ble, because a bowl of macaroni salad, a bowl of peas, and some corn had spilled down between the vegetable drawers. The food was putrid and covered with black slime. This discovery turned Ma Rivers beet-red with rage. "You call this clean?" she yelled, grabbing the mess up with her hands and putting it on a plate. "Damn your lazy hide. Maybe if you eat this mess you will learn that when I say, 'Clean the refrigerator,' I mean clean it."

My eyes immediately swelled with tears, and fear gripped the pit of my stomach as I looked at the rotten food. I vowed to myself that no matter what she did to me, there was no way I was going to eat this rotten, slimy slop. Ma continued, "You're here to work, not goof off. You're no good! No DAMN good! Just like your mother."

Of all the things someone could say to me, being compared to the woman who had killed my brother was the worst. I tried not to let her see how bad it made me feel. I didn't want to give her the satis-faction of knowing she had gotten to me.

I knew that if pa were here, he wouldn't let ma do this to me. Then, as if he heard me, pa's truck swung into the driveway. Ma did-n't hear him pull in as she continued her rampage. Pa entered the house and yelled, "What in the hell is going on in here?"

Ma, still in a rage, told him about the mess she had found, then pointed at the slime and said, "That is going to be George's lunch to teach her a lesson." Pa replied, "There is no way Georgie is going to eat rotten food!" He immediately dumped the plate of slop in the garbage.

I almost jumped for joy. I was so happy and surprised to see him stick up for me. His next words took the wind out of my sails. "What will people say if she gets sick from eating rotten food. Use your head, woman. Don't let me catch you doing anything like this again." His cold words made it clear to me that what other people thought was what was important, not my well-being.

Even the politicians knew that pa was very prominent and that his opinion counted with many people. They would always stop at our house and at the house of Uncle Norris. I never knew what pa talked about with the politicians or with other adults, for that matter. Pa had a saying, "Kids should be seen but not heard." He believed it and we lived by it, so I seldom spoke to any strangers. I was invisible to most visitors to the farm.

The one notable exception was the politicians. They usually came with a box of candy bars or a pocket full of free pencils imprinted with their name and party slogan. The nice politicians gave each of us a candy bar and pencil, without regard to whether we were foster kids or ma's and pa's natural child. I don't know which I liked better. Since school supplies were in short supply, an extra pencil was always welcome. On the other hand, the candy bars were especially sweet. For once, I was just a kid no different from any other.

After the election in November, the really cold winter weather settled in. Our home was near the Canadian border, and it was freezing cold in the room that Margaret and I shared. Frost would form on the inside of my bedroom window, and I could see my breath turn into a white fog when I breathed. Susie was originally supposed to sleep in our room, but she always slept on a twin bed in ma's and pa's room, where it was warm.

Our house was heated with a wood cook stove in the kitchen, just like it had been when pa was a boy. We also had an oil heater in the dining room, with a stovepipe that ran up through the ceiling into pa's and ma's room. Their room wasn't toasty, but it was a lot warmer than ours. I was thrilled when I heard that pa was going to have a full basement added to the house. It would hold a brand-new wood-burning furnace.

"Finally," I thought, "we would have heat throughout the entire house." When the new wood-furnace was installed, I was sure disappointed to learn that pa had the workmen put in heating ducts for his bedroom, but not for ours. I still could only get warmth into my room when they left the door to the stairway open. The frost on my bedroom window looked pretty, but I didn't appreciate it. I was too cold.

Along with the new furnace, the Rivers had a big, beautiful, modern kitchen installed. It had a a linoleum floor and a large window that faced Aunt Bessie's distant house. The walls were painted a light-beige color called "sportsman tan." I thought that it made the kitchen bright and cheery. The new kitchen was much bigger than our old one. It had many more cupboards and a lot more countertop space. We also got a wondrous frost-free refrigerator that eliminated one of my chores.

The dirty, old wood-stove was replaced with a shiny gas range. I no longer had to feed wood into a stove in order to cook a meal, and in the summer that was a very nice change. Cooking with the new stove and oven took some getting used to, but it was so much easier.

Another Christmas morning came with the usual gifts, or I should say lack of gifts. Susie received large quantities of both clothing and toys, as usual. I got my customary pajamas and school clothes, gift-wrapped with a bow on top. This year, however, there were more packages under the tree. Kenny got a toy farm set with cows, horses and chickens. It also had a red barn and fence pieces, which could be put together to make a corral. Susie, Kenny, Margaret and I all received bright-red saucer-type sleds. It was the only toy I ever received on the farm. That winter we climbed the small hill behind the house and slid down into the yard.

Cleaning was always a big task, especially during the holiday season. New Year's Day was the only day of the year when we would use the real silver. It was the biggest celebration of the year for our family. Everything had to be cleaned and polished, including the antlers on pa's trophy deer head. We would clean, polish, bake, and cook from the day after Christmas right up to the start of the New Year's Day party. It was a very exhausting time for me. I was mainly involved in cleaning and peeling the vegetables and, of course, polishing that darn silver.

When the guests arrived, I would sit at the kids' table to eat, while the adults would eat in the dining room at the big table. After dinner I had to clean up after approximately 40 people. One or two of the aunts would always offer to help, but ma would simply say, "I wouldn't hear of it. That's what Georgie and Margaret are here for."

After the New Year celebration, life settled down for a couple of months. I could tell that spring was just around the corner when sugaring time came around. The first sign of sugaring was when pa had me wash the dozens of buckets and barrels that we owned.

Then the next day early in the morning, pa, Billy and Kenny took all of our buckets into the woods. They then cut a "V" into every maple tree that they could find. They then drove a metal tap into the wood at the bottom of each "V" and hung one of our buckets from the tap. As the day warmed, the sap started to run and dripped into the buckets that the boys had hung on the trees.

By noon they were back from the woods, and pa would have Billy and Kenny shovel the snow off our heavy, wooden stoneboat. The stoneboat was a massive sled with runners made from six-by-six wooden timbers that were shod with iron skids. The stoneboat was usually used to clear rocks from the fields in the spring or to haul heavy things across the snow in the winter.

Pa and Billy would wrestle a large oak barrel onto the deck of the stoneboat, which was about a foot off the ground. Then Billy and Kenny would lash the barrel into place while pa went for the horses. A few minutes later, pa brought our matched pair of large, strong, pure-bread Morgan workhorses around, and the boys hitched them to the stoneboat. Most of the time when we used the stoneboat, we pulled it with our tractor, but for sugaring we used pa's Morgans. The tractor just couldn't get as deep into the woods as our horses could. Pa was as proud of his horses as he was of his hunting dogs or his pure-bred Jersey and Holstein cows.

In the afternoon, the men drove the horses dragging the stoneboat deep into woods on our mountain. They gathered the maple sap buckets and emptied them into the barrels. They worked late into the afternoon until they had more than a hundred gallons of sap. Pa would use the reins to slap the Morgans on the butt, and they would strain to break the stoneboat out of the snow and ice. Their load amounted to about half a ton of slightly sweet water. The trip back to the house was mostly downhill, but the load was heavy, so pa and the boys walked rather than add their weight to the burden on the horses.

They got back to the house with their barrels of sap. The next morning, we girls would build a fire under our large, black cast-iron cauldron. Then we filled the cauldron with 20 buckets of sap from the barrel. At this point, the sap was as clear and thin as water. Soon the sap was boiling, and my job was to keep adding wood to the fire. As the sap boiled down, I also had to add more sap to the cauldron. This kept me quite busy, because it took 43 gallons of sap to make one gallon of maple syrup. About noon I would ladle out the last of the sap from the barrels, so the boys could take the stoneboat back into the woods. By late afternoon, the last of the sap had been boiled down, and we had a little over two gallons of delicious maple syrup for our pancakes. After I ladled out the syrup and funneled it into quart jugs, my job was almost done for the day. The only chore left was to clean the cauldron for the next day's sugaring.

By this time, the residue on the sides of the cauldron had thickened into pure maple-sugar candy. I really loved to scrape the cauldron. It was my favorite chore of the whole year. I got to fill my pockets with these golden treasures for my sweet tooth. I hid my sugar in my room, and it lasted me for several weeks that way.

I knew the best way to minimize the abuse was to work very hard and to not cause any trouble. Margaret was still having trouble taking the abuse that was being handed out, and although she was a good worker, she would fight back if ma tried to beat her. Kenny had an attitude that was somewhere between mine and Margaret's. He worked hard and didn't complain, even when he was beaten for no reason at all.

Also, for some reason, Kenny developed a negative attitude toward church that caused him a great deal of trouble that spring. One Sunday morning, Kenny rebelled and refused to go to Mass. He got tired of being forced to belong to the religion of the people who were mistreating him and his sister so much. Pa was furious, I suppose because it reflected poorly on him if his wards weren't good Catholics. He went to get the tractor fan belt that was hanging on a nail in the barn. Kenny realized that pa would beat him with that rubber belt, so he hid in the hayloft. When pa couldn't talk or threaten him down, pa gave up and we went to Mass without Kenny.

That night, when Kenny got hungry and cold, he came down. Pa took him out to the barn and gave him the savage fan-belt beating that he had been promised. When Kenny came staggering and sobbing up to the house, I took him aside and asked, "Are you okay, Kenny?"

He bravely replied, "Yeah, I'm fine."

"You going to church next week?"

He slowly shook his head "no."

"You know pa will beat you," I continued.

"Yeah, I know, but I don't care."

I could understand Kenny's attitude. It would be so easy to give up and not even try to avoid the beatings. Heck, I wished I were dead most of the time. Why not just let them have an excuse to kill me too and just get it over with. Besides, God only loved and blessed the Rivers. I knew that God had forsaken us. Although I didn't believe that God cared for me, I felt that church attendance was an easy chore and certainly not worth taking a beating over. I was afraid of catching Kenny's attitude about church. So I shook my head, walked away, and said, "Good luck, Kenny."

"Yeah. Thanks, Georgie," he replied.

Week after week, Kenny endured his Sunday-morning fan-belt beatings. He didn't even bother to hide in the hayloft after a while. Although his thrashings were severe and left him black and blue, Kenny refused to go to church with us again. I knew in my heart that the only possible outcome would be that Kenny would give in or pa would kill him. I was very surprised when pa eventually got tired of beating Kenny every Sunday, and he gave up. After that, the only time Kenny went to church with us was several years later on the day we buried Grandma Rivers.

The Attic

IN ADDITION TO ALL of my other chores, I was ma's personal maid and hairdresser. Ma liked wavy, curly hair, so it was my job to put small pincurls all over her head every Sunday night. One Sunday evening, ma washed her short, straight black hair. Then she turned on the television and sat in her big, overstuffed chair in the living room and watched "Roller Derby." I stood behind her and went to work on her hair, as usual. I would wrap a lock of her short, coarse hair around my always-blistered and -cut index finger. I then carefully pried opened a bobby pin with my sore fingers. The bobby pin was usually missing its plastic tip.

The job was long and slow. I was almost finished when the roller derby jammer Annabelle "Slugger" Kealy jumped over the crouching Betty "Tiny Mite' McTague and punched the Bay Area Bomber Joanie "Golden Girl" Weston right in the face. Ma started cheering. Her head moved, and that sharp bobby pin scraped her scalp. Ma's hand shot up so fast that I didn't see it coming and slapped my face. "Damn you, George, be careful," she screamed.

"I'm sorry," I muttered. My cheek was still smarting as I carefully went back to work. When I finished with her hair, she had me go to work pulling out her chin whiskers with a pair of tweezers. It was actually gratifying for me to pull these hairs out and cause her to wince in pain.

The next morning before school, Kenny came into the house and asked me, "I can't find Margaret anywhere. Have you seen her?"

I replied, "No. Have you tried the barn?"

Ma interjected, "That worthless tramp ran away."

Kenny incredulously said, "Margaret wouldn't leave without telling me where she was going."

Ma Rivers said, "Well I guess she did. I told you she's worthless."

Kenny didn't believe that his sister had run away, but he had no way to find out what had happened to her. By the next morning,

Kenny was very concerned. We both hoped that Margaret would return soon. After a few weeks, it became obvious that whatever happened to Margaret, she wasn't coming back. Kenny was very upset. He couldn't believe his sister had run away without saying anything to him. He just didn't believe what ma had told him.

I knew how he felt. I had lost several siblings myself. It is the hardest thing in the world to lose that last tie with a loved one. Up until then, Kenny had always been a cooperative, hard-working boy, but now I could see that his spirit was completely broken. He was all alone now.

Kenny became very despondent and angry. He wasn't as defiant as his sister had been, but one time he stood up for himself. Kenny didn't do a chore fast enough, and ma slapped him. He slapped ma back. He was instantly sorry and apologized, but it was too late. Ma and pa both took Kenny out to the barn. Pa took down his heavy rubber tractor fan belt that he called his "Kenny persuader," which was hanging on the wall in its usual place. Ma held Kenny down, and pa beat him and beat him.

After a while, ma and pa came back, but Kenny didn't. I went out looking for him. I found him on the barn floor. He was unable to stand unaided. Kenny had been thrashed very badly. I had to help him to his feet. Kenny was a very small child, but I was quite short and small myself. I had trouble lifting him. He could hardly stand. I had to half carry him as he staggered back to the house.

The day after that beating, pa had Kenny drag a cot and a dresser down into the basement. Kenny placed his stuff next to our new wood-burning furnace. That became Kenny's room from then on. Kenny told me that he was actually happy to live in the basement, because he finally had a warm bedroom in the winter and he wouldn't have to go up and down the stairs to feed the fire. I guess that Kenny learned not to fight back ever again, because from then on, he went back to quietly taking ma's and pa's beatings just like I did. Kenny seemed very sad after that. He no longer had anyone.

I at least still had Grandma Rivers. She had been afflicted with severe diabetes for many years. This caused her foot to become quite infected. One day, one of pa's sisters came for her, and they never brought her back. I missed her very much. I heard that grandma eventually had to have her foot amputated. From that point on, her condition continued to deteriorate, until she finally died. I was inconsolable after her death. I had lost my only friend in the whole world. My world was black.

Grandma Rivers was buried just as the maple trees had turned into a patchwork of orange, yellow, red, and green. I had slipped up and fallen in love with Grandma Rivers, and now she was gone from me. There was very little love or hate left in me for anyone. I was just too exhausted to care anymore. I wished I were dead. I wished that they would beat me to death.

I guess I was lucky that ma was the only one who beat me, because ma, pa, or my older foster brother, Billy, beat Kenny virtually every day. Thrashing Kenny seemed to be everyone's favorite pastime. Ma liked to torture Kenny in other ways too. She would lay two hard dry peas on the floor and make Kenny kneel on them for hours at a time.

She also experimented with other stuff, such as rocks and sticks, but she liked dried peas the best. When I watched Kenny kneeling on stuff, I couldn't help but remember kneeling with Peter and Jill on furnace grates and broomsticks back in Chicago. These thoughts made me shudder, and I would run to my room and cry every time ma would torture Kenny. On those nights especially, I told myself, "Someday this will end. I'll either survive or I won't, but this will end." Then I would sing Peter's lullaby to myself. A few minutes of "Aah, Ah, Aaaah, AAH...Aah, Ah, Aaaah, AAH, Aah, Ah, Aaaah, AAH" would calm me down enough to sleep.

I continued to take my horrendously painful rubber hose thrashings without crying or complaining. I saved my tears for my pillow at night. I wouldn't give ma the satisfaction of seeing me cry. I tried to keep hatred and pain from consuming my life. I didn't have a master plan for how to survive, because I didn't believe that I would. I felt that I was just a dead person who hadn't fallen down yet. It was only a matter of time until the ground swallowed me up.

A foster child to replace Margaret was never brought in, so I now had to do her work as well as my own. Not only was I doing Margaret's work as well as my own, it seemed to me like I was now getting Margaret's beatings as well as my own.

As I grew older, the beatings started to taper off a little, until I was back to only receiving my share, rather than both mine and Margaret's.

Occasionally, ma still did her "punishment mess." She'd start throwing everything I owned into a heap in the middle of my floor. She snarled, "Georgie, you no-good, lazy slob. I'm going to teach you a lesson this time. You have until I get back from the barn with the hose to clean this up."

I desperately hid some of my possessions in the dirty-clothes hamper and folded the rest as fast as I could. By the time ma got back upstairs with her hose, I was done. She seemed to be satisfied. When she went back downstairs, I retrieved the rest of my possessions from the hamper and carefully put them away.

There was a room off ma's and pa's bedroom called the "attic." It wasn't really an attic, because it was on the same level as the other upstairs rooms. Until then, the only times that I had ever seen the attic was when I had to put this bag or that box into it. I would just open the door and throw things in. Eventually, I could hardly open the door. The attic horrified me. It was dark, and when the door was opened, you could hear mice scurrying.

One day, my habit of getting out of the attic as soon as possible caught up to me. My stomach jumped into my throat when I heard ma say, "George, go clean the attic."

My inner voice screamed, "Clean the attic. No, it's too scary." I was sure she could see the terror in my eyes, and this must have thrilled her because she screamed, "And I mean clean. I want everything organized. I had better be able to walk through the attic when you're done. Do you hear me?"

I mumbled a nervous "yes" as I climbed the stairs and then went through ma's bedroom to the attic.

I slowly opened the door and took a deep breath. I heard the mice scampering around, so I quietly closed the door and went back down the stairs. I went out the kitchen door and to the barn looking for a cat. I thought that if I took one of the barn cats into the attic with me, maybe I would be safe from the mice. At least having a cat with me, I wouldn't be alone. Our cats were never named because they were workers just like me. They were mousers. If they wanted to eat, they caught mice. I guess I could have named them, but at that time the concept of a pet was completely foreign to my world. I would no more name a cat than I would name the mice that the cat caught and ate.

I took the nameless barn cat back to the attic with me for protection and released him in the attic. I slowly worked my way to the center of the room and pulled the small chain that turned on the light. As I looked around, the sight that met my eyes was a nightmare of boxes, bags, and clothes of all sizes and colors. The room was hot and smelled like rot, and it was so crowded that I didn't know where to begin. "Where do I put all this stuff?" I asked myself hopelessly.

I heard the cat walking around and getting into things, and that reminder of his presence made me feel better.

At this point I thought I'd use one of ma's own tricks. She loved to throw all of my things from my closet and dresser onto my bedroom floor, so I threw all the stuff from the attic onto the middle of her bedroom floor. This brought me great satisfaction and gave me an inner feeling of revenge. I could do the same to her things that she did to mine. Soon I found myself working with great energy and zeal. As her bedroom became cluttered with junk from the attic, I began to enjoy my job.

Soon the huge, gloomy attic took on a new look. I worked through the room to the far end, where I found a window. I opened it and let the cool outside breeze filter in and freshen up the room. Opening this window, however, gave my champion an escape route. The cat went out the window, onto the roof, and down to the ground. I was on my own now. The mice had all long since gone to their hiding places, so I wasn't afraid of them any more.

I discovered a mechanical friend that day. Sitting near the window was an old Victrola. Stacked beside it were a few dusty 78-r.p.m. albums. I blew off the dust and read the labels. They didn't contain any songs I recognized, but I put an album on the turntable anyway. I pushed the button. Nothing happened. I searched around and found a crank handle sticking out of the gray, wooden cabinet. I wound the crank on the Victrola as far as it would go, then put the needle down on the old record and pushed the button again. The sound was mostly pops and scratches, but underneath I heard singing. Music filled the air. It was wonderful.

Taking a deep breath, I turned to survey the attic and contemplate my next cleaning maneuver. The attic looked great. The music and fresh air turned this scary place into a private heaven for me. I walked back to ma's bedroom door, where reality sank in.

I had been so hell-bent on throwing all of ma's things onto her bedroom floor that I didn't realize what would face me when I looked back into her room. "Wow, what a mess," I thought. A new fear crept into me as I thought of what would happen if she came upstairs and saw the carnage I had created. Box by box, I started to sort through things. I put clothes in one pile, Christmas decorations in another, newspapers in the throwaway pile, and unused dishes in yet another. Soon, everything was taking shape. I had to use the whole attic for storage, but I found a place for everything. I also made sure to leave a clear path through the middle, so I could get to the window and the Victrola.

Periodically, I interrupted my work to turn the crank on the Victrola and put on a different record. The ragtime music filled the air, and my heart lightened as I worked on my project. Throughout the afternoon, I frequently sat on the window sill to rest. I made many trips to the burn barrel, where I discarded the garbage. After many tiring hours, the attic was finally organized, and I was proud. Ma's bedroom and the attic were clean.

I had accomplished the job and had enjoyed a whole afternoon in the attic listening to scratchy old 78s. From then on, the attic with that old Victrola would become my favorite place on the farm. When I was sad and my heart heavy with despair, I would go to the attic and listen to music. Sometimes I would climb out through the window and sit on the garage roof. There, I could watch the clouds go by and think about the day when I would be old enough to get out of this place. I was desperate to be free of the sad life I was living. I would have talks with myself. "Nothing like this can last forever, Georgie. Someday you will be old enough to leave here. Please Lord, let me leave this sadness behind."

I never let ma know that I enjoyed my time in the attic. She always thought she was punishing me by sending me up there to clean. The attic looked better, and I felt good. Just knowing this private, tidy, spruced-up place was mine alone made me feel that, in some small way, I had won a battle. My little victory had a very sweet taste.

I was still in a good mood the next day when I got on the school bus. Susie wasn't on the bus to make fun of me or to tattle. So I felt free. The bus ride was a fun time for me. I always sat with Lena and Sandra on the back seat of the bus. Lena was the oldest, while Sandra and I were both about the same age. Sandra had a copy of *Hit Parade* magazine. It printed the words to all the top songs.

I already knew all the tunes, because I had heard them all on pa's barn radio. Pa had heard somewhere that cows gave more milk if they listened to music. Thank God for that theory. I'm not sure about the cows, but I enjoyed the music.

We three girls often sang the hit songs together. Back in those days, I had a rather good voice and so did my two friends. That morning we softly sang, "Blueberry Hill," "Rockin' Robin," and "Stand by Me."

Just as we pulled into Beekmantown, Sandra Bradley said, "Your foster father came over to my house last night."

"Is that right," I replied.

She continued, "He wanted my dad to sell him a thousand acres, but my father said 'no.' After Mr. Rivers left, my dad said that he would never sell Bill Rivers any land, because 'the way that son-of-a-bitch mistreats those foster kids is a crime.' "

I couldn't think of anything to say, so we sat in an uneasy silence for a few moments, then I said, "I've heard that the Beach Boys don't really surf, but I don't believe it, do you?"

Sandra, thankful to have the tension broken, replied, "I am sure that they really surf. All the kids in California surf." We continued talking about the Beach Boys until we arrived at school.

I always enjoyed the bus rides. It was our own special time. It meant that I had a life separate from the farm. During the ride, I had about half an hour to 45 minutes a day when I could just relax and act like a normal teenager. Singing on the bus was a great time, and it is my fondest childhood memory. No one at home had ever heard me sing. I never sang anything except Peter's lullaby on the farm, and I never let anyone hear me when I sang it.

The Beekmantown School was my sanctuary. There wasn't much pleasure in my life then, but this school brought me a great deal of gratification. School was the one place that acknowledged my effort and praised me for work well done.

My biggest problem at school was that sometimes I would run out of pencils or paper. I was only allowed a small amount of school supplies, and Ma Rivers would mandate how long they had to last. Unfortunately, the supplies didn't always last as long as she thought they were suppose to. The teachers didn't tolerate students not having paper for their work. Sometimes I would borrow paper from another student, but I had to be careful not to do that very often. Fortunately, I was still given my 10-cents-per-week allowance. I always took my dime to school with me so that I could buy a pencil or a ten-cent tablet of paper from the school store, if it became necessary.

This was my little taste of independence, and I felt pretty good about being able to have control over some small part of my life. I could write or draw to my heart's content. Although buying your own school supplies was a small thing to most people, to me it was a very big step. Now I could make my paper last longer. I felt like I was putting one over on ma.

On February 1, 1964, I turned 17. It was as uneventful and unrecognized as all the other birthdays before. I told myself that it didn't matter, but it hurt and it did matter. I hated it when no cake or presents appeared again that year. My life was really lonely. I knew that when I was 18 I could leave. That was a very long and lonely year away.

I Dream Of Jeanne

WEEKS TURNED INTO MONTHS and months into years. After I turned 17, mom's cruel behavior slowly changed—the beatings were less frequent. I didn't quite understand it, but I suspected that it meant the social workers were coming for one of their visits. The welfare workers would always call and make an appointment a couple of weeks before they came to the house. After the call, ma would turn all nice and sweet toward me. It would be, "Honey, do this," and, "Dear, do that," for about a week. She would also give me little hugs and affectionate pats. It was like being without water in the desert and suddenly finding an oasis. After I got a few days of tenderness, I began to think the bad was over, and I soaked up the good like a sponge. By the time the welfare worker came around, I would have done and said anything to let them know how wonderful the Rivers were.

I suspected that this sweetness was just one of ma's tricks. I was prepared this time. I had myself all geared up for the social worker's arrival. I had made up my mind that I didn't want to stay here any longer. I wanted to take my chances somewhere else, anywhere else. I was determined that I was going to tell the social worker how I felt this time, come what may.

After about a week and a half of ma's being nice to me, she came to me and said that she and pa wanted to have a talk with me. When I sat down to listen to what they had to say, I was skeptical and suspicious. Ma started out by saying that they wanted to adopt me. This was so unexpected that I was in shock. Of all the things they could have said to me, this was the last thing I ever expected to hear.

I stammered, "Adopt me. What are you talking about? Why would you want to adopt me? Why now after all these years?"

Pa answered, "If we don't adopt you, we have to send you back to your mother."

Those words sent a bolt of white fear through me. In shock, I asked, "Back to my real mother? I can't go back to my real mother."

Pa continued, "Your birth mother wants you back, but if we adopt you, you won't have to go."

I threw up my hands and said, "What choice do I have? I can stay here in hell or go back to be killed by the woman who killed my brother and beat me for years." Pa looked startled at my words.

At this point, I felt that I had nothing to lose, and I really didn't care what I said. I didn't care about the consequences of speaking my mind. This was the first time that I felt bold enough to say what I wanted. The Rivers had to know that I was not happy, but they also knew they had me right where they wanted me. I really had no viable options.

Then pa played his ace by softly saying, "You know, Georgie, we don't get to choose who we have for parents or children. We get what the good Lord gives us, but when we adopt we get to choose our child. We choose to have you for a daughter. We don't have to adopt you. We want to adopt you. We want to give you our name and have you become one of our family."

He spoke with such sincerity that I almost believed him. With all my heart I wanted to believe him. I knew that from here on, I would be treated like Susie. I would now be given all the privileges she had. When you're a foster kid, you dream of the day when you will be adopted. You picture it in your mind, and if you're not careful, it can consume you. I imagined nice people taking me away and making me a part of their family. Now it was really happening. I had paid my dues in hell for eight years, and now my hard work was going to pay off. They wanted to adopt me. I was going to be a real daughter.

Pa went on to tell me that I would be a Rivers. He also said that I could change my first name if I wanted to. "Wow!" I said. What a neat thing. How many times do you get to choose your name? I had always hated being called "Georgie Porgy" or "George," which was just as bad.

The next day, my mind raced as I thought of what I wanted to be called. The two names I liked best were "Tina" or "Connie." In the days that followed, I ran those two names through my mind, but the more I said them to myself, the more I didn't like them. I played a song on the old Victrola in the attic called "I Dream of Jeannie With the Light Brown Hair." I thought to myself that this was the name for me. Jeannie was a beautiful name and my hair was auburn! I decided to drop the "i" from Jeannie and call myself "Jeanne." Jeanne would be my choice, and it would be spelled my way. I reveled in the power of it all. I could erase the last trace of my mom Veronica's hated legacy by throwing away the name she gave me. From then on I would be called Jeanne Marie Rivers. What could be better!

I confided in my teachers at school about my upcoming adoption, and they all told me how wonderful it was to be "chosen." I hoped the work situation would change after the adoption. I didn't resent the hard work, but I was angered that Susie never had to work. I just knew that after the adoption, I would get to sleep longer in the morning.

Finally, the day of the adoption arrived, and we drove to Saranac Lake for the process. We walked into the judge's chambers, and I sat between ma and pa with my hands in theirs. The judge asked me, "Is this what you really want? Do you understand what adoption is?"

I replied confidently, "Yes. Adoption means the Rivers picked me to be their daughter."

The judge wrote on the paper in front of him and said, "Well, Jeanne Marie Rivers, you are free to go home with your parents."

"Thank you." A tear of joy rolled down my cheek.

As I stood up, my parents hugged me. This was the first hug I had received since I was seven and Aunt Bea had hugged me when I said goodbye to her. For the first time, ma called me, "Daughter."

"I am somebody today." This was a very wonderful time for me because I knew that I was finally loved and wanted. After we left the courthouse, we went out for lunch. This was quite a treat. Going out for lunch was something we never did. What a wonderful day. My heart was so light with happiness that I felt as if I was floating on air all day. I thought of all the ways my life would change now. It was a Friday, and I knew I would be able to sleep in tomorrow. I looked forward to going to school even more on Monday, because I would be riding in the car with Susie and ma, instead of going on the bus. I took a deep breath and knew I finally had a home.

Saturday morning at 5, pa stood at the top of the stairs like he did every morning and yelled, "George, it's time to get up." I couldn't believe my ears. Why was he telling me to get up? I was his daughter now. I didn't have to get up. I knew he had called me out of habit, so I just smiled and stretched under my warm covers and went back to sleep.

Ma yelling for me to get up awakened me again. "What are you doing still in bed?" she hollered at me. "Do you think you're on vacation or something? When we tell you to get up, we mean get up."

I jumped up out of bed in disbelief. Nothing had changed. Oh, my name was different, but my position in the house was exactly the same. "How could they do this to me, how could anyone be so cruel?" My heart at this moment was the heaviest it had ever been. All hope was gone. The only thing that remained was despair.

I saw no let-up in my work duties after the adoption. I also saw no change in Susie's position in the family. The saddest part was that there was no change in my position in the family either. I was still everyone's servant and ma's punching bag. I slowly came to the full realization that the adoption was just a ploy to avoid losing a good worker.

The worst sadness that I had felt in years was when my hopes of being a daughter were dashed, and I found myself still only a slave. My despondency was like a pot of bubbling black tar that swallowed me up. I was now completely broken. I felt so alone. I didn't care if I lived or died.

I believe that there are two kinds of despair:
• There is the sadness of never knowing hope.
• And the worst desperation is having hope once, and then having it dashed.

That is how I now felt. At night I hummed the lullaby that Peter had sung to me all those years before, "Aah, Ah, Aaaah, AAH...Aah, Ah, Aaaah, AAH, Aah, Ah, Aaaah, AAH." It made me feel like he was still with me, trying to keep me alive. I also talked to Peter to let him know I was still thinking of him and that I still needed him. I wanted to die, but the spirit of Peter let me know it was my responsibility to live on for both of us. We were one.

I whispered, "Peter, I love you. Help me through this." After a while, the "Aah, Ah, Aaaah, AAH...Aah, Ah, Aaaah, AAH, Aah, Ah, Aaaah, AAH" would get softer, and I would gradually drift into an uneasy sleep.

Ma didn't allow me to take part in any after-school activities. I didn't belong to any clubs or take part in any social events. I was only allowed to go to school, come straight home, and do my chores. I didn't have many friends, except for Lena and Sandra. No boys ever noticed me.

The only other girl who spoke to me was Karen. She was a popular, beautiful cheerleader, but she always had time for me in her busy life. Karen was always nice to everyone, and she spoke to me whenever we passed each other. She was very likable. We didn't hang out together or even have the same classes, but for a cheerleader to even talk to someone like me seemed very rare and special.

Cheerleaders had their own group of friends, after all. Someone plain and simple like me didn't belong in their circle. Karen just seemed to ignore the circles and was nice to everyone. We never had any great in-depth conversations. I didn't confide in her about what things were like for me at home.

My 1965 class picture. I hated being called "George," so when the Rivers adopted me, I changed my name to the more-feminine "Jeanne."

I didn't look forward to the end of school that year. I knew that summer vacation would soon begin. That meant being home all the time. I didn't know what new things Ma Rivers would come up with to make my life miserable. It seemed to me that when pa was at home working around the barn, things would go somewhat better than when ma was there alone.

In late spring, pa told me that we were going to open a new field the next day. I knew what that meant as I looked out into the new field and saw that it was strewn with rocks. Many were the size of potatoes or grapefruits. Some rocks were the size of watermelons or bigger. Everything on this damn farm was work—from seed to mouth. After I got home from school, Billy hooked the tractor to the stoneboat. Kenny and I rode the stoneboat down to the field, where we dismounted and started carrying the rocks to the stoneboat. If Kenny and I found a boulder too large to handle, Billy would stop the tractor and get down to help us with it. When we had a full load, Billy drove to the nearest wall, where Kenny and I unloaded the boat. We worked until it was too dark to see the rocks.

I spent many hot, miserable evenings after school gathering boulders behind the stoneboat that spring. My back hurt from all of the stooping. Blisters formed on my hands, and then the blisters broke. The rocks tore at the tender, exposed inner layers of my skin.

In July, pa told me that he had arranged for me to start seeing another farmer's son, Bob. Now, Bob was not ugly. Indeed he was a tall, handsome, soft-spoken man, but he was a farmer, and I swore to myself that I would never love any farmer! I was shocked! I didn't understand why pa was doing this horrible thing to me! He told me that I was expected to sit on the porch and talk with Bob on Sunday afternoons.

On Sunday, Bob showed up about 2 o'clock on his motorcycle. I had to wear my church dress and go sit on the porch to talk to him. To say that I had no idea what was expected of me is putting it mildly. Three Sundays later, after Bob left, pa came out on the porch. Bob had said something to pa about my attitude, because I could tell by the look in pa's eyes that he was real mad. I had seen him mad many times before but not at me. I didn't understand what I had done that was so wrong.

Pa started yelling at me, "What in the hell is the matter with you, Jeanne? Bob is a nice young man and a hard-working farmer. Why can't you be nice to him? Haven't I taught you anything after all these years?"

I looked pa straight in the eyes and defiantly said, "Yes, you taught me a lot of things. One of the things I learned was that I'd NEVER marry a farmer. I don't want to live like this the rest of my life." By now I was shouting shrilly!

Pa suddenly raised his hand and slapped me across the face. I was stunned, because he had never hit me before. Pa had always been the one person that didn't hit me. Pa hit Kenny, and ma hit me. That was the way it had always been. I didn't know whether I was hurt from the sting of the slap or by the fact that he had slapped me at all. My eyes filled with tears and disbelief, as I stood there just staring at the man I had considered to be a friend and a father figure.

Pa shouted, "Get upstairs to your room and stay there! I can't stand the sight of you!"

With those words ringing in my ears, I ran upstairs, crying and hurt. This incident was the turning point for pa and me. Things would never again be quite the same between us. Thankfully, Bob finally understood that I wasn't interested, and he never came back.

When school started in the fall, I was extremely happy that the summer work season had ended. Nothing much happened that fall until November. It was a blustery day that promised a severe winter ahead. I was in my last class of the day studying Business Law, when a voice came over the loudspeaker that said that President John F. Kennedy had been shot. During my ride home on the bus, many of the students were crying. I was sad that the young president had died. Although the world suffered a great loss and went through many changes as a result of this tragedy, my life remained the same. What happened in the world didn't effect my life on this farm in any way.

My First Date

ONE DAY EARLY in the next summer, ma and I went down to Ron's Four Corners Diner and ordered a couple of "Michigans." This dish was the house specialty of The Four Corners, as well as nearly every other diner in Plattsburgh. As I put some vinegar on my French fries and munched on my "Michigan"-style chili dog, I listened as ma told Ron that we would both work evenings at the diner for one paycheck if he would hire us. Ron accepted her offer on the spot.

I sighed. I had already been stacking hay all day, so I wasn't too happy to have another job. When I learned that Karen, my cheerleader friend from school, would also be a waitress at the restaurant, I cheered up a little. On the way home, Ma Rivers told me that, of course, she would keep my paycheck, but I could keep whatever tips I earned. Since I mostly did the dishes and the clean-up, my tips were sparse. However, the few coins I gathered were welcome.

The first week that I worked at the Four Corners, I met three airmen who were regulars at the Four Corners. They were stationed at the nearby Plattsburgh Strategic Air Command Airbase. Larry, Kim and James came to the diner for the "Michigans" and for a chance to dress in civilian clothes and get off base for a while. The "boys," as ma called them, would come every single weekend, when ma, Karen and I were there.

We worked at the diner on Thursdays, Fridays, and weekends all summer long. Then when I started my last year at school, ma went back to working in the school cafeteria, and we could only work at the Four Corners on weekends.

One night after work, I was lying in bed and heard pa shout at ma, "I don't like having you down at the Four Corners so much. I need you around here more."

Then he made the amazing accusation, "You're sleeping with one or all of those boys from the airbase, aren't you?"

Ma replied, "No, honey, I love only you."

I didn't have a clue as to what "sleeping" with guys meant, but I knew it must be a bad thing to do, because pa was yelling at ma about it. I was shocked to hear ma and pa arguing about our job. Although hearing angry words being voiced in our house was not new to me, it was strange to hear ma and pa shouting at each other instead of at one of us kids. I couldn't see any wrong with the way things were going at the Four Corners, but pa obviously didn't like the situation at all. Ma Rivers refused to quit working at the diner, so things were tense around our house for several months, and the "boys" kept on eating there.

One of the "boys," Airman James Robert, was a serious, solemn young man. He was tall and thin, with short, jet-black hair and a neatly trimmed mustache. He wore heavy plastic-framed glasses. James Robert always had his face buried in a book.

The only person who could get James to stop reading was a pretty 30-year-old young woman named Patty. She was a little shorter than James and had shoulder-length brown hair. Patty always wore her skirts a trifle shorter and her necklines a little more revealing than most of our customers. By looking at her you, would never believe she was married and the mother of four small children. She always came to the diner alone, so I had never seen her husband. When Patty arrived, James would put down his book, and they would get into his car. It never occurred to me why they left together.

One Friday, ma asked me to babysit for Patty, so that James could go out with her. Ma said, "Babysitting for them is a secret. I don't want you to say anything to pa about it. If he asks you, I just want you to say that you have a babysitting job but don't mention Patty. Do you understand?"

I nodded. It seemed so strange to have this type of a bond with ma. We were doing things together that no one else knew about. It was all so exciting and scary at the same time. It seemed to me that ma was becoming almost a friend. We even talked like two normal people, instead of her yelling and putting me down all the time. It felt odd for me to actually like her.

Ma took me to Patty's house around 5 o'clock on Saturday. I waited with Patty and her kids until James showed up for their "secret date." Patty had no phone numbers to give me to reach her in case of an emergency. I found this strange, but I didn't push the issue.

I knew I could call ma if something happened. When James showed up, he and Patty took off. Her kids were fun to be with, so I played with them, gave them dinner, and made the most of my time with them. After dinner, I told the children a story and sent them to bed.

While I cleaned up the kitchen, I fantasized about this being my home and those being my kids. It made me warm inside to think about all the love I had to give. I tried to imagine what it would be like to have my own home full of children. I knew my home would be filled with love, soft voices, and children that would never know the pain of not having a loving mother in their life. I had promised myself years ago that my children would never feel the pain of beatings and angry, belittling words.

When the cleaning was all done, I settled down on the couch to watch whatever I wanted on television. What a luxury. I could have watched television all night if I had wanted to, but I soon fell asleep.

After midnight, a very angry, strange man awakened me. He was demanding to know who I was and what I was doing in his house at that hour of the morning. It took me a few seconds to wake up and get my wits about me, but I told him who I was and that I was babysitting for Patty.

He demanded, "Where's Patty?"

I shrugged. "I don't know. She just asked if I would babysit, so ma brought me over here." I had an inner sense that told me not to volunteer much more information. I just acted innocent and said nothing about James. Patty's husband was very mad and told me to call ma to come and get me.

When ma's car pulled up in the yard, I saw that it wasn't ma, but pa who had come for me. I could tell by the look on his face that he was very angry. The two men talked outside for a while, and then pa gruffly told me, "Get in the car!"

I was so scared; I had never seen pa so angry. He didn't talk to me during the entire ride home. Ma was in the kitchen when we got home. The three of us looked at each other, but no words were exchanged between us. We didn't know what to say. The cold silence was broken when pa started yelling at ma. "You knew that Patty and that airman James were going off together, didn't you! How could you involve Jeanne in your trickery?"

Suddenly, pa doubled up his fist and punched ma on the side of her head. She was slammed back against the kitchen counter by the force of the blow. Ma screamed in pain. I gasped in disbelief as pa lunged at her again, and with all his might, his closed fist connected with her chin.

Ma begged, "I'm sorry. Please stop."

I slipped into the living room, where I was out of his sight, but I was still able to see what was happening to ma.

She cried, "Bill, what is the matter with you? Stop, please stop."

Pa didn't stop. Her groveling just fed his anger, and he knocked her to the floor. Then he kicked her in the side with his boot.

He snarled, "If you hadn't been fooling around with those damn worthless airmen, you bitch ..." He kicked her again and then continued, "... you wouldn't be in the mess you're in now."

Pa then kicked her again three more times—once in the stomach, once in the ribs, and a final kick to her leg. As quickly as it started, the assault stopped, and pa charged out of the house and went to the barn to start his morning chores. I was still in shock at what I had just seen. I rushed to ma to comfort her and to see what I could do for her. We hugged and she told me, "I'm okay. Just help me get on my feet."

Although I had been the recipient of this kind of treatment from ma many times, I didn't know how to react to what I had just witnessed. I was amazed to find myself actually comforting ma because pa had beaten her. I couldn't even count how many times this woman had beaten me, and not once had anyone ever held and comforted me.

She whispered through her tears, "I'm okay, Jeanne. Go get ready to do your chores."

I did what I was told, but I couldn't stop crying and feeling bad for ma. I didn't know what to expect when I got to the barn. I didn't understand pa's actions. I wondered what he would say or do to me when I saw him. I finished my house chores, then looked around for ma, but she was not in the house. I realized she had already gone to the barn to do her morning work. I went to the barn for my share of the chores, and although they were not fighting, they were not talking to each other either. They were going about their normal routine and, except for the air of tension, things were getting done like nothing had happened.

Over the next few days, life at home was not going any better for ma and pa. The fights continued, with pa resorting to hitting ma more and more frequently. It seemed like every time we got back from the diner, pa would go into one of his rages.

The next weekend, Kim and Larry came into the restaurant without James. Larry started talking to Karen. I went over to Kim, wiped my hands on my apron, and asked, "Where is James? You guys never come in without him."

Kim said, "Patty's husband contacted the Air Force about James. I think James was afraid of a court martial, so he and Patty ran off together. The Military Police found them yesterday, and they put James into the stockade. I don't know if he will ever get out."

I noticed that Karen was busy, so I said, "What will you have Kim?"

He replied, "I don't know ... a deluxe "Michigan," onions buried, and a Coke ... I guess."

I went over to the grill, gave Kim's order to ma, and told her that James was in the stockade. When the food was ready, I took it to Kim and asked, "You want vinegar or ketchup?"

He said, "Ketchup. By the way, Jeanne, you want to go the game with me next Friday night?"

I replied, "I don't think that I can, but I'll ask ma."

I had little hope that ma would let me go, because I had never been allowed to go to any after-school functions before, so I said offhandedly, "Ma, there's a big basketball game next Friday night. Kim said that he would like to take me."

To my surprise, ma said, "I guess it's okay, but not a word of this to pa. I mean it, not a word. I don't want Kim coming out to the farm, 'cause pa would have a fit. Tell him to meet us at the game, and I'll take you."

I became more and more excited as the night of the basketball game against West Chazy approached. It was almost like a date. I had heard of dates, but I had never been on one. I had never thought of Kim as a potential "boyfriend." I didn't even know that he had noticed me. Up until now, he had just talked and joked with me like a sister. I was just the shy girl who was working in the back of the diner, and he was just one of my many customers.

On the day of the game, after dinner and chores, ma and I left for the Beekmantown School.

When we arrived at the school, ma went inside, while I waited outside for Kim. I was full of butterflies as I saw his car pull into the parking lot and park alongside ma's car. Kim got out and gave me a quick hug. Then he took my hand, and we started to make our way toward the school. Suddenly, out of the corner of my eye I noticed someone running toward us in the shadows. When the runner burst into the light, I screamed, "Pa, what are you doing here?"

He grabbed my arm. "So now you're a part of ma's deception! She's using you to help her meet her "boyfriends.' "

I quickly responded, "Pa, Kim's not ma's date. He's taking ME to the game."

Pa was beyond reason and shouted, "I'll teach you both that you can't play me for a fool!" He raised his hand and slapped me hard across the face. Kim immediately jumped in to stop him, and pa punched him in the face. With all the speed I could muster, I took off running into the gym. Adrenaline pumped through my body as I desperately scanned the gym searching for ma. I found her and blurted out, "Pa is in the parking lot beating up Kim."

I ran back out of the gym with ma right behind me. When we got back, pa was holding Kim up with one hand and pounding his bloody face with the other. Kim was just standing there taking it. He couldn't or wouldn't fight back. Pa let go of Kim and glared at me for a second.

With that, Kim turned to me and said, "I'm sorry." Then he took off running for his car.

Pa said, "Get in the car." Then he pushed ma in behind me. Ma and I didn't speak a word as we took the long, slow drive back home. Tears poured from my eyes and dripped onto my dress. I looked over my shoulder and watched the headlights of pa's pickup following ominously behind us. I knew that this time he was really angry, and that there was going to be big trouble when we got home. Sure enough, pa punched ma in the face several times. He also hit her in the stomach and on the chest. His punches and kicks were relentless.

I cried, screamed, and begged for him to stop, but nothing calmed his rage. He then punched me right in the mouth, causing my teeth to cut through my lower lip. I could taste the blood. Pa then kicked me on the thigh with his boot. Finally, he screamed, "That's it. Your jobs at the restaurant are over. You're never to talk to or see those worthless airmen again, either one of you. Do you understand me?"

I stammered, "Kim was my date and not ma's. Nothing is going on between Kim and ma."

Pa shut me up by hitting and knocking me to the floor. Pa wasn't convinced. He believed what he wanted to believe, and no one could change his mind. Ma and I never went back to work at the diner, nor did we ever see Kim again.

The friendly relationship I had so carefully built with Ma Rivers for the last few months disappeared into thin air that night. I think that ma blamed me for her beating. She slipped back into her old pattern of hitting and demeaning me. The respect and love I had for pa and that he had for me was all gone. I was back to living my lonely life in a house full of angry people. I couldn't imagine my world getting any worse. I now knew that I had to try and get away, soon, somehow.

"I Can't Take It Any More"
from an oil on canvas portrait by Jeanne Fowler

Ticket To Ride

ON THE FIRST DAY of February, 1965, I became an 18-year-old adult and was faced with my first grownup decision. I could run away from the farm now or wait until the end of the school year. If I left in February, I would be going out into below-zero weather with no home, no friends, no car, no money, and no high-school degree. If I waited until the end of school, I would undoubtedly be beaten more. I knew my only ticket out of the "welfare system" was my education.

On February 9th, the Beatles were on the Ed Sullivan show, and I didn't want to miss the big event. I loved Paul McCartney the best. I thought he was so dreamy and cute, with his thick auburn hair, velvety voice, and big, brown eyes. My big problem was that ma and pa would never let me watch the Beatles on the living room television. There was a television in my room, but it belonged to Susie. I had gotten caught watching her television once before and was severely beaten. I knew that ma suspected that I was still watching Susie's television. Sometimes she would sneak upstairs to try to catch me.

I hatched a plan and waited for February 9th. That night I went to my room early and turned on Susie's TV set. When Ed Sullivan came on, I watched for a minute and then turned the television off. I waited a few minutes, then turned the television back on. The Beatles weren't on yet, so off the television went for a few more minutes. Finally, the Fab Four came on, and I was enthralled. My favorite song was "She's Got A Ticket To Ride." Any song about leaving got my vote. As soon as the Beatles finished singing, off the television went and not a minute too soon!

A short time later, ma came creeping up the stairs. I didn't even hear her, but then, I wasn't really listening anymore. She came into my room and put her hand on top of Susie's television set. Thankfully, it was stone-cold, just the way I had planned. As she walked back down the stairs, I thought to myself, "Better luck next time, BITCH!"

That spring, my entire class was buzzing about the junior-senior prom. The theme was "Shangri-La," based on Frank Capra's classic 1937 movie, "Lost Horizon." The story involved an idealistic dreamer who escapes from the war and stumbles into a beautiful, warm, enchanted Himalayan mountain paradise. Shangri-La was a utopian land of perfect peace, love, and harmony, where there was no war, greed, pain or hatred. The way of life in Shangri-La was based on one simple rule: be kind.

All the girls of my class were excitedly talking about their dates and dresses as they decorated the gym. Everyone, it seemed, except me. I was practically invisible to my classmates, and there was little chance of me being asked to go to the prom. I didn't want to go to the prom in my school clothes, and I knew that ma and pa wouldn't buy me a prom dress even if I had a date. Fortunately, no one asked me to go. No one even asked me to help decorate the gym.

The day before the prom, I noticed that the doors to the gym were open and no one was inside, so I slipped into the room. I gasped as I took in the beauty of Shangri-La. No one would have guessed that this room had once housed the best basketball team in the north state. I just stood there, frozen in my tracks, as I took in the beauty of the green and blue, twisted crepe-paper garlands. That gymnasium was the most beautiful thing I had ever seen. I closed my eyes and imagined that I was here on prom night. My gown was long and glamorous, and my hair was fixed up with flowers in it. My date was wearing a tux and he offered me his hand as we strode onto the dance floor. Then I heard someone coming into the gym. It broke my spell. I quickly dashed out of the gym with tears in my eyes.

Since I had first come to this school during the fourth grade, I had never been allowed to take part in any after-school activities. I had attended this school with the same students since I was 10 years old, but I barely knew any of them, and they didn't know me. No one knew about the life I had been forced to live. The other students didn't know the pain, suffering, and loneliness I felt. I was always left out of everything my peers did, but I didn't blame them. They were only children just like me. The other kids shouldn't have to know about such pain and loneliness, so I never told them. My heart ached every time I walked past the gym, because I would never know the joy of dancing at this prom. I felt like I didn't even exist! The night of the prom, I laid in bed crying and feeling sorry for myself. I knew that my classmates were all out having fun.

The next Monday at school, everyone was talking about the fun they had and what everyone was wearing. Pictures soon appeared, and they reflected the glamour of this once-in-a-lifetime magical night. It was hard for me to look at the photos. This was my prom, yet my schoolmates never talked to me about it. I guess it was just expected that I wouldn't be attending.

Work and more work was the extent of my life. I noticed the things that other girls my age were doing. At school I would hear them talk about what they did on the weekends. Their lives were filled with sleepovers, shopping downtown, and going to the movies. I had never done any of these things. I only knew how to work. I worked from morning until night. I couldn't call a girlfriend and just talk on the phone. I was almost grown, but I never had the chance to be a child.

I really wanted to have a "Beekmantown Eagle" yearbook just like everybody else, and I would have wanted all my friends to sign it. I even imagined myself giggling with my girlfriends over the way people looked and the funny things they wrote in my book. I sure wished that I could earn $3.95 to cover the cost. Near the end of the school year, the yearbooks were all passed out. Of course, I didn't have one. I didn't want anyone to know that I didn't have the money to buy one, so I walked away. I tried to hide whenever I saw a group of kids signing books. No one at school ever knew that I was sad or that I hurt inside. I felt like an outsider among my peers.

My only joy was still school and singing on the bus. Even these little pleasures were getting a bit thin. One song that we sang in particular was making me sad. Sometimes my eyes would glaze over when we sang Bobby Vinton's beautiful, sad love song, "Roses are Red." To me the song symbolized my girlish dreams that could never ever happen.

We dated through high school and when the big day came, I wrote into your book, next to my name. Roses are red my love. Violets are blue. Sugar is sweet my love, but not as sweet as you.

A few months after the deadline passed to buy a yearbook or a class ring, ma's sister-in-law, Aunt Shirley, called and said that she was in need of a babysitter. I needed all the cash I could get for my escape plans. Babysitting was a good way to make a few coins and get out of the house for a while. Aunt Shirley was married to Albert, one of ma's brothers. He was a nice-looking man with dark, wavy hair. Uncle Albert always worked outdoors for the electric company. His red, wind-burned winter skin was slowly turning into his deeply tanned summer skin when I first started working for them.

Aunt Shirley was a petite, soft-spoken woman who wore feminine dresses that contrasted starkly with the worn jeans that we usually wore on our farm. To me she always looked neat, clean and pretty. Her house was spotless, and although she had five small children (four girls, and a somewhat challenged baby boy), she always appeared calm and happy. Aunt Shirley was the only person in the family that I felt that I could trust enough to talk to. She was always sensitive to my situation and never betrayed my confidences. Aunt Shirley knew how unhappy I was, so we spoke many times about the issues that were important to me. Mostly, we talked about the treatment I was getting at home, but sometimes we discussed the increasing violence between ma and pa.

One day that spring, Aunt Shirley secretly helped me hatch a plan to escape from the farm. The next time she picked me up to babysit, I had a couple of pieces of clothing hidden on me, which I left at her house. My plan was starting to feel like it could really happen. Now with a few pieces of my clothes physically off the farm, the next problem was how I was going to get away and where was I going to go?

The next week, I secretly called Granddad Trombley. It had been a long time since I had talked to him on the phone, because when I would get caught calling granddad, I would always get a terrible beating. I took the risk because I had to ask for his help.

He understood and without hesitation said, "Let me know when and where to pick you up and I'll be there."

After I hung up the phone, I was more determined than ever to get away. I felt in charge of my life for the first time, and the feeling was good. I faced each new day with a strength and hope I had never experienced before.

Aunt Shirley would pick me up two or three times a week, and I soon had a brown paper bag full of clothes at her house. I had to be careful not to empty my closet too much, for fear of calling attention to my plan, so I was very selective in the things I chose to take with me. All of a sudden I didn't feel so lonely at school, because I had a very powerful secret. This gave me a new air of independence.

The remaining days of the school year just flew by. Soon, it was time to take our final exams, and because of my good grades, I only had one test to take. In the rest of my classes, I had maintained a 90% or better average, and taking the final exams was optional in those cases. This policy was both a godsend and a curse. The window for my escape was very narrow. The last day at school was my last good chance to sneak away.

Chapter Thirty-One

Dime, Clip, And Photo

I CALLED GRANDDAD from home again and told him that I was ready to leave after my one last English test. He assured me that he would be there to pick me up. I also called Aunt Shirley and told her that I was leaving and that granddad would take me to her house to get my things. Everything was set. After years of being told what to do and when to do it, I finally had managed to do something for myself. This was exciting and scary at the same time. I was about to be free of this prison I had been in since I was a child. I felt that even though my birth parents had committed the crime, I had served the hard time. My freedom was so close I could taste it. It was sweet!

Fear kept me awake most of the night. I went over and over my get-away plans in my head. If my breakout didn't work, I would undoubtedly be brought back for another rubber-hose beating. I knew that even if I got away, I wouldn't have a home, money, car or job. I didn't have anyone to count on. The stakes were high, but I was willing to take the risk because I would be free, gloriously free. The idea of liberty made my mind reel with the possibilities. I didn't care if I ended up sleeping under a bridge. It would still be better than this. I was nearly grown. I just couldn't take any more.

I was already awake and filled with apprehension when I heard pa call me, "Jeanne, it's time to get up."

Usually, I stayed in bed for a minute, waiting for the sound of the milkers to start, but on this day I was already dressed and filled with anticipation. I heard pa's heavy work boots clump down the polished stairs and out the back door. Then I could hear him calling in the cows for milking as he went down the path to the barn. Soon, the familiar humming of the milking machine motors coming on told me that pa had started work.

I was filled with adrenaline that morning and could feel my fear and excitement growing. That fear made a heavy knot in my stomach. Thoughts of freedom lightened the black dread just a little bit.

My mind was clouded as I went about the same chores I had done every day since the age of nine. I quickly did the dusting and vacuuming, and I prepared breakfast for everyone before racing to the barn to wash the milking machines. I prayed that what I had planned for this day did not show in my eyes or on my face. "Just get through the morning," I told myself. "Just get through the morning and get on that school bus."

I finished the milking, ate breakfast, and rushed back upstairs to dress for school. I took my shiny, new dime off my dresser and put it in my pocket. It was my pay for seven days of back-breaking work in the fields and the house. I quickly looked behind the mirror for my small, yellowed newspaper clipping from the year after I was separated from my birth family. I read it again quickly.

Burowsky Says, "Police Forced Confession."

Chicago, April 27 (AP)...*A small 35-year-old man testified today that police threatened him with a gun to make him "confess" that he and his wife beat to death their three-year old son. Peter Burowsky and his wife, Veronica, 28, were charged with murder. A pre-trial hearing before Judge John T. Dempsey of Criminal Court seeks to determine whether alleged confessions by the parents can be admitted into evidence. Their son, Peter Jr., was found fatally beaten in the Burowsky bathroom last July. Burowsky took the stand and identified Police Lt. Thomas Cacy as the officer he said threatened him with a gun.*

Earlier, Burowsky declared an officer with a pistol in the station said:

"I'd like to see you run so I could give you one in the back."

Two police detectives testified they heard no threats against Burowsky. Two other officers gave similar testimony Monday.

Of all the hundreds of newspaper clippings and magazine articles generated by my brother's bizarre murder, this was the only one I had. I wondered why everyone hated dad so much. I didn't care if he was as bad as everyone claimed. I had just hoped and prayed that he would come and save me from this horrible life as a foster slave. He never came, wrote or called. I didn't have time to think about dad very much on this day, so I folded the clipping, put it in an envelope, and placed it in my purse. I knew that somewhere in Plattsburgh I had many family members, but I was never allowed to visit any of them. I had no idea where they lived. The only family I could call on to help me was Granddad Trombley. I had planned each move of my getaway very carefully so as not to arouse the suspicion of my foster parents. I was terrified that I might have forgotten something important.

I removed a dog-eared, stained, black-and-white photograph that had been inserted between the glass and the banged-up, brown wooden frame of my dresser mirror. It was a picture of me as a sad-eyed three-year-old. The picture had been behind my mirror for years, but I never looked at it. Now I noticed that I could clearly see the ligature marks on my wrists from frequently being tied in my birth parents' home.

Although I didn't want to remember my birth family anymore, I couldn't throw away the photograph of me. As far as I knew, this photo of me with the scars on my wrists was the only one in existence, so I wrapped this precious artifact in a Kleenex and placed it in my pocket. Almost everything I owned was now in my pocket or burned into my soul.

Nine years of my life had been spent here on the farm, but I wouldn't miss any of it. There was nothing that I could call my own. I had no emotional attachment to anything or anyone. Nothing! Nine whole years of nothing!

As I walked out the door to catch the school bus, I stopped for a moment and took a deep breath. I ran through my mind the things I had gone through in my life. The Good (Aunt Bea), The Bad (losing my brother and sister), and the Ugly (this horrible farm). I pieced my life together at this moment with all the good things I could remember, and I left all the negative things in the kitchen with this family that deserved to carry it more than I. I muttered, "Well world, today it's you and me, and I WILL come out the victor! After today, from this moment on, no one will ever hit me again."

I made that promise to myself, and I intended to keep it. I slowly walked down the driveway to the school bus for the last time. My few clothes were hidden at Aunt Shirley's house. I had arranged with my granddad to pick me up at school. My whole desperate plan depended on granddad, a man who had carefully avoided rescuing me at every opportunity my entire life. The price of pursuing freedom might be high. If granddad did not come through this time, I knew that the thrashing I would receive would be horrendous. Whether granddad came to get me after school or not, I had to make a run for it. There was no turning back. I was finally going to save myself. All that stood between freedom and me was one English exam. Freedom! For the first time in my life, at the age of 18, I felt alive and free.

As I rode to school, my mind raced in a hundred different directions. "What if I got caught?" I could imagine the beating I would get if Ma and Pa Rivers even suspected that I was trying to escape. I was 18, and for the first time I felt like an adult. I was doing something that would alter the direction of my life. Although I felt that God had forsaken me long ago, I found myself praying to Him for guidance. I prayed to whatever powers I could call on to help me through this day. I made it through my English test and went to the back parking lot of the school.

"Please let granddad be there for me," I silently prayed. Granddad knew my situation, but he never stepped in to save me. If he failed me this time, I felt that I would be doomed. I apprehensively rounded the corner of the gym, and thankfully, there sat granddad in his new, bright-gold Lincoln Continental. It was the most beautiful sight I had ever seen! That wonderful car was my ticket out of the prison that the welfare system had put me in for the last 18 years. Tears ran down my cheek as I raced into granddad's arms to safety and freedom.

We hugged and cried for a while before I nervously said, "We need to get out of here before someone sees us. Ma is in the cafeteria working, and I can't take any chances on her seeing us and trying to stop me."

Granddad nodded.

I got into his beautiful Lincoln and away we sped. As we drove, I hurriedly gave him the directions to Aunt Shirley's house so we could get my stash of clothes. I also told granddad as quickly as I could what had been going on since I came to the Rivers' home. He already knew some of it from our brief phone conversations, but I had such a need to tell him again. It was like a dam had burst, and I was finally able to tell someone what I had been through. Tears filled granddad's eyes as he listened to me, and then he took my hand and said, "You're safe now."

I remembered some 12 years before when the policeman who came to my brother's murder scene had said the exact same words to me, and I began to sob.

By the time we arrived at Aunt Shirley's, I had regained my composure. I introduced her to granddad. After a few minutes of small talk, Aunt Shirley handed me the grocery bag. It held all of my meager belongings. I hugged Aunt Shirley and told her how much I loved her and how much I appreciated all her help. She hugged me and gave me a smile that spoke volumes. Then granddad and I left.

I had one more thing to do before that day was over. I told granddad I wanted to go to the Clinton County Welfare Office.

As we pulled up, granddad asked if I wanted him to come in with me. I replied, "No, this I can do all by myself." I walked into the building with all the strength a frightened, angry teenaged girl could muster. I asked the receptionist if I could speak to the person in charge.

"I'm sorry," she replied, "Everyone is in a meeting right now. Can I take your name and make an appointment for you?" I hadn't had a caseworker since my adoption. I didn't know who to ask for, but I was prepared for that. I was so worked up that I couldn't wait.

"No! You cannot," I stammered as I walked down the hall looking for anyone to finally listen to my small voice. There was a large room to the left of me. I saw several people sitting around a long table. I didn't know who most of those people were. I stormed into the room. All eyes looked towards me. "Hello," I said. "For those of you who don't know me, my name is Jeanne Rivers. Some of you will remember me as Georgianne Burowsky."

I was interrupted by one of the caseworkers. "Excuse me, but we are in the middle of a meeting here. Please make an appointment and come back another time." It had taken me 18 years to find a voice, and I was too worked up to leave.

I replied, "I'm not coming back at another time. You will listen to me today. You sit here with all your little folders with the names of faceless children on them," I said impudently. "I want you to remember that those names have faces."

A woman stood up and said, "Please, miss, this is not the time or the place to vent the anger you seem to ..."

I interrupted her. "This is exactly the time and place! You people put me into one living hell after another since I was three years old!"

Another lady stood up. I raised my hand as if to stop her. "I will not be silenced today!" I stared her straight in the eyes. She sat back down. I had everyone's attention. "My brother died because of you and people like you. My sisters and I were beaten because of you."

I pointed first at one and then another caseworker. "You, in your infinite wisdom put us in foster homes that continued the beatings!" A caseworker interrupted, "I did not participate in your brother's death. None of us did. I don't even know who you are."

I realized she was right, and I was somewhat embarrassed to be chastising this poor woman. I knew that the whole system had killed my brother, but how do you yell at a system? So I continued, "Yes you did. You continually put us back with our mother who beat us and beat us until Peter was dead."

"You," I said, pointing at the lady again, "are the reason my brother is dead." It was the first time in my life that I had back-talked an adult, and it was scary. I was on a roll, so I continued, "We were all safe and away from her, and you people put us back in hell. Then as if that wasn't bad enough, you put me in one brutal foster home after another. WHY?"

All the pain I had kept corked up inside for 18 years was vented toward these hapless people. The lady caseworker spoke up. "If you'll just calm down so that we can talk to you. We watched your mother very close ..."

I cut her off in mid word. "No! You did not watch her! It took her almost a year to beat my brother to death. Can you tell me just when did you check on her?" I was so worked up, that I was almost in tears. "How could you keep an eye on her and not see the bruises we all had? Don't you dare sit there and tell me that you watched out for us kids. When my sister and I did trust you and told about the abuse we were receiving, we were separated. Let's talk about the hell I just ran away from. The hell you people put me in. For nine years I have been beaten and worked like a slave after your cavalier placement. You may think that you do well by the children. I'm here to tell you that you don't have a clue about what goes on in the homes you put foster kids in. You gave the Rivers their first foster child slave years ago.

"Ma didn't come here and tell you she had a desire to give children a good home. She came here and told you she wanted a nine- or 10-year-old girl to work. You gave her children knowing full well that she only wanted kids to work. You continued to give her kids over the years to work and to beat. Well, I'm here to tell you that you have ruined enough children. I hope you can sleep at night. Every night since Peter died, I have hummed his song to help me go to sleep at night. His sad song comforted me and eased my pain, something you should have done for me. That is your job. I won't have to sing myself to sleep tonight. I know that tonight I'll sleep well for the first time in 18 years. Think of that when you go to bed tonight. Think for a minute about the kind of homes you placed me in."

With that outburst I was spent, and I started to cry. One of the caseworkers tried to comfort me. She promised me that she would look into my claims. I left the room, ran to granddad sobbing, and we drove to his house.

Another Georgie Deep Inside

I WAS SURPRISED to find that granddad no longer lived next to the Lido. He had given that house to Aunt Gerry and moved to a marvelous two-story Victorian house on Oak Street. It was trimmed in Victorian-style gingerbread. It was the most wonderful storybook refuge a girl could hope for.

Granddad introduced me to his girlfriend, Bernice, who said that I should call her "Bernie." Granddad wasn't married to Bernie, but they had been together since before Peter died. Bernie prepared a nice dinner that night, and granddad told me how he had tried to see me more, but that the Rivers never would allow it. We spent the evening talking about what I had gone through for the past nine years on the farm. I never asked about mom. Granddad never volunteered any information concerning her whereabouts.

Granddad and Bernie were gracious, but I didn't feel like I belonged there. But I was trying. I finally had a real family, and I was going to do my best to fit in. About 11 p.m., Bernie prepared the couch for me, and I retired for the night. I was surprised that she hadn't put me into one of the bedrooms, but it didn't seem very important. As I lay in bed, I thought about what Ma and Pa Rivers might have done when I didn't get off the bus that afternoon. I smiled to myself just thinking about the courage it took to do what I had done.

I slept without needing Peter's song for the first time in years. The next morning, I woke with the thought that I would live at granddad's house, and everything would be wonderful.

I hadn't really thought about what I was going to do. It was summer. I was out of school. Best of all, I was away from the Rivers. After breakfast, granddad sat at the kitchen table and said, "Jeanne, come sit with me. We need to talk about what you are going to do now that you're away from the farm."

I replied, "Well, I know I need to find a job."

"Yes," he said, "I can help with that. I have arranged for you to work at City Hall in the Civil Defense Department. They need a secretary. Do you think you can do that kind of work?"

I replied, "Oh yes. I took secretarial classes in school."

He softly continued, "Bernie and I are old, and we are in bad health. There is no room for you in this house, so you won't be able to stay with us."

I felt a knot forming in my stomach. I tentatively asked, "Where can I go?"

Granddad sensed my fear, reached for my hand, and replied, "I made arrangements for you to live at the Children's Home. You can stay there rent-free and receive all your meals at no charge. You will have to work at the Home on the weekends and at night when you get back from your office job."

The house grew quiet. He sat there and just looked at me, waiting for my response. I looked up at granddad with tears in my eyes and said, "What will I be expected to do at the Children's Home?"

Granddad smiled, squeezed my hand in approval, and said, "Let's go over and find out."

We got in his car and drove the short distance to the Children's Home.

It was a wooden two-story building. When I walked into the Home, I entered a foyer with a couple of offices on each side of the entrance. Straight ahead was a huge dining room with an industrial-sized kitchen beyond. A large living room with several couches and easy chairs was on the left. A wide, wooden staircase led to the girls' dorm. The boys' living room was to the right of the dining room. A separate staircase led to the boys' dorm. We went into an office, where I met the woman in charge. She said how happy she was to meet me and indicated that she knew what I had gone through in the years since my brother had died. She told me what would be expected of me and that, in return, I would receive three meals and would have my own room. She asked me if I could handle working with abused and neglected children.

I replied, "I can probably understand these children better than most people."

She smiled and said, "Yes, I just bet you can. Welcome to our family."

With that settled, I returned to where granddad was waiting for me and told him that I could move in right away.

We next went to City Hall, where I met the woman I would be working for. She gave me my schedule and told me to report to work at 9 o'clock on Monday morning. I left there feeling full of hope. After returning to granddad's house, I gathered my few belongings and placed them back in the brown paper bag.

Bernie asked me, "Is that every thing that you own?"

Embarrassed, I stammered, "Y...y...yes."

She said, "George, your granddaughter is a working woman now, and she needs to dress properly for her new job."

Granddad agreed. They took me to town and bought me some new clothes.

The next day, dressed in my new outfit, I felt like I looked great. I had more self-confidence than I ever had in my life.

He said, "Whenever you feel lonely, give me a call and come up to have supper with Bernie and me."

I replied, "I sure will. I ... I ... love you, granddad."

"I love you too, Georgie." I corrected granddad about my name being Jeanne. He just couldn't get use to calling me by my new name. Granddad then took me over to the orphanage to begin my new life. He drove off. I walked inside. I knew that I had no real family to fall back on, but for the first time, I had a future to look forward to.

I had my own room. The girls slept in two large dorm rooms, which reminded me of the room I was in when I was at the Children's Home in Chicago. I had 18 girls to take care of, ranging in age from five to 17. Each child had a twin bed and a nightstand to store her belongings. The children ages five to 12 were in one long room to the left of mine. The older children slept in an identical room to my right.

I slept very well in my new room and in my new life. The next morning, I woke up, showered and dressed. Then I got the children up. I asked the older girls to help the younger children, and to my surprise they did. It was the first time I could remember supervising someone. I wasn't cocky, nor did I walk around with a chip on my shoulder. I was just like these children, except for the fact that I had been where they were, had paid my dues, and had survived. I never told my story to these children, but for some reason they seemed to know that I was one of them.

I was a shy, quiet, and very unassertive girl. I tried to act confident so the older children wouldn't realize how frightened I really was. I was somewhat surprised when even the girls that were only a year younger than I showed me respect. They obeyed me when I politely asked them to do something. I tried to be gentle and understanding when I assigned everyone chores to do, including myself. I think that the children respected the fact that I worked and played alongside them. They knew that when I said it was time to do something or to settle down, that it absolutely was time to do these things.

Once everyone was dressed and their beds made, we all went downstairs to the dining hall to get our breakfast trays. We all sat together, including the boys, at the long, wooden tables. After our simple but hearty breakfast, I went back to the kitchen, picked up a sack lunch, and walked the four blocks to City Hall.

It turned out that my job at Civil Defense was mostly taking shorthand at meetings and then typing the minutes up. I also typed letters and reorganized the filing system. At noon I ate my sack lunch in a little jewel of a park across from City Hall. It was on the shore of the Saranac River, where it flowed into Lake Champlain. I fed the crust of my sandwich to the ducks. After lunch, my boss explained to me that the Strategic Air Command Air force Base on the edge of town would probably be the very first place that the Russians would destroy with their missiles. He said that people who are frightened of the communists might come in to our office from time to time for our Civil Defense pamphlets. It would be my job to hand these out.

I loved my new job at the Civil Defense office. When someone asked me to do something, there was kindness in their tone. I was treated like an adult ... I was treated like a human being.

After work, I walked back to the Children's Home for supper. The worst part of my job at the Children's Home was when the small girls would ask me questions about what would happen to them in the future. I never knew what to say. In my heart I felt that their future was bleak, but I didn't want to scare them so I would always say, "I hope everything will turn out okay for you." I never shared any personal facts about my past with the girls, and I tried to change the subject as soon as possible. I tried not to think about the future of these girls in the children's home. I mostly enjoyed coming home at the end of the day and playing with the children. It was like I was still a child myself. Many of the traumatized children at the Home wanted to be left alone. I respected their wishes.

Four small girls, however, always seemed to want to be as close to me as they could get. I tried not to have a favorite child, because I loved them all.

One very small nine-year-old girl with long blonde hair was named Penny. She had big, blue eyes that held hope, but mostly reflected sadness. She reminded me of my sister Jill. One night when I got home, I scanned the room to make eye contact with her. I gave her a wink, and she gave me a smile. It was our way of communicating without actually speaking.

At dinner we met in the dining room, and Penny sat next to me. I told her and the other girls at my table what I had done at work that day. I talked about sitting in the park to eat my lunch and feeding breadcrumbs to the ducks. The girls listened to my every word and asked a variety of questions concerning my job and my day in general. I actually felt important to these children. After dinner we helped with the cleaning of the kitchen and dining room. I taught the girls to sing several popular songs, and the singing seemed to make the time fly. In the evening, I helped get the younger girls ready for bed. Once they were in their pajamas, I sat down with them and read them a story before putting them to bed.

Several weeks after I arrived at the Children's Home, I was told that I had company. When I went out on the porch, there sat Ma and Pa Rivers on the porch swing. When I first saw them, a shock of fear went through me. I soon recovered. I knew that they could not hurt me anymore. "Hi," I said. "I sure didn't expect to see you here."

Pa spoke up and said, "I wish you had chosen a better way to leave than the way you did." Then he said something that just about summed up the kind of people they really were. "You shamed us in front of the whole community by going to the welfare like you did. I'm sorry you felt you had to do that. Now they will not give us any more children."

I just looked at them and said, "You're not sorry for the way you treated me. You're just sorry that I told the truth and shamed you."

I shook my head, turned, and walked back into the Children's Home. I never looked back.

I got so attached to the kids of the Children's Home that I just about died each time the social workers placed one of my kids in a foster home. I would have taken each and every child home with me, if I had a home. I was so distrustful of prospective foster parents that I would cry whenever a child was placed

One night while tucking Penny in, she said to me, "I am going back to live with my mother." Her eyes were teary, and she looked up at me and said, "I will miss you, Jeanne. I'm really, really scared."

I held her. "I'm sure you're a little scared, honey. You are about to enter a new adventure. When I came here, I was entering a new adventure and was a little scared too. I have had many adventures in my life. Some were good and some were not so good, but I learned from all of them. When I get scared, I sing a song that my brother taught me to keep me from being scared."

Penny looked up at me and said, "I sure wish I had a song to keep me from being scared."

"Well, maybe I can give you a song that you can sing when you are scared. Maybe it will remind you of me, and you won't be scared any more." I thought for a moment and remembered the Danny Kaye movie called "Red Nicholas And The Five Pennies," which I had recently seen on television. Holding Penny on my lap I began to sing ...

This little penny...is to wish on...to make your wishes come true.
This little penny...is to dream on...dream...of all you can do.
This little penny... is a dancing little penny...

When I looked down, Penny had fallen asleep. I put her to bed and tucked her in. Then I knelt beside her bed and asked, "God, please keep a special eye on this little Penny for me."

The next morning during breakfast, Penny's birth mother came and picked her up. I was so upset that I couldn't finish eating. I clenched my fists and chastised myself for caring about what happened to anyone. I knew better. Caring about Penny only meant that I would get hurt.

I relaxed my clenched fists and turned my shell back on. I put on my happy face. I ran all the way to work. I hated and loved the orphanage. I wanted to leave. I promised myself that I would get a place of my own as soon as possible. At noon I fed my entire lunch to the ducks and scanned the newspaper for a new place to live. I counted my money. It was less than 20 dollars.

Then I spotted a nanny's job. It didn't pay much, but it included room and board. I called the nice lady and walked across town to interview for the position. I was thrilled when I got the job. It meant that I would no longer be a part of the "system." I gave my notice at the orphanage, and soon it was time to leave. I stuffed my clothes into a paper bag and said my goodbyes. I was very sad to leave, but I was ready to go. At first, I walked slowly and looked back often, but soon the orphanage was far behind me, and I could no longer see it. I dragged my feet for a couple of blocks, thinking about the past and the future.

I knew that nothing is quite so scary if you have a smile and a song, so I put on my happy face on and I started to skip as I walked. Then in a soft clear voice, I started to sing.

Hey ... there ... Georgie Girl ...
Why do all the boys just pass you by?
Could it be you just don't try ... ?
Or is it the clothes you wear?
You're always window-shopping, but never stopping to buy,
So spread those downy feathers and fly ...
There's another Georgie, deep inside.

A Letter to Heaven

My Dear Little Brother Peter,

The sound of your somber, loving lullaby will fill my soul forever. Your song was the only thing that eased my pain as a child. Your suffering and death were not in vain. I feel your spirit standing beside me when I choke back my tears and tell our tragic story.

Now other people will hear your lullaby and maybe someone will take the steps necessary to save the life and happiness of the next small, helpless child.

As you peer down from Paradise, please watch over all of the abused little children.

You're always in my Heart

Georgie

The Need For Mommies

Your face has lines of time
Your hands are firm and gentle
You wept at the horrid crime
For you the pain was mental
But for us it is too late

Your eyes are filled with tears
And you felt our pain
You wished to calm our fears
And I know your name
I would have called you Mommy

Peter wanted to be your son
Wondered where you were
Would you ever come
But before you knew
He was gone

A tear rolled down your face
To help the helpless child
In your home to make a place
The telephone must be dialed
It's time to make the call

If your childhood wasn't like mine, please consider writing your mom and thanking her. She would probably love to hear from you.

Yours truly,

Jeanne Fowler

Where Are They Now?

I started out to find my shattered family, not to write a book. I was stunned to learn that we had all been raised in the small town of Plattsburgh, and yet we never could find each other.

In 1998 I found my older brother Pug and my two little sisters, Donna and Jill. I also visited Peter's grave. I discovered that I had two other siblings, one of whom (Debbie) I have found. I also found my foster brother Kenny and discovered what had happened to my foster sister Margaret.

Jeanne (Georgianne): I never sang Peter's lullaby again after I left the Rivers' farm. I finally quit having the frog nightmare in the late 1980s. I still have nightlights in every room of my house, so no room is ever dark. I still jump through the roof if approached from behind, even at home.

When I left the farm, I swore to never hurt anyone or let anyone hit me again. I soon married and moved to Alaska. I had two children and built a log cabin to house them. One day during an argument, my husband hit me. I divorced him. After 12 years in Alaska, I moved to California, where I worked in nursing for 20 years. I married twice more and was widowed both times.

(The Baby) Donna Burowsky: A nice Plattsburgh family adopted Donna while she was still a toddler. The scars on her wrists and ankles healed. Donna was never allowed to interact with her siblings, for fear that she would discover more about her past than her new parents wanted her to know. She is now married to an engineer and living in Pennsylvania.

Peter Burowsky, Jr.: My brother Peter was not buried in Chicago as I had been told. He was buried back in Plattsburgh, New York. His unmarked grave was in the family plot. I marked his grave in 1998.

Jill Burowsky: After I was separated from my sister Jill at the Yelle foster home, she was sent to a new foster home. Her new "father" collected young foster girls for his own sexual pleasure. She endured 12 more years of hell. She now works in the Plattsburgh area as a professional singer.

Debbie Trombley: My older sister Debbie was so badly abused as an infant that a family member adopted her. Her new parents didn't want her to mix with any of us. I never even knew that Debbie existed until I started looking for my family. Debbie has two grown children, sells Avon, cares for elderly people, and is very active in her church.

Pug Trombley: My older brother Pug went back to live with Granddad George after the murder. Pug has a wife and five grown children. He has worked in the same factory for the last 30 years.

Veronica Burowsky: My birth mother spent eight years of her 14-year sentence in prison. She never had another child. Veronica drank herself to death on January 4, 1972. She was buried in the family plot in an unmarked grave next to the son she had murdered 19 years earlier.

Peter Burowsky, Sr.: My stepdad was sentenced to spend one to 14 years in jail. Actually, he spent only one year in prison. He was paroled early so he could go back to take care of his family. Peter, Sr. eventually moved to Florida, where he worked as the manager of an exclusive yacht club. Peter quit drinking and remarried. Peter and his new wife both died of cancer within weeks of each other—Peter on November 23, 1984.

Doody and Bea Duquette: Uncle Doody died on November 6, 1984, from cancer. Aunt Bea survived the cancer that had caused her to give me up in 1954. She died at age 87 on April 18, 2000, from heart failure. I still miss her.

Margaret Franks: My angry foster sister hadn't run away like Kenny and I had been told. It turns out that Ma Rivers had called the social workers and told them to take the "unruly girl" to another home. Margaret shuffled around in the system until she aged-out at 18. She married an angry, abusive man and had two children. She was found drowned in the Saranac River on Sept 16, 1972.

It was just before her 21ˢᵗ birthday. The police suspected foul play, but no one was ever arrested.

Kenny Franks: The day after I got away from the slave farm, a caseworker went out to the Rivers' place to keep her promise to investigate. The Rivers told her that I was just an hysterical young woman. The social worker asked Kenny if he wanted to leave. My frightened foster brother was too intimidated to speak freely, so he assured the caseworker that he was happy enough. Kenny stayed for 10 more years of beatings. He was 25 years old before he finally got away. He was penniless when he left. Kenny now works for the Beekmantown School System, is married, and has children.

Susie Rivers: Shortly after I left the farm, Susie got pregnant. She was afraid to tell ma and pa, so they were surprised when the baby arrived. Susie eventually married a prison guard. She now works as a school crossing guard.

Ma and Pa Rivers: Pa Rivers died in 1994 of kidney failure. Ma Rivers died March 7, 2005 at age 82.

Abuse in Perspective

Society values family privacy and the rights of a parent to decide how to raise a child. We also value the rights of the child to be safe from abuse or neglect from bad parents. It is a balancing act, and for every case like mine where the system did too little, there is probably another case where the system did too much. I would be remiss if I didn't say a few kind words about church volunteers, social workers, police officers, and foster parents who are really trying to manage this balancing act and make a fair and safe society.

Back when I was a child, parents' rights far outweighed the child's rights. In those days, we asked untrained religious volunteers to make the decisions about where to place a child, often with disastrous results.

In those days there were no computers to track perpetrators and few laws to prosecute them. It is no wonder that the police made mistakes. When I was a child, there was little investigation before placing children in foster care and little supervision of the foster parents who were chosen. This allowed some foxes into the hen house. I do believe that most foster and adoptive parents have good intentions and that the social workers and police are doing their best to weed out the bad ones.

I have no hard feelings about any honest mistakes that were made in my case, nor do I hate the people who intentionally hurt me. It is my policy to keep people who would hurt me out of my life, but not to hate them. I feel that hate is like a cold, dark pool of acid that can destroy soul and life. I want no part of that. If others chose to swim in the acid of hate, that is their choice, not mine.

What Has and Hasn't Changed

(The following was provided by a social worker who wishes to remain anonymous.)

It was not until the definition of "Battered Child Syndrome" in 1962 that significant professional and public attention was focused on child abuse and neglect. In 1977 the state of Wisconsin passed "The Child Abuse and Neglect Act." This act mandates the reporting of all abusive acts against children. Over the years, well-meaning church and community leaders who worked as social workers in my day have been gradually replaced by college-educated professionals. Today, more effort is made to follow up on cases where parents move or have more children. However, more work needs to be done in this area.

Unfortunately, child abuse is one of the greatest health risks to our country's children. The National Center on Child Abuse and Neglect reported that caregivers abuse over one million children each year. Of these cases, about 10% are sexually abused, 20% are physically abused, and the remainder are neglected. Studies conducted from 1948 through 1953 revealed that 25% of females and 10% of males had been sexually assaulted before the age of 18.

Unfortunately, each year 2,000 to 5,000 children die as a direct result of neglect or abuse. Reports of child abuse increased 63% from 1985 to 1994. A new case is reported every seven seconds.

Child abuse is reported at a rate of four million cases per year, with one million of those cases being substantiated. This means that an average of one child in every other classroom is being abused at home.

We must all reject violence against children. Society must develop the philosophical view that every child has the right to grow in a safe environment. Children present a unique contribution to our future. Everyone shares in the responsibility of stopping child abuse before it starts. We need to change society's values and attitudes towards violence. If we want to minimize child abuse and neglect, we need to provide parents, professionals, and the community with the tools needed to combat violence against our vulnerable children.

Social workers, legislators, judges, police, and civic groups need to become more proactive and educated about child abuse. The prevention of child abuse must be tackled on a number of levels. We all need to be actively involved in social issues affecting child abuse.

We need to encourage legislators to pass laws that give children equal rights. These laws should encourage severe penalties—life sentences, etc., for the death, torture or mutilation of a child.

We have a shortage of social workers. Each worker gets an average of one new substantiated case per month to add to his or her already burdensome caseload. There are too few child welfare workers to adequately process all of these cases. It's no wonder that children fall through the cracks. Money must be provided so that social workers will have a manageable caseload. This will help ensure quality interventions and measurable positive outcomes.

Police, judges, and prosecutors need to exercise more accountability and responsibility in child abuse and neglect cases. The courts should be more sensitive to the trauma a child suffers when testifying against their parents.

Communities need to work at the elimination of child poverty and at providing child abuse and awareness programs. We need to fund more dedicated college-educated social workers.

Social workers and governmental agencies must intervene to protect the "at risk" children. Social work agencies need to promote more training, especially in tracking methods to help keep the perpetrators from changing jurisdiction to avoid surveillance.

Computers can be utilized better to manage case reviews and record audits. Annual evaluations must be kept up-to-date in order to analyze the success or failures of the service plan.

Where abuse or neglect has been substantiated, it should be the goal of child-placing agencies to provide the best solutions of intervention to protect the children. These agencies must advocate and provide the optimal services available to ensure the child is safe from present or future harm. Agency workers as well as courts must monitor these families with regular hearings, home-calls, and reviews to make the most informed decisions in regards to the safety factors encompassing the children's home environment.

Every foster care home must have a monthly review to ensure that children are not at risk for the same abuse from which they were removed.

We should advocate child placements with relatives before alternate non-relative homes are considered. This will protect the child's identity and promote the child's sense of belonging to a family unit.

The work being done in the field of child abuse varies from state to state. There are many theories about which types of interventions actually work with families. Unfortunately, there is still a substantial gap in the area of research on intervention outcomes. Although a variety of child abuse intervention strategies have been tried, few have been subjected to independent evaluations. We know little about the relative effectiveness and efficiency of child abuse programs in the United States.

Our schools should provide more conflict resolution classes and personal safety programs for our children.

Parenting is a stressful combination of environmental and personal factors. In borderline abuse and neglect cases, some carefully monitored support can lead to an improvement of parenting skills and a sense of hope in the family, whereas mere criticism can destroy the relationships in families. This in turn may lead to mistrust of the government and, worse, abuse or neglect. Stressed parents need parenting skill courses and respite care. Self-help groups such as Parents Anonymous would also help.

Even though the United States spends one billion dollars a year on foster care and each foster family receives a state per diem, there is still a shortage of foster parents. This means that for every two children who need foster care, there is only enough room for one child.

There is a great need for good, dedicated people to become active in fighting child abuse and neglect.

If you suspect a child is being abused and/or neglected, you can call your local child protective service hot line, which is listed in your local telephone directory. If you're interested in becoming a volunteer, a foster parent, or in adopting an older child, please call your local social service agency.

You can write your local congressperson and request his/her position on child abuse and neglect, as well as what they have done or are currently doing in your state or congress to address this issue. Remember to bring about change, we must become involved.

Significant changes have been made since I was a child, but children still continue to fall through the cracks and the abuse continues. Only with your help and awareness can children truly be safe.

Resources

You can contact

Jeanne Fowler
through Daisy Chain Publishing, LLC

(248) 925-5964
(248) 244-8500 (FAX)

Childhelp USA National Child Abuse Hotline
(24 hours)

www.childhelpusa.org
1-800-4-A-Child
(1-800-422-4453)

Justice For Children

www.justiceforchildren.org
1-800-733-0059

"Michigans"
(Serves 6)

Now that I have been reunited with most of my lost family, you may wonder what we talk about besides the sad, old days and the years together that we have missed. Well, for one thing we swap recipes. I hadn't eaten a "Michigan" since I left Plattsburgh, so when we had our first reunion after 45 years, my family made wonderful "Michigans" for me.

I feel that a person should have a family to have a family recipe. Now that I have a family, we can start a family tradition of eating "Michigans" when we get together. So here is my sister-in-law's recipe for that Plattsburgh favorite, "The Michigan." It tastes like home to me.

1 16-oz can tomato sauce	Tabasco sauce
¾ tsp. garlic powder	1 whole onion, diced
8 tsp. chili powder	6 premium all beef hot dogs
2 tsp. powdered cumin	6 Plattsburgh-style hot dog
2 tsp. dried diced onions	buns (you may substitute
2 tsp. black pepper	other types of buns)
2 lbs. ground beef	

1. Combine first six ingredients. Add the raw ground beef and stir. Add Tabasco brand pepper sauce to taste. Cook over low heat for 2-3 hours, stirring occasionally.
2. Place hot dogs in boiling water, return to a boil, and then place dogs on buns. Ask each family member to make a choice of onion placement: buried under the sauce, on top of the sauce, or no onions.

A family is like a recipe. It has love, responsibility, sadness, and joy, all stirred together, and the combination of ingredients tastes quite different than each individual ingredient alone. It feels odd and wonderful to have a brother and sisters, a few in-laws and some assorted nieces, nephews, aunts and uncles. They are the only people on the planet who share my blood and memories.

About the Author

Jeanne Fowler is fast becoming "the" voice for abused children, who are suffering at this very moment.

As a severely abused child herself, Jeanne experienced first-hand their feelings of abandonment, fear, shame, pain, and loss of trust. She knows and reveals an intimate look into the lives of these helpless children. To help you recognize those things that must change to help these innocent children escape their torturous struggle, she conveys valuable insights and information to make this complex issue understandable.

Jeanne is a living example of what an abused child can accomplish when at least one person cares. As a one-woman gang,

this extraordinary woman approaches the subject with dedication and the tenacity of a mother bear protecting her cubs.

Her goals are to educate and change the behaviors of parents, social workers, law enforcement, judges, legislators, foster parents, and the public in general.

This issue touches all of us. Michigan's Blue Cross and Blue Shield recognized this when, in 2003, they selected Jeanne and gave her "The Angel of the Year" award for her work with these children.